◆ Starting Points for Your Internet Exploration

The Web is like thousands of TV channels or 10,000 New York Public Libraries—it includes hours of entertainment or volumes and volumes of information. Here is a brief list of good starting places that make it easy for you to find your way to the stuff you find intriguing or useful.

Alta Vista: A big, fast, searchable database
    `http://www.altavista.digital.com`

AudioNet: A guide to audio broadcast on the Net
    `http://www.AudioNet.com`

Club Wired: HotWired's celebrity chat schedule
    `http://www.hotwired.com/club`

c|net's search.com: A one-stop starting point
    `http://www.search.com`

Excite: More than just a directory
    `http://www.excite.com`

Gamelan: Java applications sorted by category
    `http://www.gamelan.com`

HotBot: A search tool from HotWired and Inktomi
    `http://www.hotbot.com`

InfoSeek: A search service with broad coverage
    `http://www.infoseek.com`

Inktomi: A search tool using parallel computing
    `http://inktomi.berkeley.edu`

Lycos: An enormous searchable database
    `http://www.lycos.com`

Open Market's Commercial Sites Index
    `http://www.directory.com`

Yahoo: A subject-oriented index to the We
    `http://www.yahoo.com`

Surfing the Internet with Netscape Navigator 3

Third Edition

Surfing the Internet with Netscape® Navigator 3

Third Edition

Daniel A. Tauber and Brenda Kienan

SYBEX

San Francisco • Paris • Düsseldorf • Soest

Associate Publisher: Carrie Lavine
Acquisitions Manager: Kristine Plachy
Developmental Editor: Dan Brodnitz
Editor: Vivian Perry
Project Editor: Maureen Adams
Technical Editors: Peter Stokes and J. Tarin Towers
Book Design Director: Cătălin Dulfu
Graphic Illustrator: Lucka Zivny
Desktop Publisher: Bill Gibson
Production Coordinator: Kimberley Askew-Qasem
Indexer: Ted Laux
Cover Designer: Design Site
Cover Illustrator: Daniel Ziegler

Warranty

Sybex warrants the enclosed CD-ROM to be free of physical defects for a period of ninety (90) days after purchase. If you discover a defect in the CD during this warranty period, you can obtain a replacement CD at no charge by sending the defective CD, postage prepaid, with proof of purchase to:

Sybex Inc.
Customer Service Department
1151 Marina Village Parkway
Alameda, CA 94501
(800) 227-2346
Fax: (510) 523-2373

After the 90-day period, you can obtain a replacement CD by sending us the defective CD, proof of purchase, and a check or money order for $10, payable to Sybex.

Disclaimer

Sybex makes no warranty or representation, either express or implied, with respect to this medium or its contents, its quality, performance, merchantability, or fitness for a particular purpose. In no event will Sybex, its distributors, or dealers be liable for direct, indirect, special, incidental, or consequential damages arising out of the use of or inability to use the software even if advised of the possibility of such damage. The exclusion of implied warranties is not permitted by some states. Therefore, the above exclusion may not apply to you. This warranty provides you with specific legal rights; there may be other rights that you may have that vary from state to state.

Copy Protection

None of the files on the CD is copy-protected. However, in all cases, reselling or redistributing these files, except as specifically provided for by the copyright owners, is prohibited.

To L.E.M.—sister, mother, friend

and to her mother and family, with gratitude

Acknowledgments

A book is always a collaborative effort; this one has been especially so. We are indebted to the many people who have helped to make this third edition happen.

Our editor, Vivian Perry, showed the utmost professional grace and perseverance in the face of a breakneck schedule and all sorts of hurdles. We thank her for her meticulous, thoughtful work and her overall steadiness. Special thanks also go to technical reviewer Peter Stokes, friend and colleague through a couple of career changes already.

At Sybex, thanks go to Carrie Lavine, consummate marketeer and ace team builder; to Dan Brodnitz, whose urging on had a friendly quality; to Sybex heroines Barbara Gordon, Chris Meredith, and Kristine Plachy, who have stayed on track through "interesting" times; to project editor Maureen Adams; to the production team of Bill Gibson and Kimberley Askew-Qasem, who made manuscript and screen shots into an actual book; to Lucka Zivny, who transformed our scribbles into the charming line drawings; and to indexer Ted Laux, master of his craft, who compiled references with admirable compulsion.

Special thanks, too, to contributing writers J. Tarin Towers and Linda Gaus, who drove home their drafts under very tight deadlines; and to Asha Dornfest, who revised Appendix C and made the What's Out There page a reality with her usual good cheer.

At Netscape, our thanks go to Marc Andreessen and the fine people who created a remarkable product, to Marie Gunther for her help in getting the lowdown this time around, and to Jon Mittelhauser and Kipp E.B. Hickman for their good counsel and the extraordinary promptness of their e-mail answers to our many questions during the second edition.

Our profound gratitude goes as always to family and friends for their support and all the understanding they can muster. For the record, we name: Joani and Jessica Buehrle; Sharon Crawford; Jerry Doty; Rion Dugan; Fred Frumberg; Jessica, Martin, and Lori Grant; Carol Heller; Mai Le Bazner, Katri Foster, and Peter Bazner; the McArdle and Undercoffer families; Carolyn Miller; Lonnie Moseley; Wynn Moseley and her family; Freeman Ng; Gino Reynoso; Cordell Sloan; Margaret Tauber; Ron and Frances Tauber; Savitha Varadan; and Robert E. Williams III.

Contents at a Glance

Contents

Part Two:
Navigating and Publishing with Netscape
43

Chapter 3
Navigating Netscape

45

Chapter 4

Been There, Going Back

83

Chapter 5

Newsgroups and E-Mail the Netscape Way

99

Chapter 6
Communicating via CoolTalk

121

Chapter 7
Navigating Virtual Space with Live3D: VRML

143

Chapter 8
Starting Places and Search Tools

155

Chapter 9
You Too Can Be a Web Publisher

197

Part Three:
Getting Started with Netscape
243

Chapter 10
Laying the Groundwork for Installing Netscape

245

Chapter 11

Getting Netscape Navigator Going

283

Chapter 12

Get a Boost with Plug-Ins and Helper Apps

299

Appendix A
Internet Service Providers

323

Appendix B
Spots on the Web You Won't Want to Miss

327

Appendix C
What's on the CD

365

Index

Introduction

Everybody wants to get in on the Internet. If you're one of those folks, this book, written in plain English and filled with how-to know-how, is for you. It will get you started in no time exploring and using the World Wide Web, the fastest growing portion of the Internet, via Netscape Navigator version 3. Netscape is the highly popular Web browser used by more than 70 percent of all those users who are active on the Web today. It includes security and other features you won't find in any other Web browser.

◆ What's New in Version 3

Netscape Navigator version 3 adds scads of new and improved features to an already successful product. Netscape is always pushing the envelope; some of its new features enhance online security and the layout options available to those who publish on the Web; add new three-dimensional, interactive virtual reality (VRML); and offer sophisticated dynamic on-screen motion (improved Java technology). With Netscape version 3 you'll get:

- ◆ Exciting, easy-to-use interactivity with Live3D, which offers a VRML viewer so you can explore 3-D worlds online
- ◆ Seamless playing of sound and video directly from Web pages
- ◆ Jazzier communications via CoolTalk, which includes Internet telephone, chat, and whiteboarding capabilities
- ◆ Enhancements to Java and JavaScript, which enable your experience of *applets*, "small" programs that in Web pages appear as animations, games, drop-down menus, ticker-tape-style news feeds, and even sophisticated applications useful to professionals and research and business teams
- ◆ New, expanded security and enhanced page design features

This keeps Netscape way ahead of the pack, still setting the standards in the Web browser race toward new technologies.

Netscape regularly improves and updates the look of its software. The contents of this book reflect the state of Netscape Navigator 3 as of our publication date. Although the functionality we describe should not differ from the way your browser works, some of our screen captures may not match exactly what you see on your screen.

◆ Is This Book for You?

If you want to explore the beautiful, graphical World Wide Web using Netscape, or even create your own Web pages, this book is for you.

This book has been written by two Internauts with years of combined experience and professional Internet involvement. It avoids jargon and explains any necessary terms clearly. It's a great place to start for beginners, but that's not all. Because it includes information on publishing on the Internet, on the latest searching tools, and on getting and using special tools to enhance your Web experience, this book is a good follow-up for people already familiar with the Internet.

Getting and installing Netscape involves setting up a connection that is able to "introduce" your Internet service provider to Netscape each and every time you access the Internet using Netscape. Setting up this connection was quite a tricky procedure in days gone by, but don't worry. This book covers connecting via Windows 95, which includes all the software you need to make a Netscape connection through your own Internet service provider. This book also covers making your connection via some other very popular options: Netcom's Netcomplete software, America Online, and CompuServe. You'll learn how to get Netscape from the Internet itself and how to set up a working, reliable connection. With this book, you'll be up and running in no time.

 Instructions for setting up a connection and getting Netscape are in Chapters 10 and 11; information on service providers is in Appendix A.

Throughout this book you'll find the Internet addresses of dozens, if not hundreds, of sites that will provide you with additional information on every topic in this book, from getting connected and getting tech support to publishing a bang-up Web page to announcing your Web page. You'll also find the Internet addresses of fascinating sites that will get you started and keep you going in your Web travels—these sites cover topics from Art to Education, Personal Finance, Sports, and Travel, with lots of cool and useful stuff in between.

◆ What's on the CD

On the CD that comes with this book you'll find a customized What's Out There Web page, containing every Internet address mentioned in this book and then some. Through the What's Out There page you'll have access to hand-picked sites that are especially useful and intriguing; you'll also have access to literally millions of sites via especially good online directories and search facilities. You'll also have access to an online glossary that you can search via Netscape's Find feature. You can make the convenient What's Out There page your own start-up home page so you'll see its wide variety of Internet resources as starting-place options every time you start Netscape, or you can just keep it handy for reference when you want a quick route to something of special interest. You'll also get the software you need to get connected with Netcomplete, NetCruiser, or CompuServe.

Appendix C describes these items in more detail; shows you how to install the software that comes with this book, and explains how to install the What's Out There page. (Instructions for navigating the What's Out There page are a part of the page itself.)

◆ How This Book Is Organized

This book is organized into 12 chapters, beginning, logically enough, with Chapter 1, a brief introduction to the Internet. Chapter 2 goes into more detail about the World Wide Web and how Netscape can get you there. Chapter 3 shows you basic Netscape navigation, while Chapter 4 tells you in basic terms how to stay organized by using bookmarks and other tools to track your travels. Chapter 5 describes communicating with others via e-mail and newsgroups, and Chapter 6 offers even more communication options through its coverage of CoolTalk, Netscape's new chat, Internet phone, and whiteboarding program. Chapter 7 introduces you to the three-dimensional worlds enabled by VRML.

With basic navigation skills under your belt, you might want to focus your Web travels. Chapter 8 describes some good launch points for your Web travels along with how to use the new search technologies that are such an important part of maximizing your Internet experience.

Chapter 9 shows how you too can be a Web publisher—it includes a primer on HTML, the mark-up language used to create Web documents, along with tips for successful Web page design and even information on how to publicize your Web page.

Chapter 10 makes clear how you can get connected using various popular options for Internet connectivity and then how to get Netscape from the Internet itself. Chapter 11 follows up by providing step-by-step instructions for setting up Netscape to work with your Internet service.

Finally, Chapter 12 tells you how to get and use plug-ins and helper applications—special tools that will further enhance your experience of Netscape and the World Wide Web.

You'll also find three appendices: Appendix A is a listing of Internet service providers that will work with Netscape; Appendix B tours you through a variety of useful and intriguing places you might want to visit; and Appendix C, as mentioned previously, describes what's on the CD that comes with this book.

◆ Conventions Used in This Book

Surfing the Internet with Netscape Navigator 3 uses various conventions to help you find the information you need quickly and effortlessly. Tips, Notes, and Warnings, shown here, are placed strategically throughout the book to help you zero in on important information in a snap.

Here you'll find insider tips and shortcuts—information meant to help you use Netscape more adeptly.

 Here you'll find reminders, asides, and bits of important information that should be emphasized.

 Here you'll find cautionary information describing trouble spots you may encounter either in using the software or in using the Internet.

A simple kind of shorthand used in this book helps to save space so more crucial matters can be discussed; in this system, directions to "pull down the File menu and choose Save" will appear as "select File ➤ Save," and the phrase "press Enter" appears as "press ↵," for example.

Long but important or interesting digressions are set aside as boxed text, called *sidebars*.

These Are Called "Sidebars"

In boxed text like this you'll find background information and side issues—anything that merits attention but can be skipped in a pinch.

And throughout the book you'll find special What's Out There sidebars telling you exactly where on the World Wide Web you can find out more about whatever's being discussed or where to find the home page being described.

What's Out There

The URL for the home page of interest at the moment will appear in a different font, for example, `http://www.dnai.com/~vox/netscape/nsad.html`.

◆ Let's Get This Show on the Road...

Enough about what's in the book and on the CD—to start your Internet exploration using Netscape, turn to Chapter 1; to find out how to get and install the software, turn to Chapter 10.

If You Need Assistance

For answers to your questions about Netscape, call (800) 320-2099. Make sure you have your credit card handy if you have yet to purchase your copy of Netscape Navigator. You can also get help via e-mail at `client@netscape.com`.

Technical support for Windows 95 Dial-Up Networking is available at (800) 936-4200 or (206) 635-7000, help with Netcom's Netcomplete is available at (800) 353-6600 or `support@ix.netcom.com`, help with America Online is available at (800) 827-3338, and help with CompuServe is available at (800) 848-8900.

Part One:

The Internet, the World Wide Web, and Netscape

The Big Picture

You'd have to live in a vacuum these days not to have heard of the Internet. Scarcely a day goes by without some mention of it on the nightly news or in the local paper. Internet addresses are even becoming common in advertisements. Millions of people—inspired by excited talk and armed with spanking new accounts with Internet service providers—are taking to the Internet, with visions of adventures on the Information Superhighway.

But for a long time (the Internet is actually 25 years old), most access to the Internet was via text-based viewers that left a lot to be desired in the realm of aesthetics and ease of use. The Internet was trafficked only by academicians and almost-nerdy computer enthusiasts in those days.

In fact, with your old or low-budget Internet account a prompt that looks like this:

may be all you get, even if you're running the thing under Windows. Your trek into cyberspace may feel more like a bumpy ride on an old bicycle.

◆ A Netscape View of the Internet

That's why Netscape Navigator (commonly called just Netscape) is so great: It offers an elegant point-and-click interface to guide you through the Internet's coolest resources, all linked to a growing number of global Internet resources. Netscape Navigator is a *browser*—a program with which you can view graphically intriguing, linked documents all over the world and search and access information in a few quick mouse-clicks. You don't have to type cryptic commands or deal with screens filled with plain text; all you have to do is point and click on highlighted words (or pictures) to follow the links between related information in a single, giant web of linked "pages." Figure 1.1 compares a text-based view of the Internet with a Netscape view.

Within the Internet is a special network of linked documents known as the *World Wide Web*. With Netscape, you can perform point-and-click searches on the Web or just follow your whims along an intuitive path of discovery. Netscape is available for all popular computers—PCs running Windows, Macintoshes, even Unix workstations. Netscape on any of these machines looks just about the same too. (In this book, we focus mainly on the Windows version, although many of the principles we discuss apply as well to the Unix and Mac versions.) There are some differences between using Netscape on a machine that's networked and a machine that stands alone, though.

To run Netscape on your stand-alone (un-networked) PC, you need a dial-up connection to the Internet via a service provider—you need one with specific capabilities. You also need software (known as SLIP or PPP) that provides a connection between Netscape and your Internet service provider. (Don't worry. This is not difficult.)

Windows 95 comes with SLIP/PPP software; if you have Windows 95, making an Internet connection that lets you use Netscape Navigator is easy as pie. You have other options for getting connected too—for example, you can run Netscape with Netcom's Netcomplete software, with CompuServe's NetLauncher, or with any of several others. Turn to Chapters 10 and 11 to find out how to set up your Internet connection and then get and use Netscape.

```
[INLINE]
There are several minor discrepancies evident in this 1912 preliminary
drawing, evidently used for pre-fair promotion since construction was
not started until the following year. The most noticable "error" is in
the design of the Fine Arts Palace on th e left which shows the
building with incorporated rather than seperate columns.

In playing host to the Panama-Pacific International Exposition, The
Fair, which opened on February 20, 1915, San Francisco was honoring
the discovery of the Pacific Ocean and the completion of the Panama
Canal; it was also celebrating its own resurrection after the
shattering earthquake and fire of 1906.

[INLINE]
Every day was a special day at the fair. If the celebration didn't
honor the like of Thomas Edison or ex-President Taft, then it was Food
Products Day, Ohio Day, Southern California Counties Day, California
Bee Keepers Day, or some other civic, fratern al, or other special
interest group (so many that some even had to share Days). The
-- press space for next page --
 Arrow keys: Up and Down to move. Right to follow a link; Left to go back.
H)elp O)ptions P)rint G)o M)ain screen Q)uit /=search [delete]=history list
```

There are several minor discrepancies evident in this 1912 preliminary drawing, evidently used for pre-fair promotion since construction was not started until the following year. The most noticable "error" is in the design of the Fine Arts Palace on th e left which shows the building with incorporated rather than seperate columns.

In playing host to the Panama-Pacific International Exposition, The Fair, which opened on February 20, 1915, San Francisco was honoring the discovery of the Pacific Ocean and the completion of the Panama Canal; it was also celebrating its own resurrection after the shattering earthquake and fire of 1906.

Figure 1.1: Here you can see the difference between the old text-based view of the Internet (top) and the easy-to-use, graphically pleasing Netscape view of the Internet (bottom).

Let's take a quick look at the Internet first. Then, in the next chapter, we'll investigate how the Web fits into the Internet and just what kinds of stuff you can look at out there.

What's Out There

As we go along, we're going to tell you what you can find using Netscape and where that stuff is located. You'll see notes like this describing an item of interest and giving you the item's URL (its *Uniform Resource Locator*, or address on the Web). Don't worry if you don't understand this URL business yet—you will soon, and then you can look for the stuff we've described.

◆ What the Internet Is All About

So what is this Internet thing we're hearing so much about? At its most basic level, you can think of the Internet as a vast collection of even vaster libraries of information, all available online for you to look at or retrieve and use. At another level, the Internet might be thought of as the computers that store the information and the networks that allow you to access the information on the computers. And finally (lest we forget who made the Internet what it is today), it is a collection of *people*—people who act as resources themselves, willing to share their knowledge with the world. This means, of course, that when you interact with the Internet—particularly when you make yourself a resource by sharing communications and information with others—you become a part of the vast network we call the Internet.

 The Internet is a global network of networks. When your stand-alone machine gets connected to the Internet, special software on your machine (obtained from your Internet access provider) "tricks" the Internet into accepting your machine as one of the networks that make up the Internet. Your machine—and you—become literally part of the Internet.

The idea of the Information Superhighway is a convenient metaphor: information flowing great distances at incredible speeds, with many on-ramps of access and many potential destinations. In the Information Superhighway of the future, we might expect an electronic replacement for the everyday postal system (this has already begun to happen in Germany, we're told) and convergence of our cable TV, phone, and newspapers into online information and entertainment services. These possibilities become closer to reality every day.

What's Out There

The Electronic Frontier Foundation (EFF) is active in lobbying to ensure that the Information Superhighway of the future includes protections for individual rights. You can find out about the EFF, and what it is up to, at `http://www.eff.org`. Other information about the government's initiative for building the Information Superhighway is available at `http://far.mit.edu/diig`.

We're not quite up to that fully integrated superhighway envisioned by futurists yet, but the Internet as it exists today delivers plenty of power. The resources and information you find on the Internet are available for use on the job, as part of personal or professional research, or for just plain fun. No matter how you view the Internet, the idea that individuals as well as corporations can access information around the world has a particular appeal that borders on the irresistible.

The Internet does act much like a highway system. High-speed data paths, called *backbones*, connect the major networks; these actually do function much like an electronic version of the interstate highways. Through lower-speed *links*, local networks tie in to the Internet, much as city streets feed onto highways (see Figure 1.2). The beauty of the Internet system is that not all networks are, or even need to be, directly connected, because the Internet structure is one of *interconnection*. You can, in effect, hop from network to network to get where you want and what you want.

The highway metaphor begins to break down, however, when you realize that the Internet transcends geography. It's a global system, that's true, but when you use the Net, you probably won't be very conscious that the material you're viewing on your screen at one moment is actually located on a machine in Switzerland and that what you see the next moment is actually on a machine in Japan. Perhaps a more accurate metaphor for the

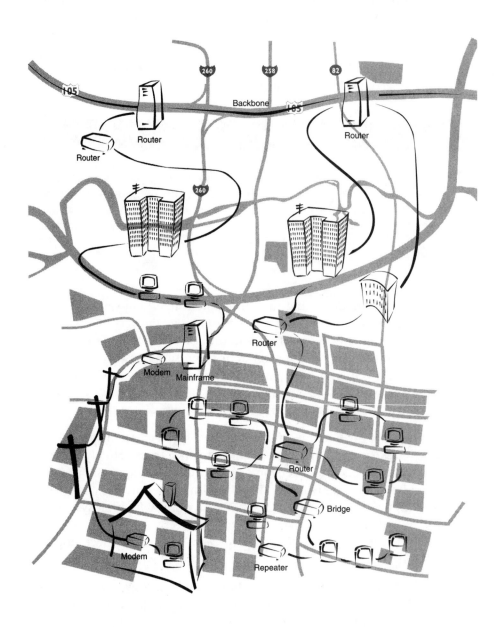

Figure 1.2: The Internet can be imagined as a system of highways and roadways, although it has no actual geography.

Internet would be having a global remote control at your fingertips, able to switch to just about any topic (channel if you prefer) of your choosing.

◆ Where It All Began

To understand how the Internet came into being, you'd have to go back 30 years or so, to the height of the Cold War era. The think-tank military planners of that age were concerned not only with surviving a nuclear war, but also with communicating in its aftermath if one should occur. They envisioned a control network, linking bases and command posts from state to state, that would remain operational despite direct attacks. With this in mind, the U.S. Defense Department's Advanced Research Projects Agency began work on a computer network called ARPAnet during the 1960s.

The principles of the network were simple. It had to operate from the outset as if it were "unreliable"—to adjust up-front for the possibility of downed communication links. Control, therefore, would be decentralized to further minimize any single point of failure. Data would be split up and sent on the network in individual Internet Protocol (IP) *packets*. (A packet can be thought of as similar to an envelope.) Each packet of data would carry within it the address of its destination and could reach its endpoint by the most efficient route. If part of the network became unavailable, the packets would still get to their destinations via an alternate route and would be reassembled with their full content intact.

Though at first this may sound inefficient, it put the burden of communicating on the computers themselves, rather than on the communications network. That was the foremost issue on the minds of the planners: that the system did not rely on a central *server* (a machine on the network that holds or processes data for the other machines on the network). This proposal linked the computers together as *peers* instead, giving each computer equal status on the network and allowing for different types of computers to communicate, de-emphasizing the communications infrastructure. Thus, even if large pieces of the network were destroyed, the data itself could still reach its destination because it was not concerned with *how* to get there. So it was that the Department of Defense commissioned the initial implementation of ARPAnet in 1969.

Perhaps you work in a business where a lot of machines are cabled together as a LAN *(local area network)*. Each of these networks is like a smaller version of the Internet, in that a bunch of machines are linked together; but they are not necessarily linked to other networks via phone lines. LANs also usually have a central *server*—a machine that holds data and processes communications between the linked machines, which is unlike the Internet in that if your LAN server goes down, your network goes down.

Throughout the '70s and early '80s, the ARPAnet continued to grow, and more developments occurred to spur interest in networking and the Internet. Other services and big networks came into being (such as Usenet and BITnet), and e-mail began to gain wide use as a communications tool. Local area networks (LANs) became increasingly common in business and academic use, until users no longer wanted to connect just select computers to the Internet but entire local networks (which might mean all the computers in the organization).

The original Internet, the ARPAnet, was replaced in 1986 by a new backbone, the National Science Foundation (NSFnet) network. NSFnet forever changed the scope of the Internet in that it permitted more than just a few lucky people in the military, academia, and large corporations to conduct research and access super-computer centers. (See Figure 1.3.) With the good, however, came the bad as well. More people using the Internet meant more network traffic, which meant slower response, which meant better connectivity solutions would have to be implemented. Which brings us to where we are today, with many companies (AT&T, Sprint, Netcom, UUNet, and more) running national backbones and demand increasing exponentially as more and more people want to connect to the Internet and discover the online riches of the '90s. (See Figure 1.4.)

◆ The Burning Issues of Control, Funding, and Use

Perhaps you've begun to wonder who runs this thing and who pays for it.

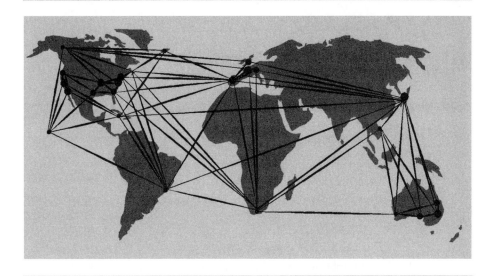

Figure 1.3: The Internet is a global resource, with servers on every continent.

What's Out There

Editor Win Treese has been compiling an extraordinary set of Internet figures and statistics in the style of Harper's Index. For a closer look, go to `http://www.openmarket.com/intindex/`.

Who Runs the Internet?

As odd as it may sound, no one person has overall authority for running the Internet. Despite this—or perhaps because of it—the Internet runs just fine, in the opinions of many people who use it. A group called the Internet Society (ISOC), composed of volunteers, directs the Internet. ISOC appoints a subcouncil, the Internet Architecture Board (IAB), and the members of this board work out issues of standards, network resources, network addresses, and the like. Another volunteer group, the Internet Engineering Task Force (IETF), tackles the more day-to-day issues of Internet operations. These Internet caretakers, if you will, have proven

Annual rate of growth for World Wide Web traffic: 341,634% (1st year)
Annual rate of growth for Gopher traffic: 997% (same year)

◆

Number of people over 16 in US and Canada with access to the Internet: 37 million (1996)
Number who have used the Internet in the past three months: 24 million
Number who have used the World Wide Web in the three months before the survey: 18 million

◆

Number of Internet-related events (conferences, workshops, etc.) scheduled for 1996: 95
Number of scheduled events to take place in Slovenia: 1
Number already scheduled for 1999:1

◆

Estimated number of U.S. newspapers offering interactive access: 3,200 (1995)

◆

Number of attendees at Internet World, April 1995: more than 20,000
Number of attendees at Internet World, December 1994: more than 10,000
Number of attendees at Internet World, January 1992: 272

◆

Date after which more than half the registered networks were commercial: August 1991

◆

Number of business listings of Web sites in the Commercial Sites Index: 15,379 (1996)
Average number of sites added to the Commercial Sites Index, per day: 73

◆

Number of online coffeehouses in San Francisco: 18
Cost for four minutes of Internet time at those coffeehouses: $0.25

◆

Estimated number of Usenet sites, worldwide: 260,000
Estimated number of readers of the Usenet group `rec.humor.funny`: 480,000

◆

At current growth rates, estimated time at which everyone on earth will be on the
Internet: 2004

◆

Amount of time it takes for Supreme Court decisions to become available on the Internet:
less than one day

Figure 1.4: These Internet statistics (courtesy of Win Treese) tell an amazing story.

What's Out There

You can find out more about these and other issues by visiting the Voters' Technology Watch at `http://www.vtw.org` and the Center for Democracy and Technology at `http://www.cdt.org`.

quite ably that success does not have to depend on your typical top-down management approach.

The Fuss about Government Regulation

As this book goes to press, there has been a lot of talk about regulation of the Internet by the U.S. government. Legislation has been discussed, proposed, and is in various stages of being voted on. The issues involved in this are many, most notable perhaps is the conflict between the international nature of the Net and the non-international nature of the legislation. Here's the dilemma: If a Web site produced in the Netherlands is acceptable by Dutch standards of "decency," but is then viewed by, say, a minor in Biloxi, Mississippi, the minor's community might not agree with the Dutch definition of decency, particularly for children. What to do?

Another issue involves whether Internet service providers should be treated as *common carriers*. Common carriers are companies in governmentally recognized businesses, like phone companies and mail delivery services, that offer service to anyone without taking responsibility for content. You may think because phone companies cooperate in catching obscene callers and because mail delivery services cooperate in discouraging use of their services for transporting illegal substances that they are responsible. But notice that in fact they are cooperating with authorities but incur no liability themselves if a user of their service breaks the law. The question in this case is whether Internet service providers fall into that category, or whether they are liable for the content that is delivered via their services.

Who Pays?

A common misconception has been that the Internet, by its very nature, is free, but this is certainly not the case. It costs a pretty penny to maintain a machine that can serve up stuff on the Internet, and someone has to pay those costs. Individual groups and institutions—such as the federal government (via the National Science Foundation), which runs NSFnet—do indeed pay to provide the information they serve on the Internet. Companies like AT&T, MCI, Sprint, Netcom, and UUNet incur costs in providing the backbones that they now maintain. And all those companies and organizations (and even plain folks) who are offering increasing amounts of Internet content are paying for content development, design, technical infrastructure, and maintenance of their sites, along with the use of high-speed communications lines of one sort or another. All this is not cheap.

At the other end, new users quickly find out that connecting to the Internet through a service provider (such as Netcom, CRL, or PSI) or a commercial online service (such as America Online or CompuServe) requires a monthly usage fee; and because it is necessary to connect through a phone line, telephone charges may also be involved.

Additionally, all these companies and people providing Internet content have now begun to look for ways to recoup their costs and perhaps even make a few bucks along the way. There are currently a few business models these content providers are trying on for size—for example, advertising on their sites, licensing their content to other companies or groups, getting paid sponsorship, and selling access via subscriptions or usage fees. Eventually they'll probably hit upon something that works and stick with it.

As you can see, the Internet is by no means free, although it is a great value. For content providers, it is an enormously successful new mass medium that takes their message out into a big world. For users, it is entrance into a universe of easy access to information, entertainment, and connection to other like-minded people.

◆ What You Can Do with the Internet

Once you are connected to the Internet, you can:

◆ View documents, browse, search for data, traverse other resources, see video and hear sound, explore interactive three-dimensional environments (via VRML), and publish your own material on the Internet via the *World Wide Web*.

◆ Send messages to friends and associates all over the world with *e-mail*. (This usually does not involve long-distance charges to you or the recipient; all you're charged for is the call to your Internet service provider, and, if that's a local number, it's a local call.)

◆ Communicate with others in real-time written conversation via *chat* and in verbal conversations transmitted over the Net via *Internet telephone*.

◆ Exchange ideas with other people in a public forum with *Usenet newsgroups*. (Note that unlike e-mail, which is more or less private, newsgroups are public. Everyone on the newsgroup can read what you post there.)

◆ Copy files from and to computers on the Internet with *FTP*. Many giant software archives, such as the CICA Windows archive, hold literally gigabytes of files you can retrieve.

◆ Connect to other computers on the Internet and use programs on them via *Telnet*.

◆ Traverse and search directories of information with *Gopher*.

Many of these tools are used (either visibly or behind the scenes) in the course of using Netscape, so we'll talk about each one as it arises in later chapters.

◆ The Internet As Medium

The Internet itself is just a medium. There's plenty of room to develop services to be used to make the most of the Internet, just as happened when the phone system was devised for simple communication and then many products and services were developed to take advantage of its potential (ranging from voice mail, pagers, and automated banking, to the 911 system and, in fact, the Internet).

Today we see many big and small companies, organizations, and just plain people with good ideas racing toward the Internet to make the most of it. As this happens, it is important for all of us to remember that the Internet is not just a big billboard system, not a table onto which one can throw a brochure. Just as when one turns on the television, one expects to see more content than advertising (and even then the advertising must have some entertainment appeal if we're actually to watch it and not change the channel), the Internet must be content-driven first and foremost.

The Internet's fundamental openness has been responsible for bringing forth a number of tools for use by the masses. A great example of this is, of course, Netscape. In the next chapter, we'll look at how you can access the best of the Internet—the World Wide Web—via Netscape.

Best of the Internet: The World Wide Web via Netscape

Before we leap head first into using Netscape, an appreciation of the World Wide Web is in order. Let's take a quick look at the Web. Then we'll glance at a typical Netscape session, and, still in this chapter, we'll talk more about what Netscape can do.

◆ How the Web Came to Be

The World Wide Web (a.k.a. WWW, W3, or simply, *the Web*) was originally developed to help physicists at Conseil Européen pour la Recherche Nucleaire (CERN), which is the European particle physics laboratory in Geneva, Switzerland. CERN is one of the world's largest scientific labs, composed of two organizations straddling the Swiss-French border—the European Laboratory for High Energy Physics in Switzerland, and the Organisation Européen pour la Recherche Nucleaire in France. The physicists there needed a way to exchange data and research materials quickly with other scientists.

The Web technology developed at CERN by Tim Berners-Lee enabled collaboration among members of research teams scattered all over the globe. How? Through a system that allows for *hypertext* links between documents on different computers.

Unlike regular documents, with static information on every page, *hypertext* documents have links built in so that readers can jump to more information about a topic by (typically) simply clicking on the word or picture identifying the item. That's why they call it hypertext—it's not just text, it's *hyper*text. (The term *hypertext* was coined by computer iconoclast Ted Nelson.) Hypertext is what makes Netscape—and many multimedia tools—possible. The term *hypermedia* is sometimes used to refer to hypertext with the addition of other data formats. In addition to text, Netscape supports graphics, video, sound, and a number of interactive formats, including VRML.

Before going to CERN, Berners-Lee had worked on document production and text processing and had developed for his own use a hypertext system—Enquire—in 1980. (According to some reports, he wasn't aware of the notion of hypertext at the time, but hypertext has been around since the Xanadu project in the 1960s.)

In 1992, the Web grew beyond the confines of CERN, and now its use and growth increase exponentially. This was all part of the plan in a sense—the Web was meant to allow for open access—but it's hard to imagine that anyone could have expected the phenomenon that's occurred.

Protocols, HTTP, and Hypertext: What It All Means

The Web's rapid expansion can be attributed in part to its extensive use of hypertext, held together by the HyperText Transfer Protocol (HTTP). A *protocol* is an agreed-upon system for passing information back and forth that allows the transaction to be efficient (HTTP is a *network protocol*, which means it's a protocol for use with networks).

Here's how this goes: If you (the *client*) go into a fast-food place, the counterperson (the *server*) says, "May I help you?" You answer something like, "I'll have a Big Burger with cheese, fries, and a cola." Then he or she verifies your order by repeating it, tells you the cost, and concludes the transaction by trading food for cash. Basically, when you walk into any fast-food place, you'll follow that same pattern and so will the person who takes your order. That's because you both know the *protocol*. The fast-food protocol is part of what makes it "fast food."

In just that way, HTTP, which is the protocol that was developed as part of the Web project, enables the kinds of network conversations that need to occur quickly between computers so that leaps can be made from one document to another. You can use other protocols to do the same things HTTP does (Netscape is *open-ended*, meaning that it's designed to support other network protocols as well as HTTP), but HTTP is terrifically efficient at what it does.

◆ Information from Around the Globe

Web servers are located in many countries around the world, providing information on any topic you might imagine; a typical session using the Web might lead you through several continents. For example, your search for information in the field of psychology may start at Yale and end up at a research hospital in Brussels, all within a few mouse-clicks that lead you along a series of hypertext links from a file at one location to another somewhere else.

The caveat here is that links are forged by the people who publish the information, and they may not make the same kinds of connections you would. That's why it's important to keep an open mind as you adventure around in the Web—just as you would when browsing in a library. You never know what you'll stumble across while you're looking for something else; conversely, you might have to do a bit of looking around to find exactly what you're seeking.

Who Makes This Information Available

Much of the information originally published on the Web existed thanks to the interest (and kindness) of the academic and research community; for a long time, almost all information about the Web (and the Internet) was available through the work of that community.

On "Mosaic" and Netscape

Maybe you're a bit confused about all the different "Mosaics" and how Netscape fits into the Mosaic picture. The short version of this story is that Netscape is Mosaic-like, but it's not Mosaic...Well, not exactly.

The first version of Mosaic, which was developed by Marc Andreessen and a team of programmers at the National Center for Supercomputing Applications (NCSA), was X Mosaic for Unix workstations. Later, versions of NCSA Mosaic became available for Windows-based PCs and the Macintosh. NCSA Mosaic was, for a time, distributed freely via the Net itself. Anyone could download and use the software without charge.

In mid-1994, NCSA began to license the rights to version 1.*x* of the software to other (often commercial) organizations. These organizations are allowed, by virtue of their licensing agreements with NCSA, to enhance the software. They can then *distribute* the enhanced software (called a *distribution*), and they can license others to distribute the software along with whatever enhancements they've included in their distribution. All distributions of Mosaic have the word *Mosaic* in their names.

In their wisdom, the folks at Netscape (Marc Andreessen again, along with some other very smart people) created and marketed a *new* Web browser— one that was faster and more reliable than Mosaic. They also made the new browser *secure*. (They wanted you to be able to conduct economic transactions, or in other words *buy* things, over the Internet without fear of someone stealing and using your credit card number.) The result of this venture, Netscape, took the World Wide Web by storm and was soon named by *Wired* magazine as one of its favorite products. Today it is estimated that over 75 percent of the people using the Web are using Netscape to do their surfing.

Increasingly, the Web has become a forum for commercial use. Given that the telephone system did not fully develop for personal use until it was seen by commerce as a tool for business, we see commercial use of the Web as a positive development. Commercial users of the Web must, however, adhere to the Internet philosophy in that they have to give to the Internet as well as use it. Along these lines, it's now unsurprising to find useful information and entertaining content that have been created as a vehicle for a corporation's advertising (in a twist on the network TV model) or sponsored by some big company (in the PBS model). Not only will you find store locators at a company's Web site, but you may find a full range of lifestyle magazines (as you do at the Toyota site), which have nothing much to do with the product being sold (Toyotas, in that case).

Actually, anyone can become a Web publisher, as you'll see in Chapter 9. You, your neighbor, or an enterprising person almost anywhere on the globe might be compelled by an impulse to publish something you think interesting to others on the Web. Many Internet service providers now offer the opportunity to publish free or cheap Web pages to all of their users. This makes the Web the ultimate vanity press as well as an extraordinary mass communications tool.

Web servers can be set up for strictly in-house purposes too. For example, a large organization with massive amounts of internal documentation or a smaller organization with shared documentation might publish that material on an in-house Web called an *intranet*. Intranets can also be made available through password-protection to outside contractors or telecommuting employees, making it possible to expand the idea of *in-house* to mean not just "in the building" but "company-wide." Just as members of a research team can use the Web to collaborate without having to be in the same location (fulfilling the original intentions of the Web's creators), so can members of a company's workgroup.

What Types of Information Exist

Internet indexes like Yahoo, which began as the project of two university graduate students, cover specific topics ranging from the entertaining to the academic. (Chapter 8 introduces some of these services.) Many, many newspapers and magazines are moving to the Web, and whole new types of publications (*Suck, the Salon, Web Review*) are sprouting up daily.

What's Out There

A growing number of high-tech companies are making information available on the Web. Some familiar names—Microsoft, Novell, and Sybex—all maintain presences on the Web. You can access these companies' Web sites at:

`http://www.microsoft.com`

`http://www.novell.com`

`http://www.sybex.com`

Consumer-oriented Web sites (see Figure 2.1) include Crayola, which provides colorful background on the making of crayons *and* the removal of crayon-based stains. Time Warner publishes news of all sorts, ranging from the hard-hitting daily stuff to more entertaining fare, at its Pathfinder site. You can tour Graceland via the Web, finding photos of the "King" and listening to sound clips of Elvis music, and you can even order a pizza using a Web order form. (This last is a pilot project so far; the pizza will be delivered only if you live in Santa Cruz, California. Solamente in California, eh?) We'll show you how to explore these and many other places in Appendix B.

What's Out There

We accessed Crayola with the URL: `http://www.crayola.com/crayola/`

◆ The Role of the Browser

So far we've talked mainly about the structure and content of the Web, describing some of the information and links that make up the Web. So how does one jump into this Web and start cruising? You need a tool called a *browser*.

Figure 2.1: Many companies see the Web as a way to put their messages in front of a wide audience.

Now, at the risk of sounding like the nerds we said you don't have to be, a browser, in technical terms, is a client process running on your computer that accesses a server process—in the case of the Web, the HTTP service—over the network. This is what's being discussed when people describe the Web as being based on *client-server* technology.

More simply put, the browser establishes contact with the server, reads the files—hypertext documents—made available on the HTTP server, and displays that stuff on your computer.

The document displayed by the browser is a hypertext document that contains references (or *pointers*) to other documents, which are very likely on other HTTP servers. These pointers are also called *links*. When you select a link from a hypertext page, the browser sends the request back to the new server, which then displays on your machine yet another page full of links.

In the same way you and a waiter at a restaurant have a client-server relationship when you ask for and receive water, a browser and the Web have a client-server relationship. The browser sends requests over the network to the Web server, which then provides a screenful of information back to your computer.

A Couple of Caveats Sitting Around Talking

Remember that the Web is ever-changing by its very nature. In this book, we attempt to guide you toward a lot of sites that seem to have stable locations and an ongoing existence. Some others are just so interesting or unusual we can't pass them up, though. If you don't find a site we've described, it may be that it has gone the way of all things. Not to worry; something even more remarkable will probably crop up elsewhere. Another thing is that in the growing, ever-expanding Web, many of the servers you encounter may not be complete—their links may be "under construction." Sometimes you'll see a warning of this, but sometimes you won't. Remember, the Web is by its very nature under construction; that's the beauty of the beast.

Before Web browsers such as Netscape were developed, all of this had to be accomplished using text-based browsers—the basic difference between them and browsers such as Netscape is just like the difference between PC programs written for DOS and those written for Windows. (DOS was text-based, so using DOS required you to type in commands to see and use text-filled screens; Windows, like Netscape, is graphical, so all you have to do is point and click on menu items and icons to see and use more graphically presented screens.) Figure 1.1 in Chapter 1 shows two views of the same information—one viewed with a text-based browser, the other with Netscape.

How HTML Fits In

In early 1993, the Software Development Group (SDG) of NCSA at the University of Illinois at Urbana-Champaign was researching an easy-to-use way to access the Internet. This led them to explore the World Wide Web and use of the HyperText Markup Language (HTML). HTML was being used for marking up documents on the Web—it's HTML that is used to *make* the document; browsers such as Netscape simply allow you to look at it easily.

HTML, a mark-up language with which text can be made to look like a page, is the coding scheme used in hypertext documents that both handles the text formatting on screen and makes it possible to create *links* to other documents, graphics, sound, and movies. Figure 2.2 shows a Netscape document and the HTML coding that was used to create the document.

```
<H1> Contents</H1>
<BODY>
<IMG Src="Cover94.2.gif">
<P>
<H4>Cover: Virtual environments for investigating
    science and engineering projects, one of NCSA's
    major technology directions, is the subject of this
    issue. Symbols from science and fine art represent
    the melding of these two knowledge bases that are
    needed in the creation of interactive, immersive
    technologies.
    <br>
    Cover produced on a Macintosh IIci using Adobe
    Photoshop, Adobe Dimensions, Aldus FreeHand, and a
    UMAX UC630 scanner. (Concept and illustration, John
    Havlik; concept and research, Fran Bond)</h4>
<P>
<H3><A HREF="http://www.ncsa.uiuc.edu/General/NCSAContacts.html">Contac
<H3> <A HREF="EdNote.html"><IMG SRC="../Icons/EdNote.gif">
    Editor's Note: Virtually experiencing science</H3></A>

<UL>
<LI> <A HREF = "VEToolset.html"> A virtual environments toolset driven by scien
<LI> <A HREF = "VROOMScientists.html"> VROOM Scientists on VR</A>
```

Cover: Virtual environments for investigating science and engineering projects, one of NCSA's major technology directions, is the subject of this issue. Symbols from science and fine art represent the melding of these two knowledge bases that are needed in the creation of interactive, immersive technologies.
Cover produced on a Macintosh IIci using Adobe Photoshop, Adobe Dimensions, Aldus FreeHand, and a UMAX UC630 scanner. (Concept and illustration, John Havlik; concept and research, Fran Bond)

Contacts Directory

Editor's Note: Virtually experiencing science

● A virtual environments toolset driven by science
● VROOM Scientists on VR

Figure 2.2: Here you can see the HTML coding (above) that makes this document (below) look the way it does.

Looking into HTML

If you want to see what HTML looks like, while viewing a Web page in Netscape, you can select View ➤ Document Source from Netscape's menu bar. A window will open showing the HTML for that page. You can't change the HTML you see, but you can copy pieces of it or even the whole thing to your Windows Clipboard (highlight what you want and press Ctrl+C) or you can save it as a text file to your local machine (see Chapter 3). Click on the Close button in the upper-right corner of your screen when you're done, and your view will once more be the document as it appears in Netscape.

Remember, though, that Netscape is not just a way to look at visually appealing pages on the Internet. It also provides dynamic linking capabilities within a hypertext document and even search options. HTML, then, is the core building block of those capabilities. We'll get into this more and more as we go along…

♦ Using Netscape to Access World Wide Web Information

Using Netscape, you can skim material quickly, or you can stop and delve into topics as deeply as you wish. Let's take a quick look at a Netscape session in action.

A Typical Netscape Session

To start Netscape, we first start our Internet connection, then double-click on the Netscape Navigator icon on the Desktop. (We'll go over starting the software again in detail in Chapter 3.) The Welcome to Netscape page (see Figure 2.3) appears on screen. From here we can traverse the Web by clicking on links, which appear on the home page as pictures and as underlined words in some special color (traditionally blue).

Figure 2.3: The Welcome to Netscape page will be your first view of the Internet via Netscape Navigator.

From Netscape's menu bar we select Directory ➤ Internet Search to open up Netscape's NetSearch page—a convenient way to search the Internet for information. You can see it in Figure 2.4.

Figure 2.4: Searching the Internet for Pamela Anderson using Netscape's NetSearch page is no trouble at all.

Netscape's NetSearch page allows you to search the Internet using a variety of high-profile indexes, directories, and search engines. See Chapter 8 for complete details about searching the Net.

What's Out There

You can get to the NetSearch page by selecting Directory ➤ Internet Search from Netscape's menu bar. There, you'll be offered a range of easy-to-use search options.

We type into the space next to the Search button a term to describe the topic of interest to us—in our case *Pamela Anderson*. Then we click on the Search button to start the search. Once the search is done, the results will appear on screen.

In the first entry we see, the phrase <u>Barb Wire</u> is in blue—it's a link to a site about the movie. We click on the link to access the Barb Wire Web site, and the server there forks up the Barb Wire home page (complete with a picture of the ever-alluring Pamela). You can see it in Figure 2.5.

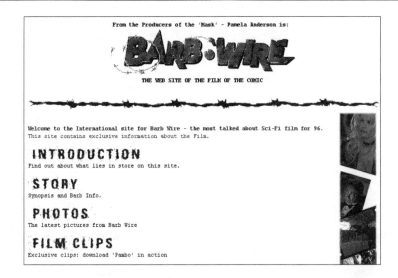

Figure 2.5: Pamela Anderson's movie, *Barb Wire,* is the subject of this Web site.

The *Barb Wire* home page is our entry point to a site with scads of information about the movie. Here we can click on links to explore pictures, video clips, information about the sound score, a puzzle, and a contest.

We can, if we like, click on a link on this page to follow it to some other page about Pamela, or we can click on Netscape's Back button to return to the list of sites the search brought up and go from there to explore another aspect of Pamela Anderson's doings. But our curiosity about Pamela Anderson is satisfied (we didn't really have much to begin with), so we exit the program directly from where we happen to be by selecting File ➤ Exit from Netscape's menu bar.

◆ Netscape Is Fast

There can be an awful lot of data involved in transferring graphics, and your 14,400 or even 28,800 bps modem acts as a bottleneck through which the data must squeeze. Many Web browsers halt all their other operations while they make you wait for images to appear. Netscape was designed specifically to get around this issue: Instead of waiting 'til the graphics appear, Netscape goes ahead and shows you the text on the page and allows you to start working with it. You can click on links in the text, for example, and move on to the next page of interest to you, before the graphics in the original page have appeared.

Further, you can decide whether you want the graphics to appear at all. Netscape, like other Web browsers, usually shows you both the text and the graphics in a given Web page. But if you find the graphics bogging you down, you can turn them off and see only the text.

To toggle off the graphics, making it so you'll see only text, select Options ➤ Auto Load Images from Netscape's menu bar. After you do this, the Web pages you view will include little markers where the graphics go. If you're viewing a page with graphics toggled off and you decide you want to see the graphics after all, just click on the Images icon on Netscape's tool bar and the page will be reloaded, this time with its graphics.

To toggle graphics back on, so you'll see them loaded a moment after the text for each page appears, select Options ➤ Auto Load Images again from the menu bar. (Note that this is a *toggle* situation, so you can go back and forth in your choice to include or exclude images again and again using the exact same process.)

Wanderers, Spiders, and Robots—Oh My!

In June 1993, there were about 130 Web sites on the Internet. One year later, the number hit 2000. Now there are over a million. So how do you find what you need in this ever-expanding haystack? Wouldn't it be great to know what's out on the Web, and where?

You can find out by consulting World Wide Web indexes and search tools that use creatures known as *wanderers, spiders, crawlers,* or *robots.* An assortment of Web robots have been developed since the beginnings of the WWW; these programs travel through the Web and find HTTP files—the files that make up the content of the Web. Some robots were designed strictly to track growth on the Web.

The more interesting and useful Web crawlers are those that dump the information they gather into a place that's readable by the rest of us browsers. The information is then collected into a searchable database that's also sometimes indexed or otherwise catalogued—Yahoo, Lycos, and Alta Vista are all examples of this technology in action. Check out Chapter 8 for information about accessing indexes, guides, and search tools that use Web crawler technology.

◆ How Data Travels

Usually you can't install Netscape on your Windows computer and expect it simply to work. You have to go through a little rigmarole to get things going. The interface mechanism between the client—Netscape—and the Web server (the machine dishing up the information you want to view) depends on the Internet protocol known as TCP/IP (Transmission Control Protocol/Internet Protocol). TCP/IP creates *packets* (see Figure 2.6)—which are like electronic envelopes to carry data on a network—and then places the packets on the network. It also makes it possible, of course, to receive packets.

The Domain Name System and Packets

There is a system responsible for administering and keeping track of domains, and (believe it or not) it's called the Domain Name System (DNS for short). DNS is a distributed system that administers names by allowing

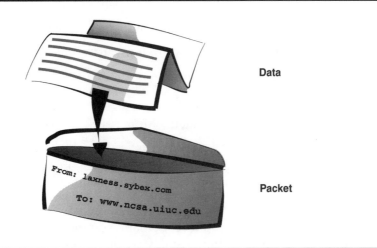

Data

Packet

From: laxness.sybex.com
To: www.ncsa.uiuc.edu

Figure 2.6: Data (e-mail, documents, video, whatever) travels across the Internet in *packets*.

different groups control over subsets of names. In this system, there can be many levels or domains, but the top-level domains are standardized.

In addition to the more familiar "English" names, all machines on the Internet have an Internet address in the form of four numbers separated by decimals; this is because, while a user might change the "English" address, an address is needed that will never change. This numeric address is organized in a system commonly called *dotted decimal notation*. An example of a host computer's address would be **130.19.252.21**. These numeric addresses work fine for machines communicating with one another, but most people find them cumbersome to use and tricky to remember. To help people out, host computers were given names, such as *ruby* or *topaz*, making it easier to remember and to facilitate connecting.

However, other factors came into play, such as making sure that each machine on the Internet had a unique name, registering the names in a centrally managed file, and distributing the file to everyone on the Internet. This system worked adequately when the Internet was still small, but as it grew in size, so did the size of the file keeping track of all the host names.

The common standard American domains are as follows:

`com`	Commercial business, company, or organization
`edu`	Educational institution (university, etc.)
`gov`	Nonmilitary government site
`mil`	Military site
`net`	Any host associated with network administration, such as a gateway
`org`	Private organization (nonacademic, nongovernmental, and noncommercial)

These domains are referred to as *descriptive* domains. In addition, each country also has its own top-level domain, commonly called a *geographical* domain. Here in the United States, we are in the us domain. Other examples of countries represented with domains include:

`au`	Australia
`ca`	Canada
`fr`	France

Just as you need not know the internal workings of the U.S. Postal Service to use the system and get your mail, you don't need to know all about TCP/IP to use Netscape. But it does help to have some understanding.

TCP/IP is not part of Netscape; it's part of your local network if you're on one. If you're not on a local network, though—if, for example, you're using your stand-alone machine at home or at work—you can still use Netscape. In that case, you have to have special network drivers loaded (not to worry, Windows 95 includes them). These drivers make things go back and forth over the phone connection using the protocol Netscape understands. We'll talk more about this in Chapter 10.

 If you're using a PC on a LAN that's already connected to the Internet, you're probably already set up with the TCP/IP software you need to run Netscape, and you can just use your company's connection. Your network administrator can clue you in to the details of running TCP/IP-based software such as Netscape.

◆ What Netscape Recognizes

Netscape has many big selling points, one of which is that it provides one-stop shopping for the Web by handling a variety of *data types*. Data types are just that—types of data. Having standard types of data makes it possible for one machine (indeed, a program) to recognize and use data that was created on another machine (and maybe even in another program). The data types recognized by Netscape include:

- ◆ HTML
- ◆ Text or Plain Text
- ◆ Graphics
- ◆ Sound
- ◆ Video
- ◆ Animation
- ◆ Virtual Reality

The data type that the Web was designed around is HTML, the type the HyperText Transfer Protocol we've talked so much about was designed to transfer.

HTTP servers, the servers that make up the World Wide Web, serve hypertext documents (coded with HTML, as we've discussed). These documents are not just what you view; these HTML documents actually guide you through the Web when you're cruising.

Netscape's Use of Plug-Ins and Helper Apps

For those data types that it can't handle directly, Netscape uses plug-ins and helper applications—these are two types of software that might specialize in displaying a graphic or playing a sound, a movie, or both. *Plug-ins* actually integrate into Netscape and allow new data types to appear right in the Netscape window. *Helper applications* (helper apps) are separate programs that launch themselves and appear in a distinct window when Netscape encounters a data type it needs help to run.

E-Mail Addressing

Electronic mail, or e-mail, is the established form of communication on the Internet. In fact, typically this is where most of us encounter the Internet for the first time. A friend tells you his Internet e-mail address at work is `kmfez@schwartz.com` and asks for your e-mail address, and you begin exchanging messages that magically pop up in your on-screen e-mail in-basket. Users around the country—for that matter, around the world— readily grasp e-mail as a quick, convenient means for conducting business or just for staying in touch (and for doing so without the expense associated with a long-distance phone call). How does e-mail work? It's actually a lot like the postal service. E-mail uses addressing and a "store and forward" mechanism. This means that there is a standard way of addressing, and the mail is routed from one place to another until ultimately it appears at its destination. Along the way, if necessary, a machine can store the mail until it knows how to forward it.

Of course, there is a little more than that to sending e-mail on its way, but not much. The address in your e-mail header, much like the address on a postal letter, contains all the information necessary to deliver the message to the recipient. In the world of the Internet, a person's e-mail address is made up of two parts: a user name and a computer name, indicating where the user's ID is located.

In the example `kmfez@schwartz.com`, `kmfez` is the user portion of the address, and `schwartz.com` is the name of the location (actually a host machine). The last part of the location's name, `.com`, is known as the *high-level domain*—in this case `.com` tells you that it is a *com*mercial organization. If `.edu` appeared instead, you'd know it was an *edu*cational organization.

An address can actually contain many domains, which you see separated by periods, like this: `joke.on.you.com`.

If multiple domains appear in an address, they move in hierarchy from right to left. As you read to the left, the domains get smaller in scope.

Netscape comes with a number of plug-ins and helper apps, for example a QuickTime movie viewer and the CoolTalk program that offers users such new features as Internet phone, chat, and whiteboarding. (See Chapter 12 for more on getting and using plug-ins and helper apps.)

Netscape Navigator also comes with very credible sound and video players integrated into it so you can play most sound and video files you come across while surfing the Net. (Assuming you have a sound card....)

How Plug-Ins and Helper Apps Work

Briefly, here's how plug-ins and helper apps work: Netscape looks at the first part (the *header*) of the file; the header tells Netscape what it needs to know to deal with the file appropriately. Text files are displayed on screen, in the very attractive way Netscape displays them. Compressed files, such as graphics, are uncompressed and then displayed. But when Netscape encounters a sound or video file, the program "knows" it needs help, and it launches the appropriate plug-in or helper app to "play" the file—if you have the plug-in or helper app on your machine, you won't see much evidence of this; you'll just hear the sound or see the movie on screen.

Many plug-ins and helper apps are available from many Internet sources (including anonymous FTP servers and the Web) and for all types of files. Netscape maintains pages at its Web site that describe plug-ins and helper apps.

 Remember that plug-ins and helper apps are separate programs from Netscape (they are often produced by companies other than Netscape, and they are actually distinct programs from Netscape) and that support in using them will come—if at all—only from their respective authors, not from the producers of sites where you got them. If you have questions about how to use any given plug-in or helper app, you must go to its author to get help.

 With the help of plug-ins and helper apps, you can play video and sound clips with Netscape, but you should avoid doing so if you have a modem connection (as opposed to a LAN connection) to the Internet. Most sound and video files are multi-megabytes in size. As a rough estimate, each megabyte takes about 15 minutes to transfer with a 14,400 bps modem (that is, on a good day with prevailing winds). It might take literally hours to access a single, relatively short video clip.

Let's talk for a minute about those types of data Netscape most commonly needs a plug-in or helper app to work with. (We'll go into more detail about how to use this stuff starting in later chapters.)

Sound   Netscape comes with a perfectly good plug-in that handles many popular sound formats, recognizing Windows audio files (WAV) and Basic audio (AU) files as linked data. Remember that sound files can be very large and take a long time to transfer over a slow connection, and that you need a sound card to use them.

Video   Netscape also comes with plug-ins that handle QuickTime movies (MOV) and Microsoft video (AVI) files. You'll need to install additional plug-ins and helper apps to view video in any other formats (such as the MPEG and VDO formats). You can find out more about installing the plug-ins and helper apps to handle these files in Chapter 12. Again, remember that many video files you'll come across as you begin to work with Netscape are, in the words of Tiny Elvis, "huge." Make sure you've got enough memory to cope with them.

Animation   You don't need a plug-in or helper app for animations that are the result of Java, server pushes, or GIF89s. (We'll talk more about this throughout later chapters.) But when you run across animation and other special effects that have been created using MacroMedia's Director, you'll need the ShockWave plug-in for Netscape, which was also developed by MacroMedia (and is given away for free). We talk about getting and installing the ShockWave plug-in quite specifically in Chapter 12.

Virtual Reality   Through the virtual reality technology known as VRML, you can view and travel through three-dimensional worlds displayed on your computer screen. These worlds can represent anything from the familiar—rooms or retail stores—to the abstract—weird landscapes or alien places. They can also include hyperlinks to other VRML worlds, or even to simpler Web pages. Netscape Navigator version 3 comes with the Live3D plug-in, which allows Netscape to display VRML worlds.

These are just some of the ways you can extend Netscape to handle new data formats. Many, many new plug-ins and helper apps are being developed for use with Netscape all the time. Keep your eye on the Netscape site for announcements and links to help you stay in tune.

◆ Netscape As a Consistent Interface to Other Internet Resources

In addition to providing a nice graphical user interface to linked multi-media information, Netscape provides a consistent interface to other information types available on the Internet. Let's take a quick look at the kinds of resources that make up the Internet and that you can access using Netscape.

E-Mail: For Fast Communications

As mentioned, most people's Internet experience starts with e-mail, the lightning-fast medium for communicating with other individuals or even (via mailing lists) with groups. In the past, some Web browsers allowed you to send e-mail, but they didn't let you receive it. Why's that? Well, basically, *receiving* requires a place for the mail to sit until you retrieve it (a mail box) and a way for you to read it (a mail reader) once you've got it.

...Receiving is more complicated than sending. Netscape includes full e-mail capability—you can both send and receive e-mail with Netscape.

 A really cool aspect of this is that Netscape's mail reader has lots of new power—it lets you view mail that includes graphics, fancy font effects, and color changes. See Chapter 5 for more on how to use Netscape's e-mail features.

We talked a lot about e-mail in earlier sections of this chapter—take a look at *How Data Travels* and *E-Mail Addressing* to find out how e-mail makes its way around the Internet world.

FTP: For Transferring Files

For transferring a file or program from one machine (a server, for example) to another (yours, for example), FTP (File Transfer Protocol) is still the popular choice, although the mechanics of FTP are now often hidden behind a Web page link.

CoolTalk: For Interactive Communications

Netscape Navigator version 3 comes with an extra nifty program called CoolTalk that offers you the chance to include chat, Internet phone, and whiteboarding in your Netscape experience. These are highly dynamic, interactive communications options. Chat lets you "talk" interactively with others by typing in your part of the conversation while they type in their part. Internet phone lets you actually speak over the Internet with other people (who, obviously, are also speaking over the Internet). In this case, the vocal transmission is of poor quality, but the idea's just terrific and has been highly popular in the form of stand-alone programs that have appeared over the course of late 1995 and early '96. Whiteboarding mimics on screen the utility of those whiteboards people draw on in meetings and classrooms, by providing an online drawing area that several people can interact with and view at once. More on this stuff in Chapter 6.

In its traditional modes FTP only lets you see a list of the files on a computer and transfer them to your machine, usually through *anonymous FTP*. (See *Anonymous FTP Explained Here*.) Still, FTP should not be overlooked for what it has accomplished and still does, namely, allowing users to bring home files, information, and software.

After retrieving a file, you may need to perform some additional steps if the file has been compressed to save space. This involves using a utility to uncompress, or unzip, the file to make it usable. There are many compression formats in use, so you may find yourself cursing sometimes rather than jumping for joy when you uncover just the file you are looking for but are unable to unzip it.

Netscape presents FTP directories as a graphical menu using icons similar to those used by the Windows Explorer. Directories are represented by a folder icon; text files are displayed as the familiar sheet-of-paper-with-its-top-corner-folded-down. These items all appear as links—they are underlined so that you can click on them to move to the place in question.

Another advantage of Netscape, over say a regular FTP session, is that Netscape reads the file type, so it can display a text file on screen when

Anonymous FTP Explained Here

Anonymous FTP permits users to access remote systems without actually having user accounts on the systems. In effect, it allows for "guests" to visit a remote site, and it permits just enough computer privileges to access the resources provided. The process involves the user starting an FTP connection and logging in to the remote computer as the user "anonymous," with an arbitrary password that, for the purposes of Internet etiquette, should be your e-mail address. The beauty of using Netscape for anonymous FTP is that with Netscape you don't have to go through all the login steps, you don't have to use a text-based FTP program on your machine, and Netscape displays all the stuff on the FTP server in an easy-to-use graphical interface. You can tell when a Web document you are viewing in Netscape comes from an anonymous FTP site because the URL starts with `ftp:`.

you click on the link. A regular FTP session involves copying the file to your computer and then opening it later using a text editor.

Likewise, Netscape will deal with sound, image, and video files that appear as links (in the FTP list) as it does in other contexts, displaying the text, picture, or movie, or playing the sound when you click on the link.

Netscape may have to be properly configured with the appropriate external player and viewer applications in order to play sounds or movies and display pictures. Also, once Netscape plays the sound or movie, it's gone. You'll learn how to save the images, sounds, and videos in Chapter 3.

Gopher: For Searching and Finding

When you use a URL in Netscape that begins with `gopher:`, your copy of Netscape is talking to a Gopher server. Originally developed at the University of Minnesota as a front-end to Telnet and FTP, for a while Gopher was one of the more important information retrieval tools on the Internet, although it has long since been eclipsed by the Web.

If you access Gopher information with Netscape, you are presented with a series of menu choices, much like the directory structure one sees in the Microsoft Windows Explorer. By clicking on icons, you can traverse the directory structure a level at a time until you come to an item. If the item is a file to download, Gopher invokes an FTP session. If the item is a link to another computer, Gopher invokes a Telnet session so you can use that computer. All this happens without the necessity of your worrying about Internet addressing schemes, domains, host names, and such.

Usenet Newsgroups: All the News You'd Ever Want

The first stop for new Internet browsers (after e-mail) typically used to be network news (also known as *newsgroups*), although with the advent of graphical tools such as Netscape, this is no longer the case.

Network news is like e-mail in that you are reading and possibly replying to messages, but unlike it in that you are able to partake of a broader scope of *public* conversations and discussions, with as little or as much participation as you want. You don't even have to take part—you can just stand back and watch if you'd prefer. (That's called *lurking*, but it's not looked upon as being as ominous as it sounds.) There are literally thousands of discussion groups on nearly every subject imaginable; you can join in or just cruise through them as you like.

Because it is organized into *newsgroups*, it is very easy to work your way through the major headings and then through the newsgroups themselves. You need a *newsreader*, a piece of software that organizes and sorts the newsgroups—Netscape provides a very capable newsreader. You can subscribe (and unsubscribe) to your favorite newsgroups, post your own articles, and read articles. We'll go over all this in detail in Chapter 5.

◆ The Human Side of Hypermedia

The Web offers a rich environment for exploring tangential or directly related information because the hypertext paradigm works the way people do when they're on the road to discovery. For example, if you were a kid in the '60s or '70s working on a book report about Native

Behind the Usenet Scenes

The major (but not the only) source of network news is Usenet, which is a free service. Usenet was actually born before the Internet, and much confusion exists as to how the two interact.

Usenet is not a network like the Internet, there are no Usenet computers per se, and Usenet doesn't even need the Internet. Rather, what drives Usenet is akin to an agreement set up between those who want to distribute and those who want to read newsgroups. Network administrators arrange with other administrators to transfer newsgroups back and forth, which usually occurs via the Internet, but only because that's convenient.

The site that provides your site with news is called a *news feed*.

Some newsgroups end up being transferred by some computers, others by other computers, and so on.

American cultures, your process might have looked like this: You began by reading the encyclopedia article on *Indians* (this, remember, is before Native Americans were referred to as such) when you came to a passage describing the dislocation of the Hopi people to a reservation near what is called today Apache Junction, Arizona.

Having never been near Arizona, you decided to find out about its climate, terrain, flora and fauna. Putting the *I* volume aside on the floor, you grabbed the *A* volume and dipped into *Arizona*. Then you wondered, "What's it like today?" You called the Apache Junction Chamber of Commerce and asked for recent industrial and employment statistics. Later that day, curious about the status of any national reparations made to the Hopi in Arizona, you made a trip to your local library and had a chat with the reference librarian, who in turn brought you copies of various federal government policy statements.

Thus, the kind of discovery process supported by hypertext—and the Web—is really modeled after the way people tend to work when they're learning new things. It's easy to see why the hypertext paradigm and the Web have really taken off. If you want more information, you can just click on a Web page link and there you are: The linked item could be a

Web page on a server 7500 miles away. If you were writing that book report today, you might travel all over the world, via the Web, without ever leaving your computer.

Moving Along...

With all this backstory in place, you're ready now to hit the highway. Starting with the next chapter, we're going to dig into how you do what you do with Netscape and the Web. Let's hit the road.

Part Two:

Navigating and Publishing with Netscape

3

Navigating Netscape

Let's get working with Netscape. In this chapter, you'll learn how to start the program, how to open and save Web documents, and how to switch between documents and other hypermedia (sound and video, for example) via *hot links*. You'll also get a good look at navigating through *frames*, which are like window panes within a document.

 This chapter assumes you already have an Internet connection and have installed Netscape on your PC. For information on making your Internet connection work and on getting and installing Netscape, see Chapters 10 and 11.

◆ Launching Netscape

Launching Netscape is easy. If you followed the instructions for getting the software and setting it up in Chapters 10 and 11, you'll have a Netscape icon on your Desktop, and you'll have a new item in your Programs menu named Netscape. To start Netscape, follow these steps:

1. Start your Internet connection. How you do this depends on the sort of Internet service you have—see Chapter 10 for details about connecting to the Internet.

2. Now start up Netscape. You can do this in one of two ways:

◆ Double-click on the Desktop's Netscape Navigator icon, shown here.

Netscape
Navigator

or

◆ From the Windows Start menu, select Programs ➤ Netscape to display the Netscape window. Then double-click on the Netscape Navigator icon.

SLIP and PPP: The Netscape Connection

Before you can start using Netscape, you must start the connection software that you use to access the Internet. This may seem a bit more complicated than starting many other programs, but it's really no big deal.

Here's how it works: You start your connection software—it can be Windows 95 Dial-Up Networking, Netcom's Netcomplete, or whatever you choose—which then connects your computer to the Internet. This software "introduces" Netscape to the Internet—it is a vital link in your Internet connection. (At one time, this could be accomplished only through special SLIP/PPP software, but nowadays there are new and different technologies, included with Windows 95, for example, that accomplish the same purpose.) Your connection software and your provider will then do a little dance together, passing back and forth the TCP/IP packets that make it possible for you to run Netscape (which is on your machine). Voilà—the Internet accepts your machine as a little network hooked into the bigger, more exciting network called the Internet, and you're on your way!

You can also start Netscape by double-clicking on any Windows 95 Internet shortcut. Internet shortcuts appear as Netscape icons and can be located on the Desktop, in folders, or even in other documents. For information on Internet shortcuts, see Chapter 4.

If all goes well (and it surely will), the Netscape window will open, and the Netscape icon in the window's upper-right corner will become animated. This tells you that Netscape is transferring data, which will appear in a second in the form of a Web page. Whenever Netscape is "working" (downloading a document, searching, and so on), the Netscape icon is animated. It stops when the action has been completed.

What's Out There

You can find out all about Windows 95 Dial-Up Networking at `http://athos.rutgers.edu/LCSR-Computing/win95.html`.

When you first start Netscape, you'll see the *Welcome to Netscape* home page, with its sleek, colorful graphics. You can change this start-up home page to something else if you like; we'll tell you how to do that later, in Chapter 5.

The *home page* is where you begin, where Netscape first lands you on your Internet voyage. Think of it as one of many ports of entry into the Web. The Web, you'll recall, doesn't just go from here to there—it's a *web*. It doesn't really matter where you start, because everything's interconnected.

You can return to the start-up home page (the one you see when you start a Netscape session) at any time simply by clicking on the Home icon on the Netscape tool bar.

You can always return to Netscape's own home page, no matter what else you've chosen as your start-up home page, just by clicking on the Netscape N icon in the upper-right corner of the Netscape Navigator window.

If you followed the steps earlier in this chapter and have Netscape running now, try clicking on the What's New button in the Netscape window's button bar. This brief exercise will test your Internet connection. The Netscape icon should become animated, and in a few seconds Netscape's What's New page should appear.

Now try clicking on the Back button. The Netscape icon will again become animated, and Netscape's home page will reappear.

Home, Home on the Home Page

The start-up home page—any home page, for that matter—may be anywhere on the Web, or it may be on your own machine. Home pages provide a lot of information and change frequently; so you may not want to zip by a Web site's start-up home page. Instead, take the time to review it when it pops up.

You are not limited to seeing the Welcome to Netscape home page at start-up—you can make it so that Netscape won't load a home page on start-up (see Chapter 5), or you can use the What's Out There page that comes with this book, or you can store and start up with one of any number of home pages that you find on the Internet. (Chapter 4 talks about storing and managing Web documents.) You can even create your own home page. (Refer to Chapter 9 for instructions on how to do so.) If you change the start-up home page and want to find the Welcome to Netscape home page again, you can use its URL, which is `http://home.netscape.com`. Or you can just click on the N-for-Netscape icon (the one that becomes animated when Web page files are arriving) in the upper-right corner of the Netscape window.

◆ What You See: The Netscape Interface

Let's look at the parts of the Netscape window. The interface shows the *document view window*. Figure 3.1 shows you what's what.

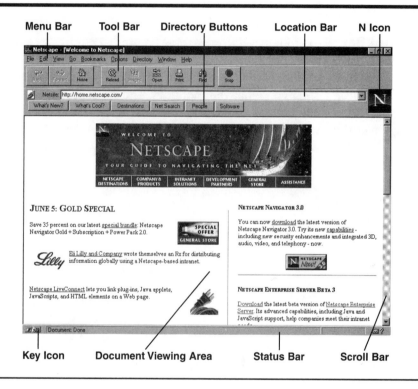

Figure 3.1: Here's the Netscape window with all its parts labeled so that you can see what's what.

Via the Options menu, you can display or hide the tool bar, the status bar, the location bar, and the directory buttons. You may want to hide this stuff if and when you want the document you are viewing to be larger.

Title Bar   In the title bar you can see the name of the page you are currently viewing.

Menu Bar   The menu bar in Netscape is similar to menu bars in other Windows applications: It provides you with drop-down menus. When you move the mouse to the menu and click on a selection, choices appear.

Tool Bar   The tool bar performs some common actions. It's like other Windows tool bars in that all you have to do is click on the icon for the specified action to occur. (If you point at a tool for a few seconds, a *ToolTip* will appear, telling you what the tool does. The ToolTip is simply a text box that displays the name of the tool to which you are pointing.) Let's quickly go over the Netscape tool bar icons.

The Tool	Its Name	What You Do with It
Back	Back	Jump back to the previous page or document in your History list (that is, the page you were viewing just prior to the current page).
Forward	Forward	Jump forward to the next page or document in your History list. (If you're on the last item in the History list, this icon is *dimmed*—it looks grayed out.)
Home	Home	Return to the start-up home page.
Reload	Reload	Refresh the currently loaded document. (You may need to do this if, for instance, you have a temporary communications problem with the Web server you're connected to and the page you want to see is incompletely displayed.)

The Tool	Its Name	What You Do with It
Images	Images	Load images into the page you are currently viewing. This icon is dimmed when Netscape is set to load images automatically (that's the default setting).
Open	Open	Open a document via its URL.
Print	Print	Print the current document.
Find	Find	Locate specified text in the current document.
Stop	Stop	Cancel the process of loading an incoming document.

Location Bar   Here you'll see the URL (the Uniform Resource Locator) of the current document. We'll get to a discussion of URLs a little later in this chapter.

Here's a sneaky trick: Click on the arrow on the far right end of the Navigation bar, and the last five URLs you visited will pop up. Select any one of them to visit that site again.

Directory Buttons   Below the location bar is a row of buttons; clicking on any of these buttons affords you fast access to some useful Web pages created by Netscape Communications to help you with using Netscape and navigating the Web.

Document Viewing Area   This is the main portion of the screen—it's where you'll see what you came to the Web to see.

Status Bar   The status bar is at the bottom of the screen. As you move the cursor about the document viewing area and come across links, the cursor changes into the shape of a hand with one finger pointing, and the status bar displays the URL for the link you're pointing to. When a document is being transferred to your machine, you'll see numbers in the status bar indicating the progress of the transfer.

◆ The key at the left end of the status bar indicates whether a document is secure.

◆ A "fractured" key indicates an insecure document—one that is transmitted between your local computer and the Web server without encryption. Or, in other words, a clever third-party with serious hacking skills can view it when it's transmitted (although most of the time, you won't be doing anything that actually would interest hackers).

Security is a topic of great concern to many users who want to protect their personal information—such as credit card numbers and bank records—from theft. Netscape has encryption and security features that make it the preferred Web client for accessing all types of commercial Web servers. Check out *A Few Quick Words on Security* and *Certificates and Enhanced Security*, both later in this chapter, for a discussion of *certificates*. (A certificate provides a unique signature that can then be verified to protect an individual from the possibility of being impersonated in Internet interactions.)

Scroll Bars   These are just like regular Windows scroll bars: They appear on the side of the viewing area, and possibly at the bottom, when the document is too big to fit in the window. Click on the scroll bars to bring into view whatever's off the screen.

◆ Opening Your First Document

You actually opened your first document when you started Netscape and the home page appeared. But let's dig around a little further and see what else we can open.

What's Out There

The Netscape Handbook, online documentation for Netscape, is at
`http://home.netscape.com/eng/mozilla/3.0/handbook`.

Following Hot Links

Moving around the World Wide Web is a snap, thanks to hyperlinks. It's as easy as a mouse-click on the link—each link points to some other piece of the Internet, just as Windows 95 shortcuts point to something on your hard drive.

As we've said before, hypertext is nonlinear. (That means you don't have to follow a straight path from point A to point Z, but rather you can skip around from one place to another to another, back to the first, round to a fourth, and so on.) Hypertext is hypertext because it has links—*hot links*, they're often called—to other sources of information. You follow these links through a document, or from document to document, document to image, or perhaps from server to server, in any way you like as you navigate the Web. (You can think of hypertext as both the text and the links—it's the navigational means by which you traverse the Web.) The great thing about the Web is that you don't have to know whether the information you're looking at is in Paris, France or Paris, Texas—all you need to do is follow a link.

If you do want information about a link before you click on it, just check the status bar at the bottom of your screen. There you'll see a URL for anything from another site to a sound or video file, to an e-mail address. For example, if you drag your mouse over the word Webmaster on any given Web page, you might see the URL for the Webmaster's home page, an e-mail address provided by the Webmaster for feedback, or the URL for a Help page about the site you're viewing. Read on, we'll tell you more about URLs later in this chapter.

How can you tell what is hypertext in a document? Words that are hyperlinks will usually be in a special color and underlined. On Netscape's home page, the special color is blue. A Webmaster (or producer) can choose any color at all to designate links, but in most cases the chosen color will be different from the color chosen for "ordinary" text. The words that stand out on a page are generally the links.

Images can also be links. Sometimes an image will have a border of color around it to designate its "linkness," but in any case, the cursor will always turn into a pointing hand when you drag it over part of a Web page that is linked to something else.

Just as both text and images on a Web page can be hyperlinks, these hyperlinks can lead you to many different kinds of information. A link could lead you through a single document, off to a different Web page, across the world to a page on a different server, or to an FTP server, Gopher site, newsgroup, or e-mail address.

Links can also lead you to images, sounds, movies, and multimedia files. We'll tell you more about how to experience the interactive Web in Chapter 6 and how to get tools to take advantage of the multimedia aspect of the Web in Chapter 12.

To Click or Not to Click?

When you click on a link on the Web, it may take a few seconds to access the information you requested. *Don't click again*; let Netscape do its job. Every time you click on a link, Netscape cancels the last order you gave it and starts a new one. So if you click on the same link four or five times, ai-yi-yi, Netscape has to start all over again each time.

If we slowed this whole business down and showed you its underpinnings, you'd see that when you click on a hyperlink, Netscape contacts the machine (or machines) on the Internet that you told it to call when you clicked on something. Then the dance between software and servers does one of these things:

◆ Gets and displays the document that the link specifies

◆ Goes to another location in the current document

◆ Gets a file, such as an image or a sound file, and through the use of a plug-in or an external viewer or player (another piece of software on your PC) displays the image or plays the sound

◆ Gives you access to another Internet service, such as Gopher, FTP, Telnet, and so on

If you still have the Welcome to Netscape home page open now, click on a few links. Don't be shy—just click on anything that looks interesting. You'll soon see why they call it the Web. Try jumping back and forth a couple of times too by clicking on those tools in the tool bar. When you've had enough, simply click on the Home button or the Netscape N icon to get back to your start-up home page.

 When you look at a document that has a link to something you've already seen, the color of that link changes. These are called visited links, and this is Netscape's way of letting you know you've been to that place before.

What's Out There

Take a look at On Internet Security for the lowdown on Netscape's security features. The URL is `http://home.netscape.com/info/security-doc.html`.

Opening a Document Using Its URL

Sometimes you're going to want to go straight for the jugular—you know where the document is, and you just want to see it without starting on a home page and skipping through a lot of hot links. Maybe your pal just sent you the URL for the Exploratorium, a really wonderful interactive science museum in San Francisco.

To open a document using its URL follow these steps:

1. From Netscape's menu bar, select File ➤ Open Location
or press Ctrl+L
or press the Open button in the tool bar.

In any case the Open Location dialog box will appear.

A Few Quick Words on Security

Keeping the data that passes across the Internet safe and secure is an issue that bigwigs in both business and government are discussing now and one that will soon become relevant even to the casual user.

You've probably noticed a lot of talk in newspapers and magazines and on TV about commercial ventures on the Web—merchants and malls all setting up shop and taking your credit card order or banks offering home services through their sites. You can even use the Web to buy and sell stocks. If this data (your credit card number, your bank balance and access code, or your stock portfolio) is not *safe*, it can be read by some eavesdropper lurking in an electronic shadow. Well, you can surely see the concern!

Fortunately, the designers of Netscape had this issue in mind when they developed the software. Netscape was the first Web browser to allow secured transactions to take place (between your computer running Netscape and a Web server running Netscape's Netsite Commerce server). In practical terms, this means that when you, running Netscape at home, connect to a home page on a special server that was purchased from Netscape Communications, the data sent back and forth can be secure from prying "eyes."

By now you've probably noticed the gold skeleton key icon in the lower-left corner of the Netscape window. Usually, the key appears "fractured." This indicates that the document you are currently viewing is *insecure*, meaning that a third party sufficiently motivated and equipped can look in on the data being sent back and forth and do with it what he or she will.

If, however, you are connected to a *secure* page—one where such eavesdropping is not possible because the data is "encrypted" before it is transferred and "decrypted" upon arrival—the key will appear unfractured. (In addition, a dialog box will appear both when you connect to and when you disconnect from that page, telling you of the secure status of the transmission.)

Netscape 3 offers even more sophisticated security with the addition of certificates to its features. Certificates are meant to "prove" your identity to Web servers through a system of verification. Look for this technology to become an increasingly important security feature as Web producers upgrade their sites to take advantage of new versions of Netscape's server software using certificates.

You can find out more about security by selecting Help ➢ On Security from the Netscape menu bar. To get a directory of sites using Netsite Commerce servers, select Directory ➢ Netscape Galleria from the menu bar. To find out more about the security of the current document on screen, select View ➢ Document Info from Netscape's menu bar.

2. In the Open Location dialog box (see Figure 3.2), type the URL of interest (in our example, `http://www.exploratorium.edu`).

 You can copy URLs from e-mail or other documents and paste them directly into either the Open Location dialog box or the location bar.

3. Click on Open, and Netscape will find the document for this URL and display it on your screen. (See Figure 3.3.)

 You can also jump quickly to a document by typing or pasting its URL directly into Netscape's location bar—that is, if you have the location bar displayed. And you don't even have to type `http://` every time you want to type in a URL. You can start with the next bit of the URL instead. Netscape assumes that the URLs you ask for are http URLs (Web pages) unless you tell it otherwise. In fact, you can often actully type just one word. For example, typing **ford** and pressing ↵ will get you straight into that carmaker's site.

The Web is *very* BIG. And it changes all the time. From time to time you might have difficulty locating or accessing a document. The original may have been removed by its owner, the machine that holds the document may be unavailable or overworked when you try to access it, or the network path between your machine and the server might be down. If Netscape has been trying for a while to access a document without success, it will display a dialog box saying it just plain cannot locate the document (See *Error Messages Demystified* later in this chapter for the dish on error messages and what to do about them.) You can go back to the document that was on screen before you tried making the jump, just by clicking on OK.

 If you're waiting for a page to arrive and you want to look at something else (another page, for example) while you're waiting, select File ➤ New Web Browser from Netscape's menu bar. A second Netscape window will open and in it you can look at something other than what you were trying for in the first Netscape window. You can then use Alt+Tab or the Window menu to switch back and forth between the two open Netscape windows. Now who said attention spans are getting shorter?

URLs Explained Here

Remember that talk about e-mail addresses back in Chapter 2? There's a standard addressing scheme with which Netscape and the Web work too. It's called the Uniform Resource Locator (URL). The URL pinpoints the locations of documents and other information on the Web so that Netscape and other browsers can find the stuff. The structure of a URL may seem complicated at first, but it's really straightforward. The components of the URL are:

◆ The type of resource

◆ The name of the machine containing the file (the document or information) to be transferred

◆ The full "path" that locates the file among the directories and subdirectories on the machine

For example, in the URL

```
http://home.netscape.com/home/welcome.html
```

the resource type and transfer protocol is `http:` (which, as you know, is HyperText Transfer Protocol); the double slashes separate the protocol from the rest; the name of the computer is `home.netscape.com`; and the path and filename of the item on the computer is `/home/welcome.html`.

You will sometimes type into a text box the URLs of pages you want Netscape to find and deliver to you. (See *Opening a Document Using Its URL.*) One thing you should keep in mind then is that, unlike e-mail addresses, URLs are *case-sensitive*—capitalization matters! This is because lots of Web servers are Unix machines; in Unix, filenames in uppercase letters are not considered the same as filenames in lowercase letters. All the punctuation marks you see in some URLs are significant too—one misplaced hyphen, period or tilde (~) will trip up the whole works. So if you're typing in a complex URL, look at it closely as you type.

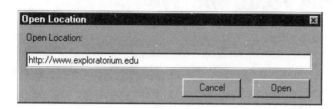

Figure 3.2: The Open Location dialog box

Figure 3.3: Here's the Exploratorium's home page. We found it using the URL a friend gave us.

◆ Changing the Size and Color of Displayed Text

If you've been working along with this chapter, you'll notice that text appears on your screen in different sizes. Usually, the text that makes up the substance of the page—the "body text"—is about the size you'd expect, while the title of the page is larger. (For a more complete discussion of the composition and elements of Web pages, see Chapter 9.)

Changing Fonts and Type Sizes

Some folks are annoyed by gigantic titles all over the page that necessitate scrolling around a lot, while others can deal with big headlines in order to make the main text of the page larger and easier to read. Whichever you prefer, you can change the font and size of displayed text in Netscape.

Here's how you do it:

1. From Netscape's menu bar, select Options ➤ General Preferences. The Preferences dialog box will appear.

2. From the tabs along the top of the dialog box, select the Fonts tab. The Preferences dialog box will be updated to reflect your choice.

3. Now, in the Fonts and Encodings area, you can make settings for either a proportional or a fixed font.

The *proportional* font is the one used for most of the text—body, head, and lists. The *fixed* font is the one used for preformatted text, which is a rarely used HTML element, but also happens to be the font that appears when you type stuff in to the forms that some pages offer, for example, for responding to surveys.

 Leave the Preferences dialog box's "encoding" set to Latin1. Latin1 is the proper setting for English and most European languages. Note too that while other choices are apparent in this dialog box, they aren't really available to you unless you have a version of Windows that's been localized to a specific language or country. Leave this stuff alone unless you know what to do with it.

4. Click on one of the Choose Font buttons, which are along the right of the Fonts and Encoding area. Each of the buttons will display the Choose Base Font window for the corresponding font— either for the proportional or fixed font. The Choose Base Font window will appear.

5. From the Font List in this window, select your favorite font. (The fonts that appear on this list are those that are installed on your system. If you've installed lots of fonts, they'll appear here. Otherwise, you'll see the fairly standard set of fonts that comes with Windows.)

6. Now select a font size, if you like, from the Size list. As a practical matter, the size you choose should probably be between 10 and 14 points.

You can now repeat steps 4 through 6 for the other font.

 Note that the Choose Base Font window's sample area changes to reflect your choice of font and size.

The changes you make will take effect as soon as you close the Preferences dialog box (which you can do, of course, by clicking on OK).

You might wonder as you go along, How does changing one font size change the style of more than one kind of text on a single page? Good question. Basically, Netscape displays different sizes of text (the title, headings, body text, and so on) in comparison to one "measure"—the basic font size. Netscape will display the title so-and-so many times larger than this base measure, and so forth. It is the base measure that you are changing in the procedure we just described.

Changing Colors

In Netscape, you have the option of changing the *color* of text. Imagine that! To do so, follow these steps:

1. From Netscape's menu bar, select Options ➤ General Preferences. The Preferences dialog box will appear.

2. From the list of tabs along the top of the dialog box, click on the Colors tab. The Preferences dialog box will be updated to reflect your choice. (See Figure 3.4.)

You can choose whether you want the selections you are about to make to override any existing settings in the documents you'll be viewing. For example, you might want all the text other than links in all the documents you view to be purple, even if the document's designer made the text black. Or you might want the document designer's wishes to outweigh your own.

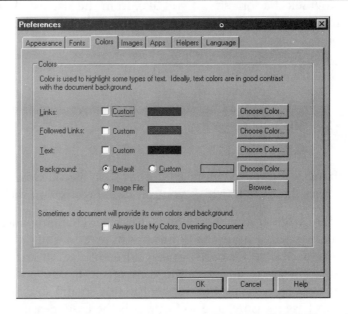

Figure 3.4: The Colors dialog box

3. To make your upcoming color choices override any other settings, select the checkbox Always Use My Colors, Overriding Document.

or

To allow the settings that exist in a given document to override the color choices you are about to make, deselect the checkbox Always Use My Colors, Overriding Document.

4. Now click on the Choose Color button for the element whose color you want to specify. Your choices are:

- ◆ Links
- ◆ Followed Links
- ◆ Text
- ◆ Background

The Color dialog box will appear.

5. In this dialog box, you can select any of a number of predefined colors by clicking on one in the Basic Colors area.

or

You can define a custom color by clicking on the Define Custom Colors button. In that case, the window will expand to include a wide range of colors. Click in the box wherever a color you like appears, and then click on the narrow panel to the right of the main color box to specify the shade (lightness and darkness) of that color. Click on the Add to Custom Colors button, The color you have specified will appear in the Custom Colors part of the Color dialog box. Click on it to make it your selected color.

Guestbooks, Surveys, and Forms—Gee Whiz!

When you see a box on a Web page that lets you type stuff in it, that's often what's called a *form*. Forms are used by Web site producers to let users like you participate in Internet surveys, order merchandise, "sign" guestbooks, and give feedback, among other fun things. The purpose of a form is usually obvious, as is the way you use it. You'll type some words in a text box, then perhaps click on a few buttons, and finally press a button at the bottom of the page that whisks that information on its way. You may be invited at some sites to fill in a guestbook with your name, e-mail address, and a message to tell the Webmaster and other Web users what you think about the Web page you just visited. Or you may be asked to fill out a survey or registration form as a prerequisite to seeing the rest of a site you've seen a smidgen of before filling in the form. Sites like HotWired (`http://www.hotwired.com/`) want to know who's using their services, and so they offer a free registration process in which you tell them who you are, and in exchange they let you visit all of HotWired's chat rooms and live broadcasts.

Sites like Time Warner's Pathfinder (`http://pathfinder.com/`) and the c|net site (`http://www.cnet.com/`) offer entertaining e-mail newsletters in exchange for your registration. Other sites may offer you contests or give-aways in exchange for your completed questionnaire.

This process is usually quick, simple, and free. However, if you're not sure exactly who might be receiving personal information, and if you don't want your e-mail box cluttered with junk from strangers, you may want to think twice about filling out every survey or questionnaire you run across. Watch for sites then that do not sell their mailing lists—they usually tell you as much, and they usually stick to their word.

6. Click on OK to close the Color dialog box. The Preferences dialog box will reappear, with the color(s) you've chosen appearing in place of the default Netscape colors that were there before.

7. In addition to controlling the color in which text appears, you can also control the color of the background—what appears behind the text. To change the background, either

   ◆ Click on the Choose Color button next to Background and choose a color as you did above, or

   ◆ Click on the Browse button and select a graphics file to use as the background. When you choose to use a graphics file instead of a solid color as the background, the graphics file is tiled to fit the window, no matter the window size.

8. When you are done specifying Netscape's colors, click on OK. The Preferences dialog box will close, and you will once again see the Netscape window.

The changes you've made will take place immediately. If you don't like the results, you can always go back and repeat the whole color-changing process, selecting something new and different.

You can also always go back to the original, default color scheme. Simply deselect any custom colors you've indicated, and be sure you've clicked on the Default button next to Background.

◆ Saving Stuff to Your Local Machine

Let's say you've been skipping around the Internet and looking at a lot of stuff and you found something really nifty you want to hold on to.

Saving takes up valuable disk space. This means you don't want to save *everything*. You do want to save things you want to keep for reference or access quickly in the future. For alternatives to saving, see Chapter 4's discussions of Bookmarks and Internet shortcuts.

You can save a document to your local hard drive in three ways. We'll get to those in a second; first, a word or two on naming files in general and hypertext files in particular.

So What If You Have a Different Browser?

One line of thinking goes that Web documents should be viewable by any person with any Web browser; so pages should be thoughtfully designed to take into account the failings of browsers other than Netscape. Another line goes that one should exploit all the wonderful features Netscape has to offer, including fancy things such as special colors and the use of columns, frames, and tables even though people using Web browsers other than Netscape might not be able to view that stuff as it was intended to appear. You can sometimes see the evidence of this "debate" on the Web in the form of messages that say something like "Use Netscape for best viewing" or "Netscape not required." Let's take a look at what all this talk is about.

Netscape, since its nascent moment, has always pushed the envelope of what a Web browser can do. Netscape 1.0 supported HTML version 1.0 and some of the proposed HTML+ extensions; at the time, all other Web browsers were offering only HTML version 0.9. Netscape 1.1 supported the newly proposed HTML 3.0 standard. Netscape 2.0 was the first commercial browser to support Java, which allows designers to add more interactive and animated functionality to Web pages. Other enhancements that became available included frames, JavaScript, helper applications, and plug-ins. (See Chapter 12, *Get a Boost With Plug-ins and Helper Apps*.) Netscape 3 adds new capabilities, allowing Web designers to create more attractive pages with new tabling techniques, providing more secure communication over the Internet via certificates, and opening up access to interactive three-dimensional experiences through VRML.

What does all this advanced thinking mean to you? Well, by using all the advanced HTML and Java features that Netscape supports, Web page authors can create state-of-the-art Web sites.

The only drawback in using these amazing features is that many Web browsers other than Netscape cannot (yet) display them on screen correctly. Netscape is usually a step or two ahead of the pack in this regard, and a document designed to take full advantage of Netscape's advanced features can look disappointingly different when viewed with some other Web browser. But you have Netscape, so you'll be just fine, right?

Naming the Files

Some of the documents you'll want to save don't conform to the
Windows 95 file naming conventions. With Windows 95, a filename cannot include a number of special characters:

> \ / : * ? <> ¦

But sometimes filenames you find on the Web may include characters that
Windows 95 does not recognize. This is because the files you find on the
Net are often created and stored on Unix machines, and their names follow the Unix file naming system. But you're using Netscape—a *Windows*
product—and that means Windows is really doing the saving. If you don't
change the filename when you save the file to disk, an error message will
appear saying you can't save the file. If this happens, go back and change
the filename using Windows 95 conventions.

Saving Stuff You Can See

Saving documents and images to your hard drive can be a good idea if you
want to look at them later without paying for connect time. You can also
use your store of saved documents as a library to jog ideas in constructing
your own home page—this may be an easier process if the page is on your
hard drive. See Chapter 9 for more on creating your own Web pages.

Saving Web Pages

To save the page you are viewing at the moment to your hard disk:

1. From the menu bar, select File ➤ Save As. The Save As dialog box
   will appear (see Figure 3.5). This is much like a Save As dialog box
   you'd see in any other Windows application.

2. In the File Name text box, type a filename. Netscape will usually
   assign either HTM or HTML automatically as the extension—these
   are the extensions for hypertext files. (If you want to be sure the
   program is assigning one of those extensions, just take a look at
   the bottom of the dialog box, where the Save As Type drop-down
   list appears.)

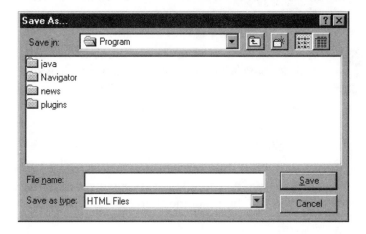

Figure 3.5: The Save As dialog box

Sometimes even Netscape can't be sure that the file you want is an HTML file. For example, if the file you're looking at is a directory, like `http://www.webpage.com/` (instead of `http://www.webpage.com/home.htm`), Netscape can't assume that the page on your screen really is a document. (This also happens with files that are generated automatically through CGI scripts and other interactive scripts.) In these cases, you can specify .HTM as the file extension.

If you want to save just the page's text, and not the HTML format, you can select Plain Text as the file type. This might be useful if you want to save, say, one of Shakespeare's plays or a lengthy magazine article—in those cases the links may be less important to you than the text alone.

3. Pull down the Save In list by clicking on its down arrow. From the list, select the drive to which you want to save the file. Below the Save In drop-down list, the contents of the drive you selected will appear as a list of folders and icons.

4. In that list, double-click on the directory into which you want to save the file.

 If you want to place the file in a subdirectory (within a directory), first double-click on the directory that contains that subdirectory so that you can see it. For sub-subdirectories, repeat this process as needed until you find the target subdirectory.

5. Click on the Save As dialog box's Save button.

Perhaps this is obvious, but you won't see the document you've saved on screen when you save it. You'll know it's been saved when you check the Directory list and see the filename there.

Saving Images

You might want to save one special image to your hard drive instead of a whole Web page. ...What for? Well, you can use that image as Desktop wallpaper for your computer, send it as a map to a friend who's coming to town, or print it to hang over your desk at work. If the image is clip art (or otherwise in the public domain), you can also use it on your own home page. (See Chapter 9 for more on creating Web documents.)

Saving an image to your hard drive is easy. Just do this:

1. Using your right mouse button, click on the image of interest. A pop-up menu will appear asking you what you want to do.

 Your other choices from this menu include viewing the image on a separate page, or if the image is a link, creating a Bookmark or Internet Shortcut to the page it's pointing to. See *Pop-Up Menus and You,* later in this chapter, for more on how to use your handy right-mouse-button tool.

2. From the pop-up menu, select Save Image As. The Save Image dialog box will appear.

3. Now follow steps 2 through 5 in the section titled *Saving Web Pages* earlier in this chapter. Netscape will automatically detect and choose the correct file format (usually either GIF or JPEG) for the image.

4. To verify that the save was successful, you can use the Explorer to look in the directory to which you just saved the file. You should see the file listed.

Saving Stuff That's Not in View

Let's say the page you are viewing at the moment includes a link to something (maybe to a sound or to an image) that you want to save to disk to check out later. You can save the stuff at the other end of the link without first having to travel that link. Just follow these steps:

1. Pointing to the link that goes to the stuff you want to save, click the right mouse button. A pop-up menu will appear.

2. From the menu, select Save This Link As. The Save As dialog box will appear.

3. Now follow Steps 2 through 5 in the section titled *Saving Web Pages* earlier in this chapter.

To verify that the save was successful, you can use the Explorer to look in the directory to which you just saved the file. You should see the file listed.

 When you save an HTML document to your hard drive, what you get is the HTML code and the text—not the images. When you load the page later into Netscape, the images won't be there. This is because HTML documents tell Netscape where to find images, but they don't actually contain any pictures. An image in a Web page is really a link to a picture located on the Internet—but Netscape loads the pictures onto the page instead of just linking to them.

◆ Viewing Documents You've Saved

You can view a document you've saved to your local hard drive by selecting File ➣ Open File from Netscape's menu bar.

 You don't have to be running your Internet connection to use Netscape to look at files on your computer.

The File Open dialog box will appear; again this is a standard Windows dialog box. Select and open the HTML file of interest by double-clicking on it. By the way, saving a file and then viewing it this way is a lot faster than accessing and viewing it when it's somewhere else in the world; the drawback is that if the owner of the document has made changes to it, you won't know about them. A really cool aspect of this, though, is that when you view a document that's been saved to your local machine, *the links have been saved with it,* and you can simply click on those links and start up your Web travels again.

Pop-up Menus and You

Netscape offers a lot of handy shortcuts that are no further away than the rightmost button on your mouse. Try these:

◆ Point at some white space or non-linked text, click the right mouse button, and a pop-up menu will appear offering options for going back or forward and for adding a bookmark or Internet shortcut for the page you're currently viewing.

◆ Point your mouse at a link and click with your right mouse button and a pop-up menu will appear offering options to copy the link's URL to the Clipboard; to add a bookmark or an Internet shortcut; to save the document behind the link to your hard drive; or to open the link in a new window instead of the one the link is in.

◆ Point at an image and click with the right mouse button, and a pop-up menu will appear offering options for saving the image to your hard drive, copying the image's URL, or viewing the image in a separate window.

◆ Jumping Back and Forth While Viewing a Document

The Back and Forward icons on the tool bar provide a convenient way to jump back and forth among the hot links you've followed.

This is because Netscape tracks the documents you visit in a History list. The Back and Forward icons actually let you travel through the History list. If you have Netscape running, try clicking on the Back icon to jump backward along the links you just followed, and then try clicking on Forward to jump forward.

There is an end to this—if you jump back to the first document you viewed in a session, or forward to the last one, you reach the end of history. The Back or Forward icon, depending on which end of history you reach, will be grayed out. (You can, as always, create more history—click on another hypertext link to explore further.)

Nothing's Showing Up! What to Do?

Sometimes the N icon will be animated, its comets flying along, and either nothing shows up, or the text arrives *sans* any images. What's going on?

When a Web server is busy, overloaded, or just plain slow, you'll get the text and basic HTML from it first and the images last. Images are a lot bigger (file-size-wise) than text, so they take longer to load. You can:

Stop   Press the Stop button. Often, the images that were trying to load are mostly there, and hitting Stop will say, "Hey images! Hurry up and load!" Many times, they will.

Reload   If that doesn't work, press the Reload button. In fact, if a Web page ever looks funny or incomplete in some way, try Reloading it.

Load Image   If a single image hasn't shown up, but the rest of them have, click the right-hand mouse button over the *placeholder* (that funny-looking picture that represents an image that should be there, but isn't). When the pop-up menu appears, select "Load Image." Netscape will then try to retrieve that single image and load it onto the page you're viewing.

Give up   Sometimes Webmasters goof up, and sometimes, particularly if the Web server you're trying to access is halfway around the world, the connection is just too danged slow. Oh, well. If you really want to see that picture of Joe Namath as a baby, try your luck again some other time.

At the bottom of many documents, you'll find a hot link that says something like <u>Go Back</u>. If you click on this link, you won't necessarily go back to where you came from; instead, you'll visit the page that the Webmaster assumed you just came from (usually another page at the same site). If you want to go back to where you were before, click on the Back icon on the Netscape tool bar.

◆ Getting Around in Frames

Frames are popping up all over, ever since they became a design option (in version 2 of Netscape Navigator). Frames appear on a Web page looking like a bunch of panes within the larger viewing area window; these "panes in the window" each hold some piece of the larger whole. Like everything else in life, frames are good when used purposefully, and not so good when they're used gratuitously. In Figure 3.6, you can see News of the Day, a Web page that uses frames to enhance the organization of the page by offering a navigation frame on the left and a larger frame in which various news sources appear on the right.

Having too many frames in a Web site is like putting too many bows on a dress—too much. Frames are best used when used judiciously, and when no other option will do. To be fair, many sites use frames quite well—one of the most practical applications of frames are pages that offer a table of contents in one of the frames. That index stays put (in some form or other) the whole time you're navigating the rest of the site.

Whatever their purpose in a Web site, each individual frame has its own URL. They also can have their own scrollbars, various background colors, images, text, Java or Java Script elements—anything, in short, that a non-frame Web page can have.

When you click on a link in one frame, often another frame on the page will change to reflect that click. That means you can easily get lost trying to find some information that was in a frame you saw five clicks ago.

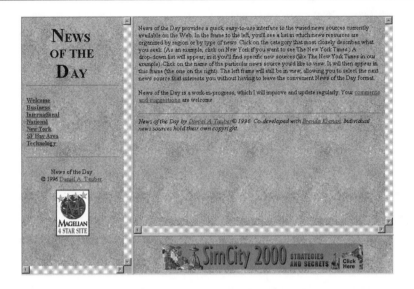

Figure 3.6: The News of the Day page uses frames to enhance navigation of its contents.

What's Out There

Two of HotWired's sites use frames really well: Cocktail is located at `http://www.hotwired.com/cocktail/`, and Net Surf is at `http://www.hotwired.com/surf/`.

News of the Day is at `http://www.dnai.com/~vox/news`.

For a lesson in creating frames in your Web pages, check out Netscape's Frames Tutorial at `http://home.netscape.com/assist/net_sites/frames.html`.

There are two ways you can get back to where you once belonged. The easiest is to use the Back button—in Netscape 3, the Back button sends you back one frame at a time until you reach the beginning of a framed-up site. You can also use the right mouse button to navigate backward—click and, when the handy pop-up menu appears, select Back In Frame.

You can bookmark a document or a frame; this is much like putting a bookmark in a book in the sense that it helps you find where you've been without having to retrace your steps. See Chapter 4.

◆ Caching and Reloading

Netscape stores the pages you visit in what's called the *cache*. A *cache* (noun) is just a chunk of storage—it can be RAM or the disk drive—on your computer that's been set aside as a temporary storage place. Your PC *caches* (verb) parts of the programs that you're running in its cache to make them run faster. Similarly, Netscape caches the Web pages you look at so that when you go back and forth between pages, you don't have to access the Internet anew every single time you look at the same page. Instead, your machine accesses the copy of that page that's in the cache.

Netscape actually maintains two caches of documents—one in your computer's memory that goes away when you end your Netscape session, and another on disk that it uses between sessions. When you access a Web page, Netscape first checks to see if you have a current copy of the page either in the memory cache or in the disk cache. If a copy of the current page is located in either of these places, that copy is displayed instead of a fresh copy, relieving Netscape of the slow process of downloading the page from the Internet anew. (This is also true of images, sounds, video—in short, anything on the Net you access via Netscape.)

As you continue to visit new sites on the Web, old stuff in the cache is flushed out, and the newer stuff you visit in your travels is added. Sounds reasonable, eh?

There is a big drawback to this scheme: When you click around from page to page, you may not be seeing the most current version of a Web page; you may instead be seeing the cached version. This can be a drag if the page changes a lot and it's the fresher version you want. Certain pages, like weather maps, newsfeeds, and live camera links, for example, change minute by minute and you want the freshest view of them.

If you ever doubt that you're seeing the most current version of a page, just click on the Reload button, and the page will appear from scratch, rather than from the cache.

Specifying How Often to Check the Cache

You can specify that Netscape approach this matter by checking the cache Every Time, Once per Session, or Never.

The default is Once per Session. It's best not to mess with this unless you have some compelling reason and know what you're up to, because it'll slow down other operations. But here are the details:

1. From Netscape, select Options ➤ Network Preferences. A Network Preferences dialog box will appear, with the tab marked Cache selected. (Figure 3.7.)

2. Locate the Verify Documents label. To the right of the label you'll see three radio buttons, one for each option:

Option	What It Means	When It's Good
Every Time	Netscape will not look at your disk cache and will always retrieve from the Internet (instead of locally)	When you're viewing lots of pages that change frequently, and especially if you're on a high-speed line
Once per Session	Netscape will go looking for each page once (the first time you access this particular Web page in this particular session).	During your usual activities; this is the default, and it's best to call this a keeper
Never	Netscape will always go for the copy in your disk cache unless it becomes unavailable (or unless you click on the Reload button).	When you're not connected to the Net and you want to look at pages in the cache

Click on the button of choice. Then click on OK to close the dialog box. Netscape will hereafter comply with your choice.

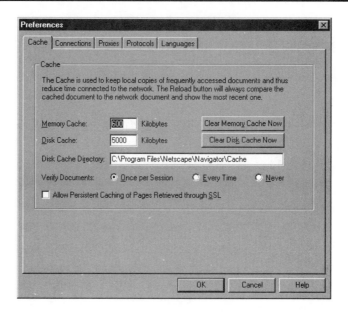

Figure 3.7: The Network Preferences dialog box displaying information about the cache

Increasing the Size of Your Disk Cache

As a default, Netscape sets the disk cache at 5000K. This is a good minimum, but you may want to increase it, depending on how much disk space you want to dedicate to Net surfing. The more disk space you allocate to Netscape's cache, the more stuff it will hold.

It makes a lot less sense to increase the size of the memory cache than to increase the size of the disk cache. The other programs you're running, including Windows 95, need all the memory they can get. Don't shortchange Windows for the sake of Netscape or other applications that rely on Windows.

To increase your disk cache, follow this simple procedure:

1. From Netscape's menu bar, select Options ➤ Network Preferences. The Network Preferences dialog box will appear, as shown previously in Figure 3.7, with the tab marked Cache selected. (If its not selected, just click on the Cache tab.)

2. In the Disk Cache text box, type the number of kilobytes (K) you want to reserve for Netscape's disk cache. The default is 5000K (or 5MB); 20000K (20MB) is a better choice if you have that much disk space to spare.

3. Click on the OK button. The dialog box will close and you'll find yourself in the familiar Netscape window.

From this moment forward, you should find accessing the pages you visit most often a lot faster than it was before.

◆ Error Messages Demystified

The Internet works really well most of the time, but both computers and humans are fallible, and sometimes you'll click on a link or enter a URL and you'll get an unhappy message from Netscape instead of the Web page you wanted. See Table 3.1 for a listing of error messages and what they mean.

A few general tips:

◆ Most errors aren't permanent. If you get an error, try a few minutes, hours, or even days later, and the page you want will usually come back.

◆ You're more likely to get *Busy* or *Connection Refused* messages during peak hours, like lunch time and right after the workday ends. Try accessing busy pages during off-peak hours.

◆ Good Webmasters do routine maintenance on Web pages fairly often, and this can increase the chances of certain parts of a server being off-limits. If you try accessing the site a day or two later, you'll usually be able to access the page you want, or you'll be given a pointer that says the site has moved.

◆ If a page disappears inexplicably or permanently, check your favorite search engine to see if it can locate an alternate address for the page.

◆ There are probably lots of other error messages you could get, and a good rule of thumb is to try the page again later, especially if you know you've been there before, or to check the spelling and format of the URL.

 As always, when in doubt, click on Reload and see what happens.

Table 3.1: Netscape Error Messages We Know and Love

Error Message	What It Means	What To Do
Too Many Users	This Web site may restrict the number of accesses allowed per day or per hour.	Try again later.
A Network Error Occurred. Unable to Connect to Server	Either the host is busy, or the URL is spelled wrong, or something else is funny.	Make sure you actually put the forward slashes in after http:. If so, just try again later.
Broken Pipe	Something went wrong en route and some data got lost..	Click on the Reload button, or try again later.
Connection Refused	The line is "busy" and this is the Web's busy signal.	Try again later.
Document Contains No Data	The Web page you tried to link to is there, but there's nothing on it.	Forget about it. Whoever pointed you there made a mistake.

Table 3.1: Netscape Error Messages We Know and Love (continued)

Error Message	What It Means	What To Do
The Location (URL) Is Not Recognized.	You asked for a type of URL that doesn't exist.	Look for typos in the URL you entered, especially the `http://` part.
The Server Does Not Have a DNS entry.	This server doesn't exist right now, at least not the way you spelled it.	Check your spelling of the domain name. If it's spelled correctly, try again later.
Netscape Is Out of Memory	Boy, you've been looking at a lot of huge Web pages today!	Quit Netscape, and then launch it again.
403 Forbidden	The part of the Web server you're trying to access is off limits right now.	Try it again tomorrow or next week. If that doesn't work, forget about it. Someone doesn't want you there.
Please Enter Username and Password	If you don't have an account on this server, it won't let you in.	Try visiting the site's home page to see if they require you to complete a registration process.
404 Not Found	The page you tried to link to may be gone forever, or there may be a typo in the URL you entered.	Try it again tomorrow or next week. If that doesn't work, the thing's probably gone.
409 Fire, Flood, and Pestilence	This is a joke.	Ignore this geek humor and go on with your life.

◆ Printing a Document or a Single Frame

To print a Web document, you must first have it open. Then, follow the usual printing procedure:

1. From the Netscape menu bar, select File ➤ Print. The Print dialog box will appear.

2. Fiddle with the dialog box to specify what you want exactly, and click on OK.

The whole document will pop out of your printer. Note, however, that the document probably will not be a single page long (unless it's a very brief home page, for example). This, of course, is because Web pages do not have the same physical boundaries as paper pages. So a single Web page may be several paper pages long. Also, perhaps obviously, if you want to print other pages linked within a single site, you'll have to go to those pages and print them separately. (Of course, you can't click on a printed-out Web page. But you already knew that, right?)

With frames, the matter gets a little stickier. You can't print out an entire Web page full of frames, because each pane in the window is technically a distinct document. To select the frame you want to print, again with the page (with frames) open,

1. Click on some blank space within the frame, and that frame will appear highlighted.

To see how this works, try clicking from frame to frame in a site that uses frames. Try News of the Day, which is located at **http://www.dnai.com/~vox/news**. You can see how each individual frame gets highlighted as you go from frame to frame.

2. From Netscape's menu bar, select File ➤ Print Frame. The Print dialog box will appear.

3. Fiddle with the dialog box to specify what you want exactly, and click on OK.

To make sure you're printing the frame you want, you can select File ➤ Print Preview from Netscape's menu bar before you print. A window will appear showing you what you're printing, how many pages long it is, and other nifty things about the page. To exit Print Preview and return to the Navigator window, click on Close from Print Preview's tool bar. To go ahead and print, click on the printer icon.

The frame you selected will pop out of your printer. Now, the thing to remember is that it's *one frame* that you've printed, and a whole Web page can be made up of several frames. If you want to print an entire Web page with all its frames, you'll unfortunately have to print each frame individually.

◆ Quitting Netscape

You can quit Netscape any ol' time—even when the Netscape icon (the N) is animated. To leave Netscape, simply do the following:

1. If the N is animated, click on the Stop button on the tool bar. This will cancel whatever Netscape is trying to do at the moment. (If the N is not animated, skip this step.)

2. To actually quit the program, double-click on the Control button in the upper-left corner of the screen, *or* select File ➤ Exit from the menu bar. The Windows Desktop will reappear.

3. Remember, even if you aren't running Netscape, you are still connected to your Internet Service provider, and you must break this connection, using whatever techniques are specifically appropriate. (Check with your Internet service provider to find out about that.)

Now, with your basic skills in place for navigating the Web via Netscape, let's take a look at how you can more closely track where you've been by using Internet Shortcuts and Bookmarks, and how you can manage your bookmark list as it grows and grows.

What's Out There

Want to be hip to what's happening on the Net? The latest Net Happenings are the topic at `http://www.gi.net/NET`. And you can get advance information about new versions of Netscape and other Web browsers via the Browser Watch site at `http://www.ski.mskcc.org/browserwatch/`.

Certificates and Enhanced Security

As the next generation of Netscape servers become more widely used, certificates and other enhanced security features will come into use. The use of certificates, which "prove" your identity by means of a verification scheme, will help in enabling secure economic transactions and may make unnecessary the use of a password to gain access to protected sites or areas. They'll also be a key tool in preventing forged e-mail messages.

To get your own personal certificate, follow these steps:

1. From the Netscape menu bar, select Options ➤ Security Preferences. The Security Preferences dialog box will appear.

2. Click on the Personal Certificates tab and the dialog box will update to reflect your choice—it will include a listing of the personal certificates you already have (the list will be empty on your first go-round). Click on the Obtain New Certificate button. The Certificate Authority Services page will appear in a new window.

3. On this page you'll see a list of all the *certifying authorities* (organizations that provide certificates) that issue certificates to work with Netscape Navigator. Each certifying authority has different rules governing its certificates—some may allow you to obtain your certificate entirely online, while others may require you to send a photocopy of your driver's license or even a notarized application. Some may charge fees. Select one and follow its directions to get your certificate.

Watch Netscape's Certificate Authority Services page and updates to this book for further developments.

Been There, Going Back

In your Web travels, you're bound to come across some sites you see as worth visiting again. It's just not smart to think you'll be able to remember where this stuff is or follow a trail of bread crumbs back to it—you need to mark your favorite places on the Web, so you can go back easily. Alternatively, you can use the History window, the Go menu, or even an Internet shortcut to track the sites you've seen.

◆ You Can Get There from Here in a Snap: Bookmarks

A big part of managing your Netscape tour of the Web is tracking what you found and liked. One way you can revisit what's worthy is to save files to disk, a process we described in the preceding chapter. But you don't always want the stuff on your disk—it takes up valuable space. When you stumble across something on the Web that you want easy access to in the future, you should mark it with a *bookmark*. In the menu bar you'll find a drop-down menu devoted entirely to bookmarks. Let's take a look at it.

What's Out There

Get the latest on bookmarks from the Netscape Handbook: Mail, News, and Bookmarks page at `http://home.netscape.com/mozilla/3.0/handbook/mnb.html`.

Bookmarking Documents

When you're viewing a page or a document that you like so much you want to view it again later, bookmark it. There are three very easy ways to add a site to your Bookmark list.

◆ From Netscape's menu bar, select Bookmarks ➤ Add Bookmark. *Poof!* The site is bookmarked.

◆ Press Ctrl+D. *Poof!*

◆ Press the right mouse button, and a pop-up menu will appear. Select Add Bookmark. *Poof* (again)!

When you're using the right-mouse-button trick, you have two options. If your mouse is pointing at a link, you can bookmark that link whether you've visited it or not. If your mouse is pointing at white space, you can bookmark the page you're looking at right now.

The name for whatever page you're so taken with will appear immediately on your Bookmark list, which you can access by clicking on Bookmarks in the Netscape menu bar. A drop-down menu will appear, with all your bookmarks listed. Any bookmarks you add later will also appear there, directly below the Add Bookmarks option.

Keep in mind that you're not saving the page itself when you create a bookmark—you're saving the page's URL. This means that when you revisit the page you found so interesting, it may have changed. This can be both an advantage, in that you may find even more interesting stuff there next time, and a disadvantage, in that whatever you liked so much the first time might be gone on your next visit.

Quickly Jumping to Documents on the Bookmark List

Any time you are using Netscape, regardless of where you are or what you're viewing, you can jump to any page you've bookmarked. To do this, with your connection going and Netscape running, simply select Bookmarks from the menu bar, and in your Bookmark list, click on the name of the page that interests you. The N icon will become animated and presumably the page will appear.

What's Out There

Bookmark this: 24 Hours in Cyberspace (`http://www.cyber24.com/home.html`). And: Yahoo Internet Life (`http://www.zdnet.com/yil/`).

Bookmark Management

After a while, when you've bookmarked a lot of pages, you'll find the list growing to unwieldy proportions. The bookmarks themselves might seem to be in no particular order. (Actually, bookmarks are listed in the order you created them, but that's not very helpful when you're digging through a long list.)

Fortunately, Netscape allows you to impose some order on all this seeming chaos. You can toss out the old and unused stuff if you want, but you can also shift things around so that they make more sense. You can put related pages next to one another on the Bookmark list; and you can even group related pages under folders, which then appear as submenus of the Bookmarks menu.

Rearranging Bookmarks

You can easily rearrange items in your Bookmark list. Let's say we've created three bookmarks: One is the Exploratorium home page, which we saw in Chapter 3, the second is the Pamela Anderson page shown in

Chapter 2, and the third is the home page from the National Center for Earthquake Engineering Research (NCEER) at SUNY Buffalo.

The first and the third pages might fit nicely together into a *science* category. Here's how to put them next to each other on the Bookmark list:

1. From Netscape's menu bar, select Window ➤ Bookmarks. The Bookmarks window will appear, as shown in Figure 4.1 (where the three bookmarks are displayed).

Bookmarks now have their own separate window in Netscape. From Netscape's menu bar, select Window ➤ Bookmarks, and a separate window will appear that lets you do whatever you want with your bookmarks. To visit a bookmark from this window, just double-click on its icon.

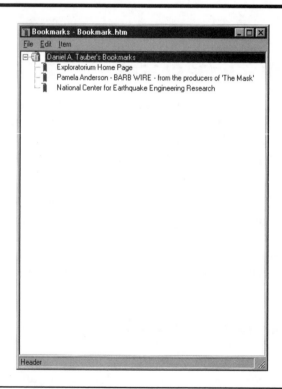

Figure 4.1: The Bookmarks window

2. Highlight the bookmark you want to move by clicking on it and then drag (by holding down the mouse button as you move the mouse) it up or down to its final resting place. Once you have moved the mouse pointer to the bookmark's final location, release the mouse button. You'll now see the bookmark in the new location.

That's all there is to it.

Creating Folders

When you've created a long, long list of bookmarks, rearranging them may seem tedious. In the end, it's also a poor solution to your organizational woes—you'll still find yourself searching line by line through the list. Worse yet, you'll end up with a Bookmark list too tall for Netscape to display. A better way to deal with the problem is to group bookmarks in *folders*, which will appear on the Bookmark list as submenus. (Bookmarks grouped under a folder will appear as options on these submenus.)

Here's how to create folders:

1. If it's not already open on your screen, open the Bookmarks window by selecting Window ➢ Bookmarks from the menu bar.

Netscape conveniently provides useful information about any highlighted bookmark in the Bookmark Properties dialog box. To view the Bookmark Properties dialog box for the highlighted bookmark, select Item ➢ Properties from the Bookmarks menu bar. You'll find the name of the highlighted page, its URL, and the dates when you created the bookmark and when you last visited the page. There's even a text box into which you can type your own description of the bookmarked page.

2. From the Bookmarks window's menu bar, select Item ➢ Insert Folder. The Bookmark Properties dialog box will appear (Figure 4.2).

3. In the dialog box's Name text box, give the new folder a descriptive name—one that will help you find this stuff when it appears on the Bookmark list. (We'll call our new folder here *Science*.) Once you have entered a name, click on OK. The dialog box will close, and the Bookmarks window will reappear, with your new folder listed.

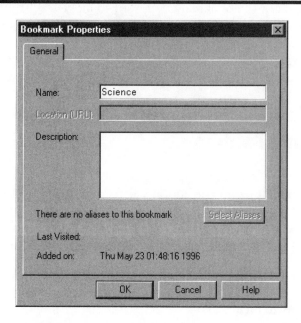

Figure 4.2: You'll see information about a particular bookmark in the Bookmark Properties dialog box.

4. Highlight and drag the folder to a position above the bookmarks you want to appear in the folder. Following our example from the previous section, we moved the new folder to a location above Exploratorium and NCEER.

5. Now that you've created and named a new folder, you'll have to group bookmarks under it. Highlight and drag a bookmark to the folder. As you move the bookmark over the folder, a highlight will appear over the folder. When this highlight appears, release the mouse button. The bookmark will appear as an item in the folder—the bookmark's title will be indented under the folder's title.

6. Repeat Step 5 for each bookmark you want to place in a folder. When you've finished, close the Bookmarks window by selecting File ➢ Close from the menu bar.

Now if you pull down the Bookmarks menu, the folder you created will appear as a submenu (marked on its right side by an arrow), but the bookmarks you placed in it won't be listed there. Not to worry—simply select the new folder, and the bookmarks grouped in it will appear.

Choices, Choices: Displaying the Bookmark List

Suppose you're doing research on Mad Cow Disease or the geological origins of the Grand Canyon. While you're doing research, you may want to place all your bookmarks directly into a specific folder instead of sorting them later on. Or say you have a lot of bookmarks already, and you're surfing for information on your favorite bands—you might want to make it so your Music folder appears temporarily in place of Bookmarks on the menu bar. Here's how you can customize the delivery and appearance of the Bookmarks feature on the menu bar.

New Bookmarks Folder   Once you've created a folder, you can tell Netscape to put any new bookmarks in it. By default, you see, Netscape will put a new bookmark at the top level of the Bookmark list, which means directly on the Bookmark list and not in any folder you've created. To change this and to put any new bookmarks automatically and directly into a folder, first open the Bookmarks window. Then, highlight the folder you want to use, and from the menu bar, select Item ➢ Set to New Bookmarks Folder. It's that simple.

Bookmarks Menu Folder   Netscape also allows you to "shrink" the Bookmark list so that when you pull down the Bookmarks menu, only the bookmarks contained in one folder are displayed. This may be useful if you've got a *lot* of folders and you're only going to be using one group of bookmarks in a given Web session. To do this, highlight the folder you want to see on the Bookmarks menu in the Bookmarks window. Now, from the menu bar, select Item ➢ Set to Bookmark Menu Folder. To change the list back and display all bookmarks (and folders) again, highlight the topmost folder in the Bookmarks window, and from the menu bar, select Item ➢ Set to Bookmark Menu Folder.

Renaming Items in Your Bookmark List

When you bookmark a Web page, the title of that page appears in your Bookmark list, the Bookmarks menu, and the Bookmarks window. (They're all the same list, of course.) This is usually just fine, but sometimes you'll

The Ol' Bookmark-List-Becomes-a-Web-Page Trick

Here's a nifty trick. You can make your Bookmark list into a Web page that links you to all your favorite places. This is possible because Netscape stores your bookmarks in an HTML file that can be viewed and navigated like any other Web page. With Netscape running, follow these steps:

1. From the Netscape menu bar, select Window ➣ Bookmarks. The Bookmarks window will appear.

2. From the Bookmarks menu bar, select File ➣ Save As. The Save As dialog box will appear.

3. In the dialog box, type a filename—something like FAVES.HTM or whatever you like that will remind you that this is your own personal Bookmark List page. Click on the Save button. The Bookmarks window will reappear. From here, you can close the Bookmarks window, or you can click on the Netscape window to leave the Bookmarks window open in the background.

Now you can open up FAVES.HTM (or whatever you called it) just as you would any other HTML file you've saved to your local machine (by selecting File ➣ Open File from the menu bar, for example). The first cool thing is that you'll find you have created a Web page version of your Bookmark list, which you can use as your own home page or pass on to friends and colleagues for their use. The second cool thing you'll find is that all the headings and organization you've done in your Bookmark list will be included in the page (Figure 4.3). The third cool thing is that any descriptions you've provided for individual items (in the Bookmarks window's Description box) will appear as text describing those links. Yes, we said links. Because, of course, all the items you've bookmarked appear in this page as clickable links to those resources you found so appealing or useful that you just had to bookmark them.

want to rename the item—to clarify what the page is about, for example, or perhaps because the page's creator gave it no title in the first place. You can easily change the name of any item that appears on your Bookmark list (including folders). Just do this:

1. From the Netscape menu bar, select Window ➣ Bookmarks to open the Bookmarks window.

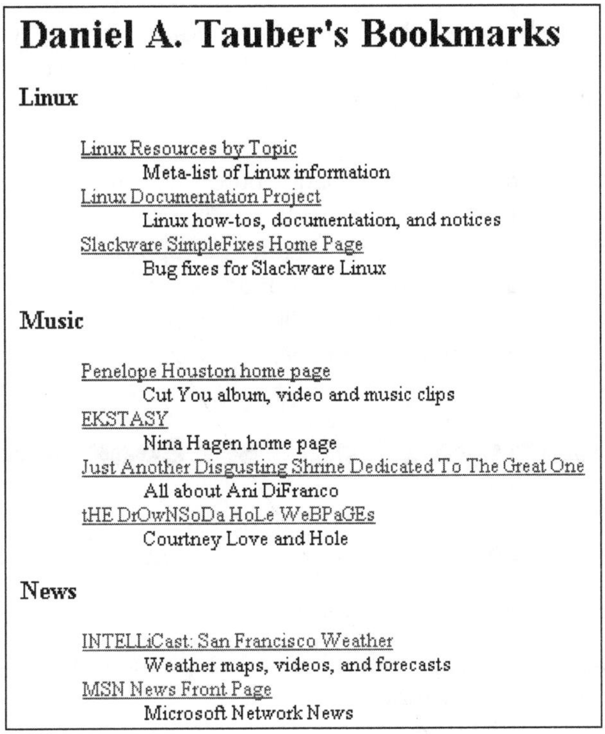

Daniel A. Tauber's Bookmarks

Linux

Linux Resources by Topic
          Meta-list of Linux information
Linux Documentation Project
          Linux how-tos, documentation, and notices
Slackware SimpleFixes Home Page
          Bug fixes for Slackware Linux

Music

Penelope Houston home page
          Cut You album, video and music clips
EKSTASY
          Nina Hagen home page
Just Another Disgusting Shrine Dedicated To The Great One
          All about Ani DiFranco
tHE DrOwNSoDa HoLe WeBPaGEs
          Courtney Love and Hole

News

INTELLiCast: San Francisco Weather
          Weather maps, videos, and forecasts
MSN News Front Page
          Microsoft Network News

Figure 4.3: This somewhat simple home page began life as a Bookmark list.

2. In the window, highlight the bookmark or folder you want to rename.

3. From the menu bar, select Item ➤ Properties. The Bookmark Properties window will appear.

4. In the Name text box you'll see the name of the bookmark or folder you highlighted. Type the new name you want to assign to this item into the text box.

5. Click on the OK button. The Bookmark Properties window will close (and your change will take effect).

6. If you want to rename another item, repeat steps 2–5.

7. When you've finished renaming bookmarks and folders, select File ➤ Close from the Bookmarks window's menu bar to return to the Netscape window.

To rename the Web page you created from your Bookmark list (as described in the section titled *The Ol' Bookmark-List-Becomes-a-Web-Page Trick*), just rename the topmost folder of your Bookmark list—usually you'll find your actual name there; you can rename the folder anything you like, then open the list as a Web page and it'll have the new name you gave it.

Removing Items from Your Bookmark List

Out with the old and in with the new! You can remove any bookmark or folder from your Bookmark list, making room for fresher material.

To delete items from your Bookmark list, follow these steps:

1. From the Netscape menu bar, select Window ➤ Bookmarks to open the Bookmarks window.

2. In the window, highlight the bookmark or folder you want to remove.

3. Press Delete.

or

From the Bookmarks window's menu bar, select Edit ➤ Delete.

If you delete a folder from your Bookmark list, any bookmarks under that folder will also vanish.

4. When you've finished removing bookmarks and folders, select File ➤ Close from the Bookmarks window's menu bar to return to the Netscape window.

The items you deleted will no longer appear in the Bookmark list (that is, on the Bookmarks drop-down menu).

Netscape includes a great feature that allows you to see which of your bookmarked Web pages have changed since the last time you visited them. To get the latest, highlight the page(s) of interest in the Bookmarks window (or highlight nothing if you want to check all the bookmarked pages), and from the menu bar, select File ➤ What's New. Netscape will venture forth to check the Web pages and report which of them have been modified since your last visit. The title of any page that has changed will appear as usual in the Bookmarks window, but its icon will have little yellow "Hey! Lookee!" lines beaming from it. Pages that Netscape can't verify will appear with question marks—for example, some pages that use interactive scripts may be impossible to verify and will appear with question marks. (You'll have to check into them manually.)

Bookmarking a Single Frame

You may have noticed that no matter where you go in a site that uses frames, the URL that appears in the Location bar changes not a bit—until you move on to a different Web site, that is. This is because, while each frame technically has a different URL, the *entire page* has just one URL— the one that appears in the Location bar.

Suppose you like one part of this framed Web page, and you want to bookmark the contents of just that specific frame. There are two ways to do this:

◆ Right-click in the frame containing the material of interest, and from the Netscape menu bar that appears, select Add Bookmark. Then you can open and check the Bookmarks window to make sure that you bookmarked the contents of the frame you wanted instead of the whole page.

◆ Go back to where you saw the link to what you like. Point and click the *right* mouse button on this link, and a pop-up menu will appear. Select Add Bookmark from the menu. The bookmark will then appear on your Bookmark list.

◆ The History Window As Bookmark List

You might think of the History window as a pseudo-Bookmark list. The History window, which appears in the Netscape menu bar under the Window option, is a log of every move you make in your Netscape session. Each time you launch Netscape, the History window starts empty; then it fills up with a list of your moves as you go along. To see the History window, select Window ➣ History from the menu bar (a highlight appears over the name of the current page). You can then double-click on any page listed there and jump to that item, or click on the Go To button. Thus, you can use the History window as a kind of short-term Bookmark list.

To add items from the History window to your Bookmark list, highlight the item of interest in the History window, and then click on the Create Bookmark button. The next time you check into your Bookmark list, you'll find a new bookmark there.

◆ Go Gets You There, Too

The Go feature on the menu bar is one of the most useful—and most overlooked—features of Netscape. After you've gone a lot of places during a Netscape session, select the Go menu from Netscape's menu bar. You'll see a list of places you've been since you started surfing the Web this particular time. Of course, there is a limit. If you've visited hundreds of pages in a particular session, only the last dozen or so of those pages will be available from the Go menu.

Oddly enough, when you visit a page that you've already visited, and then you branch off somewhere else, all the items in the Go menu that you visited after that point will disappear and the list will start anew.

To take advantage of the Go feature, from the Netscape menu bar, just select Go. From the menu that appears, you can go Back, Forward, or Home, or (here's the true value) you can select any of the pages listed— the pages you've visited most recently. Between this and the History window, you're pretty much covered.

◆ Using Internet Shortcuts to Web Documents

As an alternative to bookmarking Web pages or saving them to your local machine, you can create Internet *shortcuts*. These shortcuts are a Windows feature; they look just like files on your local machine—appearing as icons on your Desktop, files in folders, or the like, but instead of *being* a document (like a word-processed document, for example) they *point* to documents on the Web. Internet shortcuts offer you the advantage of having direct access to Web documents whatever else you happen to be doing on your computer. You can embed an Internet shortcut in any application that takes advantage of current OLE technology (that means most Windows 95 applications) or on your Desktop; so it'll be there for your convenience when you want it.

The difference (to the user) between an Internet shortcut and a bookmark is that the shortcut can appear on your Desktop or in another Windows application document, whereas a bookmark appears only on the Bookmark list in Netscape. Assuming your Internet connection is going, when you click on an Internet shortcut, the shortcut will launch Netscape and load the page of interest in one fell swoop.

The big advantage to having and using an Internet shortcut as opposed to saving the actual Web document on your machine is that the shortcut takes you to the Web document of interest as it exists "live" on the Net. When you save and view a document, on the other hand, you'll be viewing the document as it existed when you saved it—you may not be seeing the most current version, and you won't have the images unless you saved each one.

 Shortcuts conserve disk space—a shortcut takes up only a few bytes of disk space regardless of the size of the original document, while saving a whole document may take up tens of thousands of bytes.

The drawback to shortcuts (it isn't much of a drawback) is that you must be connected to the Internet to view documents with them. (They're *shortcuts* to documents as they exist on the Web, not the documents themselves, remember.) This means that the best use of shortcuts is for getting to Web documents you need to see "live." If you want to save a document you don't expect to last long on the Web, or if you don't want to pay for connect time to view a document, you may want to save the document instead of using a shortcut to get to it.

Creating an Internet Shortcut

You can create an Internet shortcut to the document you are currently viewing in Netscape by following a few simple steps.

Creating an Internet Shortcut on Your Desktop

Creating an Internet shortcut on your Desktop is an end in and of itself and is the means to creating one in a Windows application. Here's how to do it.

1. With Netscape running and the Web page of interest in view, point your mouse any place on the Web document that is not a graphic or a link. (White space is a good choice.)

2. Click the right mouse button. A pop-up menu will appear.

3. From the menu, select Internet Shortcut. The Create Internet Shortcut dialog box will appear (Figure 4.4).

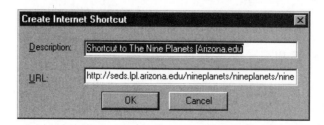

Figure 4.4: The Create Internet Shortcut dialog box allows you to enter the URL and title of the Internet shortcut you are creating.

4. In the dialog box's description text box, type a description of the Web page of interest to help you identify it in the future. Leave everything else alone.

5. Click on the OK button.

You won't see any immediate difference on screen, but the next time you minimize or close Netscape, you'll see your new Internet shortcut appearing as an icon on your Desktop. It'll look like the classic Netscape icon you're so used to seeing, with the name of the Web document under the icon.

 You can also create an Internet shortcut by clicking on a hypertext word or phrase (or any other link) in a Web document and then dragging that link from Netscape's window to the Desktop. When you release the mouse button after this clicking and dragging procedure, an Internet shortcut will appear where you placed it.

Placing a Shortcut in a Windows Program

Having created an Internet shortcut for the Web document of interest on the Desktop as described in the section before this one, you can now pick up the shortcut there and place it in a Windows application. It's easy.

1. Follow the procedure for placing an Internet shortcut on your Desktop, as described in *Creating an Internet Shortcut on Your Desktop*.

2. Open the Windows application *and the document* (or spreadsheet, or whatever) where you want the shortcut to conveniently be at your disposal.

3. Resize or otherwise position the application's window (containing the document into which you want to place the shortcut) so that you can see both it and the shortcut that appears on your Desktop.

4. Click on the Internet shortcut of interest and drag it to the document in the application's window, dropping it where you want it to appear.

5. Save the document as you would if you'd made any other changes to it, using the familiar File ➢ Save or Save As feature you know so well.

In the future, when you open that Windows application document (whether it's a word-processed document, a spreadsheet document, or whatever), and you then double-click on the Internet shortcut you've created, Netscape will start and load the URL, taking you automatically to the Web page of interest.

 If you have an e-mail program that uses OLE technology—the Windows 95 Inbox, for example—you can drop one of these shortcuts into an e-mail message, and when the recipient of your message clicks on the shortcut (assuming he or she has Netscape), Netscape will do its thing, and the Web page of interest will appear.

Activating an Internet Shortcut

Any time you see an Internet shortcut, you can double-click on it, and Netscape will launch itself and display the page to which the shortcut points. Remember, your Internet connection must be active for this procedure to work.

What's Out There

Visit **http://www.msn.com/** to find out how to customize the Microsoft Network's Start page.

Away We Go!

You now have basic Netscape navigation skills, and you know a thing or two (or three or four) about keeping track of sites you've seen, too. Now let's take a look at how you can communicate with others (via newsgroups and e-mail) the Netscape way.

Newsgroups and E-Mail the Netscape Way

Before the advent of the wonderful World Wide Web and its attending browsers, there was an Internet, and it was already a happening place. Much of what went on via the Internet then took the form of talk— typed talk, to be sure, but talk nonetheless, in the form of newsgroup articles and e-mail. For a long time, many people thought newsgroups *were* the Internet—the whole Internet. Even today, e-mail is one of the most popular features of the Net, and newsgroups are a highly viable forum for discussion on all sorts of topics.

In earlier versions, Netscape provided a competent newsgroup reader and the ability to send e-mail (but not receive it). Among the stellar accomplishments of Netscape are an improved newsgroup reader and a full-featured e-mail program that lets you send and receive e-mail using either Netscape or Microsoft Exchange—your choice. Let's take a look.

◆ Reading and Writing Usenet News with Netscape

Unlike many other Web browsers, Netscape provides you with fully workable access to Usenet. Usenet is a collection of discussion groups, called *newsgroups*, each organized around a specific topic or area of interest. Access to Usenet is through a feature of Netscape called Netscape News. Using Netscape News, you can read and post *articles* (messages) to those newsgroups that interest you.

Before you can start using Usenet with Netscape, you must set up Netscape to work with the way you access the Internet, whether that's via an Internet service provider, an online service such as AOL or CompuServe, or whatever. This is a special aspect of installing Netscape. See Chapter 11 for details.

What's Out There

To find out all about Usenet newsgroups get the FAQs. What Is Usenet is at `ftp://rtfm.mit.edu/pub/usenet/news.answers/usenet/what-is/part1`, MIT's RTFM archive is at `ftp://rtfm.mit.edu/pub/usenet/news.answers`, and the Ohio State archive is at `http://www.cis.ohio-state.edu/hypertext/faq/usenet/`.

Starting Netscape News, the Newsgroup Reader

Netscape News is quite easy to start up. Simply follow this single step:

1. From Netscape's menu bar, select Window ➤ Netscape News. The Netscape News window will appear.

That's all there is to it. Now you can start reading and writing Usenet news.

Reading Usenet News for the First Time

At first glance you may find the Netscape News window a bit confusing. Don't worry—we're going to tell you how to use it. The window has a number of sections—each displays different information. A list of Usenet news servers appears in the upper-left side of the window (you told Netscape the name of your Usenet news server when you got Netscape working with your Internet connection). Clicking on any of the news servers (most likely you'll only have one server listed) displays a list of newsgroups located on that server to which you are subscribed. In the upper-right side of the window is a list of articles in the currently selected newsgroup. The actual articles appear in the bottom part of the window. Use the scroll bar on the right side of the bottom part of the window to see the complete text of the currently selected article.

What's Out There

DejaNews keeps a giant archive of past Usenet news articles that you can search at http://www.dejanews.com. You'll find a no-nonsense, searchable, browsable listing of newsgroups at http://sunsite.unc.edu/usenet-i/. And Zippo Dot Com, at http://www.zippo.com, selects the best newsgroups for you, telling you, among other things, where there are postings about software you can get via FTP.

One Way to Get into a Newsgroup

Netscape News lets you *subscribe* to groups you read or participate in regularly. When you subscribe to a newsgroup, its name appears in the Netscape News window, and you can start using the newsgroup just by clicking on its name.

 Subscribing to a newsgroup involves no money changing hands and no particular commitment. It's just a way of informally "joining up" to listen in or actually participate in the newsgroup.

To subscribe to a newsgroup, follow these easy steps:

1. If the Netscape News window is not already open, from Netscape's menu bar, select Window ≻ Netscape News. The Netscape News window will appear, looking something like it does in Figure 5.1.

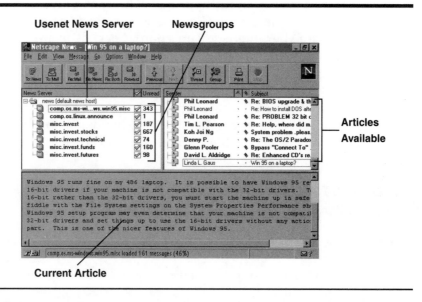

Figure 5.1: The Netscape News window gives you access to Usenet news.

2. From the Netscape News menu bar, select Options ≻ Show All Newsgroups. A dialog box will appear warning you that it may take a while to get the list of all newsgroups.

3. Click on OK to dismiss the warning dialog box. Netscape News will start downloading the list of newsgroups from the news server to your machine. While the list of newsgroups is downloading, the mouse pointer will be an hourglass. You can follow the downloading progress in the status bar along the bottom of the Netscape News window.

4. When the list of newsgroups has been downloaded to your computer, it will appear in the Netscape News window, listed under the news server. Locate the newsgroup to which you want to subscribe, and select the checkbox that appears to its right.

The newsgroup to which you've subscribed will appear with a checkmark to its right in the list of newsgroups. The two numbers that appear next to it tell you how many articles in that newsgroup you have yet to read and how many articles are available in total. In Figure 5.2, you can see that we've subscribed to a newsgroup called `comp.os.ms-windows.win95.misc`, which is a hotbed of talk about Microsoft Windows 95.

---

news (default news host)		
comp.os.ms-wi...ws.win95.misc	☑	192
misc.invest	☑	200
misc.invest.stocks	☑	652
misc.invest.technical	☑	80
misc.invest.funds	☑	182
misc.invest.futures	☑	113

Figure 5.2: The newsgroups to which you subscribe will be listed in the Netscape News window.

Another Way to Get into a Newsgroup

The URLs for newsgroups start with `news:` rather than with `http:`. Knowing this handy fact, you can access a Usenet newsgroup by selecting File ➤ Open Location from Netscape's menu bar and, in the window that appears, typing the newsgroup's URL (which is just the name of the newsgroup preceded by `news:`) into the text box and clicking on Open. This is a quick way to get into a newsgroup, but it does not preserve your access to the newsgroup—next time you want to go there, you'll have to repeat this procedure.

Once you've accessed a particular newsgroup using this technique, you can read articles and, using the skills described in the sections that follow (check out *Posting a Reply* and *Posting a New Article*), you can write to the newsgroup.

Unsubscribing from Newsgroups

You won't always want to remain a subscriber to a particular newsgroup. Your interests will change; the newsgroup will grow dull. You'll want to move along.

In fact, Netscape automatically subscribes to three newsgroups for you. They provide helpful information for new Usenet users but aren't really necessary once you've become accomplished. After a while, you'll probably want to let them go. Unsubscribing is really easy. Click on the checkbox to the right of the newsgroup name to remove the checkmark. When you do this, the name of the newsgroup will disappear from the list of newsgroups to which you are subscribed. You can always resubscribe if you want to pick up that newsgroup again.

Reading Articles in Subscribed Newsgroups

To read articles once you've subscribed to a newsgroup, click on that newsgroup's name in the Netscape News window. All the "unread" articles in the newsgroup will appear in a list along the right side of the window (see Figure 5.3). To read an article, simply click on it in the list. When you do this, Netscape transfers the contents of the article to your computer and displays it in the bottom part of the window.

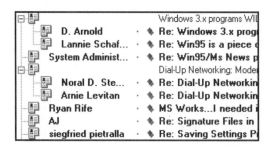

Figure 5.3: A few of the unread articles listed for a group called `comp.os.ms-windows.win95.misc` (a general discussion group about Microsoft Windows 95)

Reading Along a Thread

Notice also in Figure 5.3 that articles are listed by authors' names and that some articles appear indented below others. Some less-capable newsgroup readers display articles only in the order they were posted, but Netscape arranges articles by *subject* in the order they were posted. A message that is not indented is the beginning of a discussion on a particular topic. A message that appears indented below another is a later message about the same subject; often it is a reply.

By ordering the messages in this way, Netscape allows you to read all the articles about a subject, one right after the other. Messages grouped by subject in this way are called *threads,* and reading messages this way is called *reading along a thread*. A thread is essentially a string of related articles—they're related in that they are usually responses that follow the original article.

To read along a thread, first open any article you want by clicking on its name. (Because Netscape lists the articles in each thread in the order they were posted, it's probably a good idea to start with an article that begins a thread—in other words, one that is not indented.)

When you're done reading the first article, you can read the next article in the thread—this can be the next contribution to the discussion or a reply to the message you just finished—by clicking on the Next button. If you're in the middle of a thread, you can read the article posted prior to the one you're looking at by clicking on the Previous button. This button and all the others you need to read newsgroup articles are at the top of the Netscape News window.

Let's quickly go over all the buttons Netscape News provides for reading articles.

The Tool	Its Name	What It Does
To: News	Post New	Posts a new article
To: Mail	New Message	Sends an e-mail message

The Tool	Its Name	What It Does
Re:Mail	Reply	Sends an e-mail message to the author of the article you are currently reading
Re:News	Post Reply	Posts a reply to the article you are currently reading
Re:Both	Post and Reply	Posts a reply to the current article and e-mails the reply
Forward	Forward	Forwards the current message to someone else via e-mail
Previous	Previous	Moves to the previous article in the thread you are currently reading
Next	Next	Moves to the next article in the thread you are currently reading
Thread	Mark Thread Read	Moves to the first article in the next thread, marking the current thread as read
Group	Mark All Read	Marks all the articles in the current newsgroup as read
Print	Print	Prints the current article
Stop	Stop	Interrupts the transfer of an article to your computer

Posting a Reply

If you want to post a reply to an article you've read, follow these easy steps:

1. With an article open (presumably the one to which you want to reply), click on the Post Reply button. A window will appear, as shown in Figure 5.4.

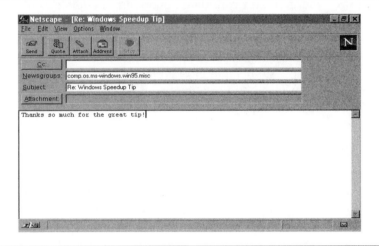

Figure 5.4: This window is your door to writing newsgroup replies.

In the window's Subject box, the subject of your post (taken from the original article) will appear. In the Newsgroup box, the newsgroups in which the original article appeared will be listed.

2. If you'd like to include the original message in your reply, click on the Quote button at the top of the window. The original message (the one to which you are posting a reply) will then appear in the window. To make it easy for you to see what's what, each line in the original message will be prefixed with the > symbol. You can delete any part (or all) of the original message if you like.

The original message will be quoted automatically if you've checked the appropriate box (which is located on the Composition tab that you can call up by selecting Mail ➤ News Preferences from Netscape's Options menu).

3. Type your reply to the original message in the text box along the bottom of the window, and click on the Send button at the top of the window.

Your reply will be posted automatically to the groups in which the original article appeared.

You needn't feel compelled to quote the entire original article in your reply. It's considered good form to delete as much of the original message as necessary 'til you get down to the part that is immediately relevant to your response. Further, you can add or delete newsgroups listed in the Newsgroup text box as you wish. This is a simple matter of typing in the names of any newsgroups you want to add or of highlighting any you want to delete and then wielding your Delete key.

Posting a New Article

You can post new articles to start new threads as well. Simply click on the New button at the top of the Netscape News window. The procedure after this point is exactly the same as that for posting a reply, except that the subject of the article is not filled in and there is no text in the Message text box. Refer to the preceding section (*Posting a Reply*) for more information.

Do You Need Help?

For answers to your questions about using Netscape, call (800) 320-2099 or e-mail `client@netscape.com`. Keep your credit card handy if you haven't paid for Netscape just yet.

◆ Sending and Receiving E-Mail the Netscape Way

Netscape offers a full-featured e-mail program, Netscape Mail, that allows you to send and receive e-mail using either Netscape itself or, if you prefer, Microsoft Exchange. This is relatively new to the world of Web browsers and is quite a nifty feature. Heretofore, most Web browsers allowed you to send e-mail but not to receive it. That was because receiving e-mail involved much more complicated issues of, for example, storing messages 'til you read them. Netscape has licked this challenge, and now (since version 2) you have the e-mail capability in your Web browser to prove it.

Before you can use Netscape Mail, you must set up Netscape to use your Internet service provider's POP3 mailbox and SMTP mail server. This is not difficult; turn to Chapter 11 for more information.

Using Netscape Mail with Microsoft Exchange

If you use Microsoft Exchange (the full, expensive version, not the scaled-down version that comes with Windows 95) as your regular e-mail client, you may prefer to use Exchange rather than Netscape for sending and receiving e-mail while you're out there surfing the Web. To designate Exchange as your e-mail interface of choice, follow these steps:

1. From Netscape's Options menu, select Mail ➢ News Preferences. The News Preferences dialog box will appear.

2. On the Appearance tab, click in the circle next to Use Exchange Client for Mail and News to select that option.

3. Click on the OK button to save your changes. The dialog box will close and the Netscape window will be visible.

Now, whenever you send an e-mail message or post an article to a Usenet newsgroup, you'll be doing it through Exchange rather than through Netscape Mail.

Starting Netscape Mail

To start Netscape Mail, take these simple steps:

1. From the Netscape menu bar, select Window ➢ Netscape Mail. The Password Entry dialog box will appear (see Figure 5.5).

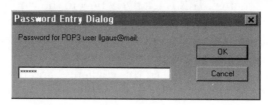

Figure 5.5: In the Password Entry dialog box, you must enter your e-mail password.

2. Type the password assigned to you by your Internet service provider, and click on OK. In a few seconds, the Netscape Mail window will appear. You can see it in Figure 5.6.

With the Netscape Mail window open, you are ready to start getting and sending e-mail.

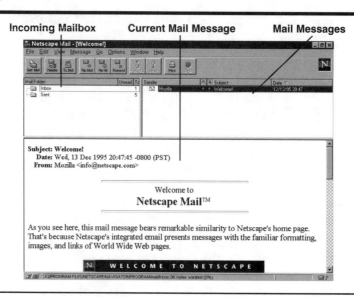

Figure 5.6: The Netscape Mail window allows you to read and send e-mail to anyone on the Internet.

Reading Your Mail

The Netscape Mail window is divided into several sections, much as the Netscape News window is. Along the upper-left side of the Netscape Mail window you'll see a list of folders—it should include an Inbox and Sent Mail folder. (You may also see an Outbox and a Trash folder; Netscape Mail creates these when they are needed.) Along the upper-right side of the Netscape Mail window (see Figure 5.6) is a list of messages from the current folder. The current message is displayed in the bottom part of the Netscape Mail window.

The buttons that appear along the top of the Netscape Mail window are shortcuts to many commonly used and popular features.

The Tool	Its Name	What It Does
Get Mail	Get Mail	Retrieves mail waiting on the mail server
Delete	Delete	Deletes the highlighted message
To:Mail	New Mail	Creates a new message
Re:Mail	Reply	Replies to the author of the current message
Re:All	Reply All	Replies to all the recipients of the current message
Forward	Forward	Forwards the current message to someone else

The Tool	Its Name	What It Does
Previous	Previous	Moves to the previous message
Next	Next	Moves to the next message
Print	Print	Prints the current message
Stop	Stop	Stops transmission or whatever activity is occurring

 When you click on the Delete tool to get rid of a message, it doesn't actually vanish. Instead, it's moved to a special Trash folder. To permanently dispose of messages in the Trash folder, select File ➢ Empty from the menu bar.

Sending a Message

Sending a message with Netscape Mail is easy. You can do it while you're connected to the Net, or you can write up a bunch of messages when you're not connected and send them along later, which is a boon if you're not near a phone line or are interested in saving online time.

Writing and Sending a Message Online

So you're already connected and just want to dash off an e-mail or two? Just follow these steps:

1. On the Netscape Mail tool bar, click on the New Mail button. The Message Composition window will appear. In Figure 5.7 you can see one into which we've entered all the necessary info, but when this window appears it will be empty, waiting for you to fill it in.

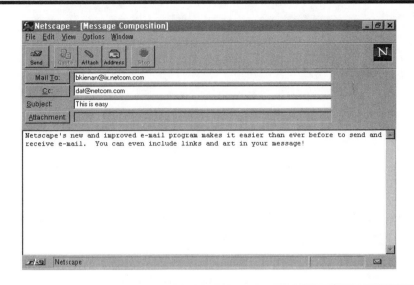

Figure 5.7: In the Message Composition window, you'll enter all the stuff that makes up your e-mail message.

2. In the Mail To text box, type the e-mail address of the person to whom you want to send an e-mail message.

 You can also get the e-mail address from your Address book; click on the Address button to gain access to it. See *Creating Your Very Own Address Book* (later in this chapter) for more details about this handy feature.

3. Now in the Subject field, type a subject for the message you are about to write.

4. Click in the big text box along the bottom of the window, and start typing your message.

5. When you are done typing your e-mail message and are ready to send it, click on the Send button along the top of the window. Your message will go off in a matter of seconds, and you will be returned to the Netscape Mail window.

What's Out There

Find your favorite star's e-mail address with the search options and listings at `http://oscar.teclink.net/~chip1120/email.html`.

Writing a Message Offline and Sending It Later

Sometimes, especially if you're using a laptop that's nowhere near a phone line and you'd like to write e-mail, it's convenient to be able to compose your messages while you're *offline* (not connected to the Internet). Luckily, Netscape Navigator 3 is flexible enough to let you do this by following these simple steps:

1. On the Netscape Mail tool bar, click on the New Mail button. The Message Composition window will appear.

2. Before you begin composing your first message, in the Message Composition window's menu bar, select Options ➤ Deferred Delivery. This will cause Netscape to store this and any subsequent messages you write during this particular offline session in a queue which you'll later be able to send on its way (when you are connected to the Internet).

3. Now in the Message Composition window's Mail To text box, type the e-mail address of the person to whom you want to send your message.

4. In the Subject field, type a subject for the message you are about to write.

5. Click in the big text box along the bottom of the window, and start typing your message.

6. When you're done and satisfied that you've said it all, click on the Send button (along the top of the Message Composition window). Your message won't be on it's way—it'll be stored in the Outbox folder instead.

7. To send this and other queued messages, get connected to the Internet, then from the Netscape Mail window, select File ➤ Send Messages in Outbox.

At last, all your queued e-mail messages will be on their merry way.

Creating Your Very Own Address Book

Netscape provides you with the convenience of keeping an address book in which you can organize and store the e-mail addresses of all the people with whom you correspond. The Address book works and is useful both in Netscape Mail and Netscape News—any time you need to enter an e-mail address you can use your handy Address book. But first you have to get the addresses in there.

What's Out There

A very nifty list of mailing lists, Liszt (cute, eh?), is at `http://www.liszt.com`. Liszt grows like a weed, and it offers descriptions of the mailing lists, so you can easily pick those of interest. Once you subscribe to a mailing list, you'll get messages on the topic of interest delivered to your inbox on a daily or even hourly basis.

One Way to Add People to Your Address Book

Adding new e-mail addresses to your Address book is as simple as most other Netscape tasks. Usually, you'll find you want to add the e-mail address of someone to whom you're replying. To do this, you'll of course start with either an e-mail message or a Usenet article from the person whose e-mail address you want to add to your book appearing on screen.

1. With the e-mail message or Usenet article from the person you want to add to your Address book on screen, right-click your mouse (preferably and most safely in some white space in the message). A menu will appear.

2. From the menu, select Add to Address Book. The Address Book Properties dialog box will appear.

3. This dialog box has in it text boxes where you can type information about the person you are adding to your Address book. In the Nick Name text field, type a nickname for the person. (In the old days we called this a "handle." You can just use the person's given

name if you like.) Nicknames must be single words and contain only lowercase letters.

4. In the Description text box you can enter a description or notes about the person whose e-mail address you are adding. For example, you might want to make notes about how you met this person, why he or she is of interest, or what you mean to be in touch about in the future.

5. You'll find that the Name and E-Mail Address text boxes are already filled out—this is a result of the message from the person being open. Now finish up by clicking on the OK button to add the e-mail address to your Address book. The Address Book Properties dialog box will close.

Next time you open the Address Book window you'll see the new e-mail address listed.

Another Way to Add People to Your Address Book

If you know someone's e-mail address and you just want to add it to your Address book without being in mid-reply to a message, follow these steps:

1. From the Netscape menu bar, select Window ➤ Address Book. The Address Book window will appear.

2. From the Address Book window's menu bar, select Item ➤ Add User. The Address Book Properties dialog box will appear.

3. This dialog box has in it text boxes where you can type information about the person you are adding to your Address book. In the Nick Name text field, type a nickname ("handle") for the person, or just use the person's given name. Nicknames must be single words and can contain only lowercase letters.

4. In the Description text box you can enter a description or notes about the person whose e-mail address you are adding. For example, you might want to make notes about how you met this person, why he or she is of interest, or what you mean to contact him or her about in the future.

5. In the Name and E-Mail Address text boxes, type the name and e-mail address of the person whose address you're adding to your book.

What's Out There

Lost track of old pals? You can track down friends and lost relatives using Yahoo's People Search gizmo. Pop over to `http://www.yahoo.com/search/people` and type in a name to find that person's snail-mail address and phone number, their e-mail address, or the URL for their home page. Another resource for investigating the e-mail addresses of others is Okra Net Citizen Directory at `http://okra.ucr.edu/okra/`.

---

6. Now click on the OK button to add the e-mail address to your Address book. The Address Book Properties dialog box will close.

Now you'll see the new entry you just created in the Address book window.

Using Your Address Book for Sending Mail

In the section titled *Sending a Message* earlier in this chapter, we told you the basics for sending e-mail, but it can be a more convenient process. Once you've got people listed in your Address book, you can start using it to make sending e-mail easier. To send e-mail to someone who's listed in the Address book, follow these steps:

1. From the Netscape menu bar, select Window ➤ Address Book to open your Address book.

2. In the Address Book window, locate and double-click on the name of the person to whom you want to send mail. The Message Composition window will appear, with your intended recipient's name and e-mail address filled in.

3. Go ahead—write and send an e-mail message as you usually would.

That's all there is to using Netscape's multifunctional, convenient Address book.

Replying to a Message

Replying to a message is very much like writing a new message. Just follow these steps:

1. With the message to which you want to reply on screen, click on either the Reply or the Reply All button. (Remember, the Reply button will address your reply only to the person who sent the message; the Reply All button will address your message to everyone involved—including all the people who were "Cced.") Regardless of which buttons you click on, the Message Composition window will appear.

2. In the Message Composition window, you'll see that the Mail To, Cc, and Subject fields are already filled in, based on information that came from the message to which you are replying. You can modify any of these fields if you like, or you can leave them "as is."

3. In the text area near the bottom of the window, type your message. You can include the contents of the original message in your reply by clicking on the Quote button.

4. After you type your e-mail message, click on the Send button. In a matter of seconds, your message will be transferred from your computer to your Internet service provider's mail server—it's on its way!—and the Netscape Mail window will reappear on your screen.

Now you know how to send a reply.

You can embed HTML (hypertext, images, and more) into your e-mail messages—effectively making your messages into documents. See Chapter 9 to find out how.

The Coming Days of Secure Mail

The current generation of Netscape servers offer increasingly enhanced security features that you may find helpful in preventing e-mail "forgeries." See *Certificates and Enhanced Security* at the end of Chapter 3 for more information.

Changing the Look of Netscape News and Mail

Netscape Navigator 3 lets you change the look of Netscape News and Mail to suit your taste. Here's how:

1. With Netscape running, pull down the Options menu and select Mail and News Preferences. The Mail and News Preferences dialog box will appear.

2. Click on the Appearance tab, and the contents of the dialog box will change to display options for changing the fonts, quoted text style, and the window pane layout of Netscape News and Mail.

3. To use a fixed-width font for displaying messages and articles in Netscape News and Mail, click in the circle next to Fixed Width Font. Alternatively, to use a variable-width font, click in the circle next to Variable Width Font. (Most of the time it's advisable to use a fixed-width font for displaying messages and articles in Netscape News and Mail because this ensures that you'll see the whole message in the most legible layout. But maybe you have your own reasons for changing this.)

4. To change the style (appearance) of text you've quoted from other e-mail messages and articles in e-mail messages and news articles you write, click in the circle that corresponds to the way you'd like quoted text to appear. You have four options here: quoted text can be plain, bold, italic, or bold italic (bold and italic at the same time).

5. To change the size of text quoted in e-mail messages and news articles, click in the circle that corresponds to the size in which you'd like quoted text to appear. You have three options here: quoted text can be plain (the same size), bigger, or smaller than the text of your message.

6. For both Netscape News and Mail, you can choose to display window panes in any one of three ways: split horizontally (the default setting), split vertically, or stacked. We've found that the horizontal panes are the most convenient, but you may want to experiment a bit and see which layout suits you best.

7. Once you are done making changes to the Mail and New Preferences dialog box, click on the OK button to make your changes take effect, and you will return to the Netscape window.

Quitting Netscape Mail

When you're finished reading and replying to your mail, quitting Netscape Mail is a quick, standard procedure you can accomplish in just one step.

1. From the menu bar, select File ➤ Close.

or

Click on the × in the upper-right corner of the Netscape Mail window. Either way, the Netscape window will appear.

Now you can practice any of the skills you picked up in this chapter, or if you're done for now, you can quit Netscape altogether.

We're on Our Way!

Now that you know how to use Netscape's basic features, the newsgroup reader, and the e-mail program, let's turn our attention in Chapter 6 to CoolTalk, Netscape's new plug-in for interactive communication, and then, in Chapter 7, to that other new plug-in, Live3D.

Communicating via CoolTalk

CoolTalk is *plenty* cool. It makes communicating about as interactive as it can be without seeing or sitting in a room with other folks. CoolTalk lets you use the Internet as a telephone, "chat" with your friends via interactive typed messages, and collaborate using a whiteboard (Figure 6.1) on which you and your compadres can draw or write material while you can all see it. CoolTalk also includes an answering "machine" that will take messages for you if you miss a CoolTalk call. CoolTalk is simple to use and doesn't require sophisticated hardware, so you don't have to be Joe Megabucks Genius to make it work for you.

 When you download Netscape Navigator, you have the option of getting the standard version, which includes CoolTalk and Live3D, or a more stripped-down version that doesn't. See Chapter 10.

What's Out There

Kevin Savetz maintains a Net telephone guide at
`http://www.northcoast.com/~savetz/voice-faq.html`.

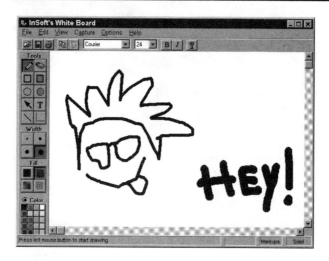

Figure 6.1: You can use the CoolTalk whiteboard to share a drawing space with associates.

◆ Starting Up CoolTalk for the First Time

CoolTalk can be installed automatically with the standard version of Netscape. All you have to do is tell the installation utility that you would like CoolTalk put on your system by clicking on Yes at the appropriate time. (We cover this in Chapter 11.) Do make sure you've got the right stuff—you need just three pieces of easy-to-get hardware to use CoolTalk:

◆ A sound card (it's possible to use CoolTalk's Chat tool and white-board without one, but what fun is that?)

◆ An inexpensive microphone

◆ Inexpensive speakers

Don't bother shelling out for a microphone or speakers for the sake of your CoolTalk experience; expensive equipment doesn't improve CoolTalk's performance. The primary problem for most of us in using this sort of thing is still bandwidth, not the hardware on our desks. Go for economy in this case, and spend your money on memory and a good sound card.

The first time you start up CoolTalk, you'll have to do a bit of setup. Not to worry, you'll be in the sure hands of the Setup Wizard, which will lead you through the process. Here are the steps to follow:

1. From the Windows 95 Start menu, select Programs ➤ Netscape. The Netscape window will appear with the CoolTalk icon in it (along with a bunch of other stuff).

2. Double-click on the CoolTalk icon. A dialog box will appear telling you that the Setup Wizard has been invoked.

 If for any reason double-clicking on the CoolTalk icon doesn't invoke the Setup Wizard, go ahead and start CoolTalk by double-clicking on its icon, then pull down the Help menu and select Setup Wizard. Go on to step 3; you'll be fine.

3. The Setup Wizard will inquire as to whether you've got a sound card in your computer. If you do have a sound card, make sure it's installed properly and check to see that your microphone and speakers are connected and turned on. Click on Next to continue. If you don't have a sound card, you're not completely out of luck; although you won't be able to take advantage of CoolTalk's telephony features, you'll still be able to use the Chat and Whiteboard tools. Click in the checkbox labeled *I don't have a sound card in my computer*; then click on Next to continue. In either case, a dialog box will appear with information about modem speeds.

4. Click in the circle next to the speed that corresponds to the speed of your modem:

- ◆ 9600 baud or lower
- ◆ 14400 baud
- ◆ 28800 baud or higher

Click on Next to continue. A dialog box will appear informing you that the Setup Wizard is about to detect the audio devices in your computer.

5. Click on Next. A dialog box that contains the results of the Setup Wizard's search will appear, showing three pieces of information about your sound card:

- ◆ *Record* info indicates which sound card you have and the speed at which it's set to record.

◆ *Playback* info indicates (again) which sound card you've got and the speed at which it's set to play back recorded audio.

◆ *Sound card mode* info should specify Half or Full Duplex.

This dialog box also includes a note about an impending test of your sound card's capabilities.

If your sound card didn't come with what's called a *full-duplex driver*, or if you didn't install one when you put your sound card in, you may want to check with your card's vendor to see whether such a driver is available. Having one of these babies will improve your sound card's performance significantly, so it's probably worth asking the question.

What's Out There

If you have one of the popular SoundBlaster boards and don't happen to have a full-duplex driver, you can download one from Creative Labs' Web site. Check out `http://www.creaf.com`.

Check your equipment—are your microphone and speakers connected and turned on?

6. Click on Next. A dialog box will tell you what message you'll hear. If you do hear it, that's dandy. If not, check your connections again.

7. Click on Next to continue. A series of dialog boxes will appear testing the various aspects of your sound system's capabilities to deliver and record sound. The messages and responses are very intuitive—just follow the Wizard as each sound test is performed, and click on Next to move on to the next one, until all of the playback and recording tests are complete.

 As you go along, you'll be judging the sound. If you judge it to be off in any of the tests, click on *No, the pitch was wrong* and then on the Next button to continue the test. Don't fret over whether the pitch is perfect—this isn't piano tuning. Just make sure it sounds good to you.

8. When the playback and recording tests are done, a dialog box will appear telling you that Setup has completed audio configuration and it's about to perform a test of your system's performance. Click on Next to continue, as usual. A progress indicator will appear; hang on until it's done.

9. A dialog box will then appear congratulating you that your computer has enough CPU power to run CoolTalk. Click on Next yet again. The CoolTalk business card form will appear (looking something like Figure 6.2 except that it won't have been filled out yet).

 If by chance your hardware comes up short in the performance test, don't waste your time trying to use CoolTalk—you'll only be disappointed.

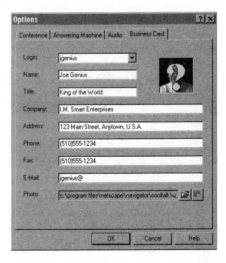

Figure 6.2: Your CoolTalk business card will tell others who you are.

The business card form defines the content of your online "business card," which will tell other people who you are and, if you like, show them your photo or some other image. Let's fill out the form now:

1. Click in the Login box and type your complete login name, for example, jgenius.

2. In the Name box, type your real name or any name by which you'd like to be known while using CoolTalk.

3. In the Title, Company, Address, Phone, Fax, and E-mail boxes, supply any information you wish to make available to your fellow surfers.

4. In the Photo box, specify the location of the image file that contains the picture or graphic you want to appear on your business card. If you've got a scanned photo on hand, you can use that (CoolTalk supports most of the common graphical file formats). Be sure to specify the complete path for the location of your image file, for example, C:\IMAGES\HEADSHOT.BMP. Or, if you prefer, you can use a graphic stored on the Windows 95 Clipboard by pasting it in.

5. When you're finished, click on Next to continue. A dialog box will thank you for using CoolTalk. Click on Finish. The main CoolTalk window, shown in Figure 6.3, will appear. Close the window for now by clicking on its Close box (in the upper-right corner).

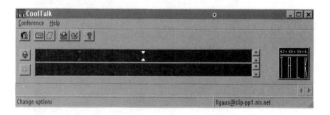

Figure 6.3: Here's the main CoolTalk window.

 To modify your CoolTalk options once you've got the program up and running, just run the Setup Wizard again, changing what you like as you go along.

It's time to do the Internet equivalent of dropping that dime. Here we go!

◆ Using CoolTalk to Talk

Turn on your speakers and microphone and fire up that computer so you can talk, talk, talk. You can yak with a pal (it's usually best to set up an appointment beforehand to make sure you're both online), or you can find a friendly and, presumably, talkative stranger.

What's Out There

Cycor Marketing Services, a Canadian Internet Service Provider, maintains a list of public Internet phone servers on their Northern Lights server. The URL is `http://www.cycor.ca/iphone/serv.html`.

Start Talking

Here's how to start yakking it up:

1. Connect to the Internet as you usually do. (See Chapter 10 if you don't know how.)

2. From the Windows 95 Start Menu, select Programs ➤ Netscape. The Netscape window will appear with the CoolTalk icon in it (along with the usual other stuff).

3. Double-click on the CoolTalk icon to start up CoolTalk. The main CoolTalk window (which you saw in Figure 6.3) will appear.

4. From the menu bar, select Conference ➤ Start. The Open Conference dialog box will appear.

5. If there's someone in particular you'd like to talk with, click on the Address Book tab. To talk to your friend I. M. Smart, type her address, `imsmart@mensa.com`, in the text box labeled *Enter or select a conference participant* (Figure 6.4) and click on OK. CoolTalk will ring your pal, and assuming she answers and that your equipment is configured properly, your repartee can begin.

    or

    If you'd prefer to talk to a stranger, click on the IS411 Directory tab in the Open Conference box. A list of other Internet phone users who are currently connected to the same server you are will appear. To ring someone, double-click on his or her name.

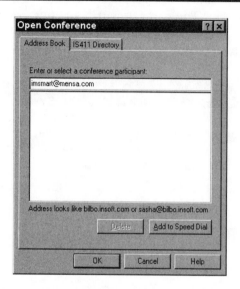

Figure 6.4: Calling someone you already know

CoolTalk comes set to use an IS411 server provided by Netscape. You can change to a different IS411 server (some corporations run their own IS411 servers for their employees, for example) by selecting Conference ➢ Options to display the Options dialog box and type its name in the Host name text box.

As they say, *now* you're talking (well, almost). Be aware that you may be rejected, but if you don't succeed, try, try again—it's a free-for-all and someone out there will want to talk to you. If you'd like to see the business card of the person you're talking to (this is especially useful if you're talking to a stranger), pull down the Conference menu and select Participant Info. The caller's business card will appear, so you can see who he or she claims to be.

If you're having trouble hearing each other, first fiddle around with the volume settings on your speakers and microphone. Sometimes just finding the right volume level does the trick. If not, while you're talking, slide the Silence Level (red) and Echo Suppression (white) slide controls on the main CoolTalk window to the left and right until you find the optimal setting for your computer. Finally, try leaving the present conference (see *Ending a Call*) and then run the Setup Wizard again to make sure that your audio settings are configured properly.

Ending a Call

When you're finished talking, *say goodbye*. Then, from the CoolTalk menu bar, select Conference ➤ Leave Conference. The main CoolTalk window will be visible.

Handling Incoming Calls

To accept an incoming call, click on the Accept button on the dialog box that pops up when somebody rings you. To reject an incoming call, just click on the Reject button on the same dialog box. The person who was ringing you will simply go away.

The Bandwidth Follies

The primary problem with CoolTalk can be summed up in a single word: *bandwidth*. Especially if you're connecting to the Internet through a modem rather than a LAN with a fast line like a T1, you'll notice that transmission quality could be a lot better, and it often takes several seconds for your computer to produce what the person you're talking to has just said. Until more of us are working with equipment that can keep up with the immense data flow necessary to support real-time voice communications, there will be problems with sound quality and voice lags. At times, this can be frustrating, which is one reason why the phone companies don't seem to feel overly threatened by Internet phone services quite yet. Telephony on the Net is still in its infancy...watch (or *listen*) for improvements in the future.

Blocking Unwanted Calls

If you'd rather not make yourself available to be phoned by others through the IS411 server, you can block incoming calls. Just follow these steps:

1. From the CoolTalk menu bar, select Conference ➤ Options. The Options dialog box will appear.

2. Click on the Conference tab to examine your conference settings.

3. Remove the checkmark next to the label *Make me available through server*.

4. In the Accept Invitation area of the dialog box, select the setting you prefer:

Select	If You Want
Never	All incoming calls rejected
Ask	To be asked whether you're accepting calls
Always	To allow others to call you at will

5. Click on OK to save your settings. This will return you to the main CoolTalk window, from which you can access any of CoolTalk's features.

What's Out There

Netscape maintains a CoolTalk phone book that lists all the CoolTalk users who are online at any given time. The URL for this handy service is `http://live.netscape.com/`.

◆ When Talking Won't Do: Chat

Talking is all well and fine, but while CoolTalk is a great concept, it's not always as good in the execution as it was in the planning. You may prefer the more reliable method of interactive conversation known as *chat*, which involves conversing in real time via typed messages rather than via actual talk. Cooltalk's chat feature lets you communicate with others in print (either to type what you're "saying" or to share text files). Let's take a look.

Using Chat to Communicate

To use the chat tool, first follow steps 1 through 5 in the *Start Talking* section to find a chat partner. Then,

1. Click on the Chat tool button on the CoolTalk tool bar. (It's the one with the little typewriter on it.) The Chat Tool window will appear (Figure 6.5).

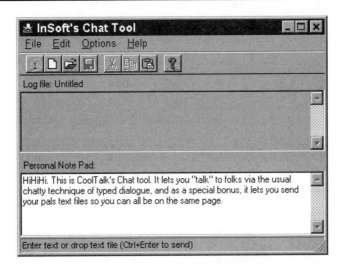

Figure 6.5: Type whatever you want to say in the big text box.

2. To start chatting, type whatever it is you want to "say" in the big text box, then click on the Send button on the Chat tool's tool bar to post what you've typed to the conference. You have these tools at your disposal during your chat:

The Tool	Its Name	What It Lets You Do
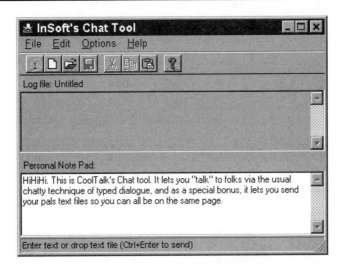	Send	Send whatever you've typed (or a text file you've included) to the person you're chatting with

The Tool	Its Name	What It Lets You Do
	New	Start a new chat log
	Include	Send a text file to the person you're chatting with
	Save	Save the contents of your "conversation" to a file called a *chat log*
	Cut	Cut selected text
	Copy	Copy selected text
	Paste	Paste selected text
	?	Get access to the Chat tool's Help file

3. When you're finished chatting, from the CoolTalk menu bar, select Conference ➤ Leave Conference. This will terminate your CoolTalk chat session and leave you at the main CoolTalk window.

What's Out There

For group chats, tune your Web browser (Netscape, not CoolTalk) to SonicNet Chat Central (`http://www.sonicnet.com/sonicore/chat/`), or to HotWired's Club Wired celebrity schedule (`http://www.hotwired.com/club/`), or to Parents Place (`http://www.parentsplace.com`).

Using Chat to Send Files

If you'd like to try sending a text file to your chatty pals, follow these steps:

1. Create a text file using your favorite text editor. If you're running Windows 95, you can use WordPad or your favorite word processor (don't forget to save the file as text only, rather than as an MS Word DOC file).

2. When you're ready to send the text file you've created, click on the Include button on the Chat tool bar. The Include File into Pad dialog box will appear.

3. Browse through folders until you find the file you want to send. Click on Open and the contents of the text file will appear on the Chat tool pad.

4. Click on the Chat tool bar's Send button to send the text file you've just included to the person you're talking to.

That's really about all you need to know. Happy chatting!

◆ When You Need to Present Visuals: The Whiteboard

Sometimes it's convenient to be able to eyeball the thing(s) you're hearing about, and sometimes you just have to draw a picture (which is, after all, worth a *lot* of words). CoolTalk's whiteboard lets you and anyone you're talking to via CoolTalk share images and even mark on them. If you like, you can use CoolTalk's whiteboard while you're talking to someone, but using it while you're chatting with someone is tough because you have to keep switching back and forth between the Chat and Whiteboard windows. And, just in case you're interested, it's possible for both people talking to mark up the whiteboard at the same time. Sometimes there's a lag when you're doing this, but so what if it takes a few seconds for your mark-ups to appear?

The CoolTalk whiteboard (Figure 6.6) resembles many PC paint programs.

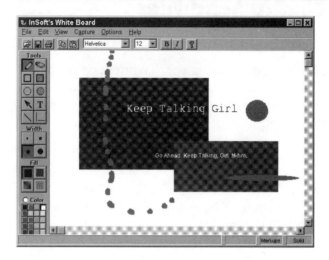

Figure 6.6: The CoolTalk whiteboard offers a drawing area that can be seen by others thousands of miles away via the Internet.

Using the buttons on the tool bar at the top of the Whiteboard window, you can import graphics files (scanned photos, logos, etc.) and save and/or print the contents of the whiteboard. Here's a quick overview of the tools on the whiteboard's tool bar:

The Tool	Its Name	What You Can Do with It
	Open File	Open a graphics file so that the person you're talking to can see it on the whiteboard
	Save	Save the contents of the whiteboard to a file
	Print	Print the contents of the whiteboard
	Copy Bitmap	Copy a Windows bitmap file to the whiteboard

The Tool	Its Name	What You Can Do with It
	Paste Bitmap	Paste a Windows bitmap file to the whiteboard
Courier	Font Box	Change the typeface of text on the whiteboard
24	Point Size Box	Change the size of text typed onto the whiteboard
B	Bold	Make text on the whiteboard appear in boldface
I	Italic	Make text on the whiteboard appear in italics
	?	Get access to the whiteboard's Help file

Using the markup tools in the whiteboard's tool box (we'll introduce you to these shortly), you can mark up an existing image by drawing or painting on it, adding text to it, or pointing to a part of it. You can also draw on the whiteboard, doodling to your heart's content.

Getting the Whiteboard Up and Running

Getting the whiteboard up and running will seem quite natural if you've already checked out CoolTalk's telephone and chat features.

1. Connect to the Internet as you usually do.

2. From the Windows 95 Start menu, select Programs ➣ Netscape. The Netscape window will appear with the CoolTalk icon and other items in it.

3. Double-click on the CoolTalk icon. The main CoolTalk window (Figure 6.3) will appear. If you'd like to use the CoolTalk white-board while you're talking to someone, first start talking to him or her. (See the section called *Start Talking* earlier in this chapter.)

4. In the CoolTalk main window's tool bar, click on the whiteboard button (the one with the picture of a palette) to kickstart the whiteboard.

5. Doodle away, using these nifty tools:

The Tool	Its Name	What It Lets You Do
	Freehand Line	Draw a line in any shape you like
	Eraser	Erase the area specified by your click-and-drag motion
	Rectangle	Draw a rectangle
	Filled Rectangle	Draw a filled rectangle
	Circle	Draw a circle
	Filled Circle	Draw a filled circle
	Pointer	Point to something in particular on the whiteboard
	Text	Type text onto the whiteboard

The Tool	Its Name	What It Lets You Do
	Line	Draw a straight line
	Vertical/ Horizontal Line	Draw a straight (vertical or horizontal) line

Especially if you've used a PC paint program, these controls probably feel pretty natural under your fingers.

Importing and Marking Up an Existing Image

If you've got a graphics file on hand that you'd desperately like your CoolTalk buddy to see, you're in luck—it's no sweat to import an existing image and then, if you like, mark it up. The whiteboard is comfy with these graphics file formats: Windows bitmap (BMP), CompuServe GIF (GIF), Zsoft Paintbrush (PCX), TIFF Revision 5.0 (TIF), JPEG (JPG), Sun Raster, and TARGA. If your image is in another format, convert it to one the whiteboard supports before importing it.

Follow these steps to share your favorite images:

1. Start the whiteboard by following steps 1–4 in *Getting the Whiteboard Up and Running.*
2. From the whiteboard menu bar, select File ➤ Open. The Open dialog box will appear.
3. Locate the graphics file and click on Open. The file will appear in the CoolTalk window, first as a dotted-line image.
4. Click and drag the outline to where you'd like the image to appear and then click the left mouse button. (Alternatively, you can press Shift to preview the image where it will appear, or you can click the right mouse button to cancel this operation altogether.)

Feel free to use those handy markup tools to alter the image.

Closing the Whiteboard

When all is said and done, to close the whiteboard, follow this simple step:

1. From the whiteboard menu bar, select File ➤ Close.

You'll still have CoolTalk open—you can talk or chat or close up shop.

◆ CoolTalk's "Answering Machine"

Can't miss that important incoming call, eh? CoolTalk's answering machine feature acts just like an actual answering machine—it will play an outgoing message and then record incoming messages for you. A quick caveat: CoolTalk must be up and running *and* connected to an Internet phone server for the answering machine to work. Unless you've got a constant connection to the Internet going, you probably don't want to leave CoolTalk running all the time, so there's a limit to its usefulness. It's not so much a good thing for when you're out as for when you're talking to someone and don't care to be interrupted, or maybe when you're briefly away from your desk. It is a very clever thing, however—let's take a look.

Turning the Answering Machine On and Off

The CoolTalk answering machine doesn't have to be turned on for you to set it up, but you must turn it on before you can use it. Turning it on and off is as easy as this one step:

1. With CoolTalk running, click on the Answering Machine button (the one with the cassette tape on it) on the CoolTalk tool bar. This is a toggle switch, so if it's off your action will turn it on, and vice versa. You can tell that the answering machine is active because the button on the tool bar will looked depressed.

…Nothing to it.

Preparing an Outgoing Message

You don't have to be online to set up the CoolTalk answering machine; in fact, you may find it easier to prepare your outgoing message before you log on to the Internet. Your outgoing message can be something you've recorded ("Hey folks, I'm not available...") or an audio clip stored as a WAV file. (If you record your own message, the sounds that make it up also will be stored as a WAV file.)

To record an outgoing message, first make sure you've run the CoolTalk Setup Wizard to configure your audio settings. (See *Starting Up CoolTalk for the First Time.*) Then check to see that your speakers and microphone are connected and turned on, and finally, follow these steps:

1. From CoolTalk's menu bar, select Conference ➤ Options. The Options dialog box will appear. Click on the Answering Machine tab and the contents of the dialog box will change to reflect your choice (Figure 6.7).

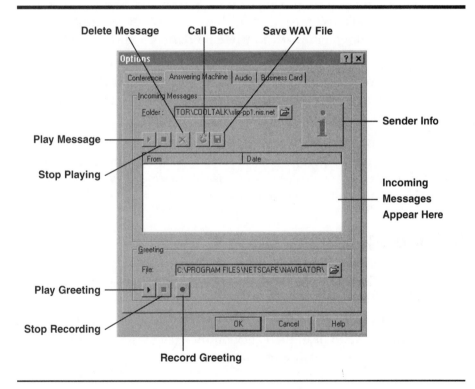

Figure 6.7: Just about all answering machine functions take place here.

2. In the Greeting area at the bottom of the of the dialog box, click on the Record button (the one with the red circle on it).

3. Say what you have to say. Speak clearly into the microphone. When you've said it all, click on the Stop button (the one with the square on it) in the Greeting area of the dialog box.

   or

   In the File text box, specify the path and filename of the WAV file you want to use—William Shatner singing, perhaps?

 Audio clips are very commonly stored as WAV files; browse through your Windows 95 files, and you'll probably find that you've already got a bunch on hand.

4. To check your greeting, click on the Playback button (the one with the right-pointing triangle on it). You should hear the message you've just recorded. (If not, check the volume controls and make sure your equipment's all wired up right. Then re-record.)

5. When you're happy with what you've done, click on OK to close up shop. The dialog box will close and the main CoolTalk window will be visible—you can ring someone up, chat, use the white-board, or quit out altogether. It's up to you.

Whether you've chosen to record your voice or a bugle or just use a nifty WAV file, your outgoing message is ready to rock. Time to turn your answering machine on (see *Turning the Answering Machine On and Off*) so that someone can leave you a message.

Getting Messages from Others

Once you've got an incoming message or two on your answering machine, follow this simple step to play one back:

1. In the Incoming Messages area's list of messages, highlight the one you'd like to hear, then click on the Play Message button (the one with the right-pointing triangle on it). *Voilà*.

You can stop the message before it's through by clicking on the Stop Playing button, then resume by clicking on Play Message again. You can phone the person back by clicking on Call Back, and hey, guess what? If they aren't receiving calls but have their connection running and their answering machine on, you can even play phone tag!

Another nice feature of the CoolTalk answering machine is that it can store the business card photo of anyone who's left an answering machine message for you. To see a caller's business card photo, just highlight the message from the person whose business card photo you'd like to see, and click on the button with the big *i* in it.

Saving an Incoming Message As a WAV File

We don't care to speculate on why you might want to save a CoolTalk answering machine message as a WAV file (to use as your own greeting to confuse people, maybe?) but if you do, follow this single step:

1. Highlight the message you'd like to save, then click on the Save button (it's the one with a picture of a floppy disk on it). The familiar Save dialog box will appear, prompting you to specify where your new WAV file should be saved. Type a filename in the Save box and click on Save. With that, the message you've selected will be saved in the location you've specified, with WAV as its file type.

Deleting Messages

Sooner or later, if you're an active CoolTalk user, you'll have a big bunch of messages and you may want to clear things out a bit. To delete a CoolTalk answering machine message, follow this step:

1. Highlight the message you'd like to delete, then click on the Delete button (it's the one with an × on it). A dialog box will appear asking if you really, truly want to delete this message. If you do, click

on Yes and the message will go away. If you'd rather not delete the message in question, click on No and the message will remain.

With that, you're set. Remember to turn your answering machine on when you're online; otherwise all these fancy answering machine features won't do you much good. Have fun.

Talk, Chat, Draw!

Now that you know how to use CoolTalk's telephone capabilities and you've been introduced to its chat tool, whiteboard, and answering machine, it's time to take a look at another plug-in that comes with the standard version of Netscape, Live3D. Hold onto your hat, because we're off to explore the wild world of virtual reality. VRooM.

Navigating Virtual Space with Live3D: VRML

Imagine, if you will, entering three-dimensional worlds in which you can interact with what's happening on your screen, perhaps by walking through a representation of a house you're considering buying. Imagine playing a multiuser online game that's not just visually stunning but navigable—imagine that in this game you traverse a three-dimensional universe. Imagine virtually touring the inside of your computer!

Okay, now stop imagining, and get real, because the standard version of Netscape Navigator 3 comes with Live3D, a happening VRML viewer, and that's what this chapter is all about. Take a look at Figure 7.1 to see a freeze-frame representation of a VRML site. We'll show you around VRML in coming sections, and we'll define terms so that you'll understand all the technical jargon that comes along with virtual reality. By the time we're through, you'll be able to amaze and amuse your friends with your knowledge of the latest and greatest technological innovation out there on the Internet.

What's Out There

One of the first VRML sites, Virtual SOMA, is still one of the best. Stroll through the streets of San Francisco's South of Market district by visiting `http://www.planet9.com/vrsoma.htm`. Incidentally, this part of San Francisco is where a good portion of the multimedia content on the Internet is produced.

Figure 7.1: San Francisco's South of Market district, a.k.a. Multimedia Gulch, is the subject of this VRML site.

◆ A Short Lowdown on Virtual Reality

Live3D is your ticket to the amazing world of virtual reality. But what *is* virtual reality? Virtual reality, or VR, is what you get when programmers use computers to *model*, or re-create, reality as we know it. This results, of course, in 3-D images. The thing is, those wacky virtual reality programmers don't just confine their efforts to *re*-creating reality—they sometimes *create* alternative realities. Fans of the latest Star Trek series are undoubtedly familiar with holodecks, which are places where members of the crew can go to unwind by living out a fantasy of their choice. Well, virtual reality is supposed to be the same kind of thing, and although Live3D can't yet equal the experience of being in a holodeck (where you're surrounded by the sights, smells, and sounds of your fantasy), it's as close as most of us are likely to come, at least for now.

Actually, virtual reality philosophers would say that virtual reality is much more than cool 3-D images—that it represents a fundamental change in the nature of a computer's user interface, moving it to a more human-centered design. They believe that the space around the user should become the computing environment and that the entire *sensorium* (a fancy word for all five senses) should be engaged in the interface. They go on to say that virtual reality was created in an effort to make computers more responsive to the humans who used them and that it focused around a basic realization: If something is represented sensually, it is possible to make sense of it. Perhaps this is true; we'll let you be the judge of that once you've had a chance to experience virtual reality for yourself.

Let the browser beware: VRML sites, like all Web sites, vary widely in quality. A badly coded VRML site may crash your browser inexplicably, and unfortunately, you may not know that a site is unwieldy until it's started loading. As a safeguard, you shouldn't try surfing VRML sites unless you have 16MB of RAM or more.

◆ Just What Is VRML?

In the words of its creator, Mark Pesce, VRML (which is an acronym for Virtual Reality Modeling Language) is a language for describing multiuser interactive simulations. Say *what*? Put in terms that we can all understand, VRML is the computer language used by clever programmers who've got lots of time to fiddle around (and lots of expensive computer equipment for fiddling) to create the 3-D images that characterize so-called virtual worlds. In Web-speak, a virtual world (sometimes just called a "world" by those in the know) is a Web site that contains 3-D images of places and/or things created using VRML. Some virtual worlds also include an audio component that you can access if you've got a compatible audio plug-in, but at the moment, these sites are relatively few and far between—sound, as we say elsewhere in this book, takes mucho memory and the amount of information necessary to provide both 3-D images and sound is incredibly huge.

What's Out There

You can catch Mark Pesce all over the Net. He moderates the VRML mailing list. To join, send mail to `Majordomo@efn.org` with the command `info eug_vrml` in the body of your message. Mark's home page is at `http://www.hyperreal.com/~mpesce/`. And he's got lots to say about VRML in HotWired's VRML Hypermail Archive (`http://vrml.wired.com/arch/`).

As long as we're defining terms, let's add one more to the mix: a WRL (pronounced "whirl") file is the collection of data (that is, of VRML code) that describes a virtual world. That's enough technical mumbo-jumbo for now; let's get on to what VRML and virtual worlds are good for.

What's Out There

If you do want more in the way of tech talk, as well as a bunch of virtual places to visit, then check out VRML.org, a resource page at (guess what?) `http://www.vrml.org/`. Or try the VRML Repository at San Diego Supercomputer Center, one of the premier resources for VRML. The central URL there is `http://www.sdsc.edu/vrml/`.

Techies who want lots o' links on this topic should hop on over to 3DSite's VRML Links page, which we found at `http://www.3dsite.com/cgi/VRML-index.html`.

What VRML Is Good For

Okay, so VRML is terribly cool, the freshest idea since word processing, but what the heck can you actually do with the thing? Let's take a look at areas of human endeavor that lend themselves easily to this new medium.

Education   Simulations of objects or situations that are otherwise difficult to see may become an important component of education. For example, medical students can brush up on their anatomy and "practice" surgical procedures using 3-D images of the human body. And let's not forget flight simulators and even *driver* education!

What's Out There

A visit to `http://www.nas.nasa.gov/NAS/Vislab/` (not a VRML site per se) will clue you into different kinds of visualization techniques now being developed by the science community. For an outstanding example of VRML in Chemistry, examine `http://ws05.pc.chemie.th-darmstadt.de/vrml/`.

Design, Architecture, and Art   Rather than making models out of paper and wood, architects, industrial designers, and the like are already likely to use CAD (computer-aided design) programs to model their creations on the computer. VRML offers them the opportunity to take this to the next (three-dimensional) step. And although virtual art is still in its infancy, there are some highly creative people out there. (Figure 7.2).

What's Out There

An illuminating site highlighting both lighting design and architecturally inspired art, Lightscape's Walkthrough Library, is at `http://www.lightscape.com/models.html`. Be aware, however, that these .WRL files are enormous—they range from 2.5–10MB apiece, so they won't move at the speed of light.

WaxWeb demonstrates how art and technology can be yoked to create an interactive and thoroughly enjoyable educational experience. This site, which is located at `http://bug.village.virginia.edu/`, contains a VRML version of David Blair's feature-length independent film *WAX, or the discovery of television among the bees*.

Figure 7.2: Join the hive and give WaxWeb a try.

Entertainment   For those who are looking for yet another way to procrastinate, or those who are looking to unwind through new gaming experiences, VRML is a revelation. Interactive virtual reality games are becoming increasingly popular and may ultimately prove to be big business too.

What's Out There

For a different kind of 3-D environment, look into AlphaWorld. Worlds, Inc., which you'll find at the URL `http://www.worlds.net/`, claims that AlphaWorld, is the first true online society. You can even build your own site in this multiuser virtual reality land. Visit Worlds, Inc. to download AlphaWorld, WorldsChat, and other trendy interactive stuff, including product demos in Java and VRML.

Marketing   Advertising has already become part and parcel of the Internet. It's everywhere, just as it is in the print and broadcast media. And it's expected to pay for a lot of otherwise free content. Whatever your own feelings may be about the issue of advertising on the Internet, it seems likely that advertising and sales companies will seize on virtual worlds to create virtual showrooms and 3-D advertising. You may be able to preview a home for sale, a certain model of car with various interior options, or a vacation resort, all from the comfort of your computer screen. Figure 7.3 gives you a glimpse into Intel's clever use of VRML.

What's Out There

Intel's Intel Inside site combines a slick advertising gimmick with actual education by leading you on a tour of your computer's insides. Look for this computer innerspace wonder at `http://www.intel.com/procs/ppro/intro/`.

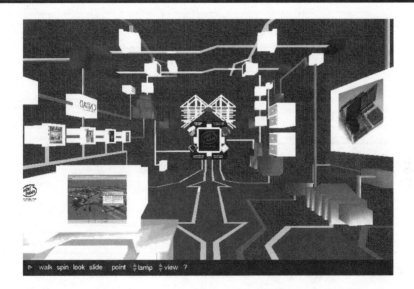

Figure 7.3: Intel takes you on a virtual reality tour of the inside of a computer.

 If you're connected to the Internet via modem, you'll have to be patient while viewing VRML sites. As with CoolTalk, the problem is bandwidth. That is, if you're using a modem (even a fast one), it may take a good while for the huge amount of information necessary to create 3-D images to get from a remote machine to the computer on your desktop.

◆ Getting Live3D Going

You must have the full version of Netscape Navigator 3 installed to use Live3D; it does not come with the minimal version of the program. If you're unsure whether or not you've installed Live3D on your system, follow these steps (note that it doesn't matter whether or not you're online when you do this):

1. From the Netscape menu bar, select Help ➤ About Plug-Ins. A list of the Netscape plug-ins that are installed on your computer will appear (Figure 7.4).

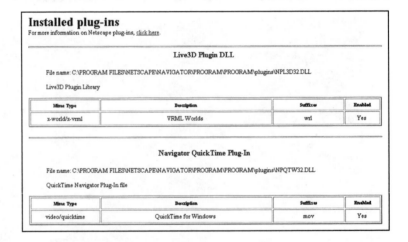

Installed plug-ins
For more information on Netscape plug-ins, click here.

Live3D Plugin DLL

File name: C:\PROGRAM FILES\NETSCAPE\NAVIGATOR\PROGRAM\PROGRAM\plugins\NPL3D32.DLL

Live3D Plugin Library

Mime Type	Description	Suffixes	Enabled
x-world/x-vrml	VRML Worlds	wrl	Yes

Navigator QuickTime Plug-In

File name: C:\PROGRAM FILES\NETSCAPE\NAVIGATOR\PROGRAM\PROGRAM\plugins\NPQTW32.DLL

QuickTime Navigator Plug-In file

Mime Type	Description	Suffixes	Enabled
video/quicktime	QuickTime for Windows	mov	Yes

Figure 7.4: These are the Netscape plug-ins on our machine.

2. Scroll down the list to see if you see an entry that says something about x-world/x-vrml and files with the suffix .WRL. If the entry is there, proceed to step 3; if it isn't, you probably haven't installed Live3D. To remedy this, reinstall Netscape, making sure you install the standard version (including Live3D).

3. After figuring out that you have Live3D, click on Netscape's Back button to get back to what you were doing or looking at.

The About Plug-Ins file appears in the regular Netscape viewing area, instead of in a separate window. If you close the viewing area, you will exit Netscape. Use the Back button to return to what you were doing.

Now that was easy, right? Let's move along to using Live3D.

◆ Navigating through Virtual Space

Once Live3D is installed on your computer, you don't have to do anything special to activate it; it will start up automatically whenever you come across a virtual world. Furthermore, navigating through virtual space is very easy because most VRML sites provide you with the same basic set of controls. When you enter a virtual world, you'll see a row of buttons appear at the bottom of your screen as the WRL file is loading.

 Because Netscape is working extra hard to get WRL files and load them, you might find that clicking on that ol' familiar Stop button won't do what it's supposed to do until it's too late. Netscape may keep loading those huge files against your will—just grit your teeth and bear it.

At all the sites we've seen so far, you've got eight buttons at your disposal, which you can use to examine all or part of a virtual world. Here's an overview of what each of the buttons can do for you.

The Button	What It Does
Walk	"Walks" you closer to or farther from the object you're viewing (when you click and drag with the left mouse button)
Spin	Rotates the object you're viewing in the direction you indicate by clicking and dragging with the left mouse button; (left = clock-wise, right = counterclockwise, up = toward you, down = away from you)

The Button	What It Does
Look	Allows you to activate a link (by clicking on it) whose presence is indicated by text that appears on or near the object you're viewing
Slide	Slides the object you're viewing in any direction you indicate by clicking and dragging with the left mouse button
Point	Zooms in on any part of an object you click on
Lamp	Adjusts the "lighting" of a virtual world; that is, the virtual light source within the world will get brighter (with the up arrow) or darker (with the down arrow) as you choose
View	Zooms in on or pans out to show different (fixed) views of an object; you can click on the object to stop these moves
?	Toggles this display of helpful information in the lower-left corner of the window

 Point the rightmost button on your mouse at a virtual world on your screen and click. A pop-up menu will appear; select Navigate from that menu and you'll have quick access to navigation commands.

If you'd like to practice getting around before you encounter a full-fledged virtual world, follow these steps. (Note that you don't have to be online to test your navigational skills.)

1. From the Netscape menu bar, select File ➤ Open File. The Open dialog box will appear. Here, in a moment, you'll specify the name and location of the file you'd like to open.

2. The file we're looking for is a 3-D rendering of the Netscape icon, which is stored in a file called NETSCAPE.WRL. To point Netscape at the proper file, in the Open dialog box's File Name text box, type the full path name: C:\PROGRAM FILES\NETSCAPE\ NAVIGATOR\LIVE3D\NETSCAPE.WRL. Once you've specified the file and pathname, click on Open. The dialog box will close and the file should appear on your screen.

 Alternatively, you can browse through folders until you locate the file. If you choose this route, you may have to pull down the list labeled *Files of type* (in the Open dialog box) and select All Files (*.*) to see the VRML files listed there.

3. Soon you should be looking at a big white 3-D "N" on a dark background. The buttons at the bottom of the screen are the controls to which we introduced you just a moment ago. Use them until you feel comfortable with what they do, then you're ready to begin your next journey.

Now that you know how the VRML controls work, there's just the small matter of how VRML links work, and then we're off.

◆ Using VRML Links

Using VRML links couldn't be simpler, especially if you're already familiar with their cousins, HTML links. The main difference between VRML links and HTML links is that while HTML links usually appear highlighted in a special color and underlined, VRML links appear as light-green text that appears and disappears depending on where on a virtual world you've positioned the mouse pointer. As soon as you move the mouse pointer to a place where light-green text appears, you're ready to use the VRML link. To follow a VRML link, just follow these steps:

1. While you're viewing a virtual world, move the mouse pointer until you see some light-green text appear on the screen, superimposed over the 3-D images. This text is a VRML link.

2. Click on the text. You should then be transported to the destination specified by the link you've chosen. It may take a while for you to see where you've been transported, so be patient.

Generally, VRML links lead to one of two things: another virtual world or a Web document containing information related to the virtual world you're currently viewing.

Links in a virtual world can take you any place links in a Web document can. For example, a virtual world can contain links to HTML documents, still images, sounds, and other virtual worlds stored on servers all over the world.

VRML links between worlds do tend to be a *lot* slower and more cumbersome than HTML links. VRML files tend to be quite a bit larger than HTML files and, as such, take much longer to load. Have patience. That's often the price you pay for being among the first to use a new technology.

What's Out There

See where it all began…Silicon Graphics, Inc., known to those in the know as SGI, does VRML proud with a Web site called VRML Moving Worlds, at `http://webspace.sgi.com/worlds/`.

Construct's Web site, which evolved out of the Interactive Media Festival and the VRML Arc Gallery is at `http://www.construct.net/links/projects.html#vrml`.

Netwatch's Top Ten Links site (`http://www.pulver.com/netwatch/topten/topten.htm`) includes links to good VRML sites, electronic publications, and forums on VRML.

"Terminal Reality," a cool 3-D "terminal" that can lead you all kinds of hip places, is at ZDNet's 3-D site (`http://www.zdnet.com/zdi/vrml/`).

Next Stop: Starting Points

Now that you've got the skinny on Live3D, Netscape's new plug-in, as well as VRML, virtual worlds, and all that good stuff, let's go out on the Web and explore some good and useful starting points that map the whole Internet.

Starting Places and Search Tools

You won't always want to *wander* the Web; sometimes you'll want to focus your travels or gather information in ways that aren't so willy-nilly. Fortunately, there are some great comprehensive starting points on the Web that can really help get you going. Many Web sites—Netscape's included—provide listings of interesting sites, usually by category. Several really terrific directories focus on organizing sites by specific subjects; while a growing number of search engines can be used to find facts and opinions on focused topics. There are even some nifty all-in-one search pages that gather up a lot of search options for your convenience.

In this chapter, we'll cover comprehensive starting places and search tools. There are also plenty of starting places that focus on certain subject areas (biosciences, handicrafts, travel, etc.) or on certain Internet activities and experiences (audio, VRML, chat). But here we'll concentrate on the starting places and search tools that will get you started in an overall way.

◆ Directories and Search Engines: An Industry Is Born

Imagine TV without the benefit of those handy programming guides that come with your Sunday paper, or imagine a really huge library without a card catalog—whether it's in a file cabinet or on a computer. You wouldn't know what's where when, or how to find anything.

...That's the Web without the tools you can use to show you around. An entire industry of Web indexing has arisen from this need; today there are lots of well-known Web directories and search tools, all competing to be the biggest, the best, or both.

Let's start by defining terms. A *directory* in this context is really a large database filled with references to Internet sites; the organization of this database is overseen by editorial types who (presumably) keep it intelligently organized. Yahoo is of the *index* type of directory; its main feature is a browsable, subject-oriented listing of sites (though the listing is also searchable).

Some directories go further by also offering reviews and rating systems so that you can pick and choose among what some "expert" thinks is best before you spend your time wandering around online. These days, directories generally are searchable, adding another dimension to their usefulness, and many are beginning to offer editorial content in the form of features such as Best of the Web awards, articles, and informative material such as newsfeeds.

A *search engine* (in this context) differs from a directory in that it offers no editorial content, and its main feature is an enormous, searchable database of sites that's been gathered in an automated process using a Web crawler or robot, with little or no regard to any sort of indexing or reviewing. Search engines typically perform faster searches of more stuff than the search aspect of indexes or guides can do, but they offer you uncategorized lists, which may be less useful in some circumstances (say when you're trying to find the "best" site on a given topic) or more useful in some others (like when you want a comprehensive listing of everything available on your subject of interest).

In this chapter, we're going to cover the major directories (both the index-type and the guide-type), and the major search engines. We'll also show you some great all-in-one places that offer you the choice to search all these gizmos from one convenient location.

◆ The Big Picture

The first time you start Netscape, the Welcome to Netscape page will be the default home page—the page you see automatically. (Later, you can display a different home page on start-up, if you like.) The Welcome to Netscape page is a perfectly good place to start—we'll look a little more closely at what it has to offer in a second—and there are many other good starting places as well. Before we look at these in detail, let's go over some general information about Web sites and home pages.

What Is a Web Site? And a Home Page?

A *Web site* may be a single page on the Web or a collection of pages. Often you'll enter a Web site by starting at its *home page*. You can look at this in a couple of ways. To you, the user, the home page can be a starting point for exploring a single site or the whole World Wide Web. You can think of a home page as a kind of "main menu." This analogy breaks down a bit because the Web is neither hierarchical nor linear and Netscape is by no means menu-driven; but a home page does outline your options—at least the options for moving along the links from this site to other points of interest both within and beyond this site, as imagined by the site's producer. To whomever publishes it, the home page is a cross between a magazine or book's cover and its table of contents. Producers of a Web site's home page have to think through its construction completely to make clear what the site is about and what can be found there.

 Just to clarify a bit, a *Web site* may be a single page or a collection of pages. The main page among a number of pages in a Web site is the *home page.* A *Web server,* by the way, is the machine and software that houses the Web site.

In reality, a home page is any hypertext document that has links to other points on the Web and acts as a starting point. Your start-up home page, the one that is automatically loaded each time you launch Netscape, should be one that helps you get going. It may be the default Welcome to Netscape page, some other home page that provides a general starting point, or one that is specialized to your interests. You can even set up Netscape not to access and display a home page if you want to start your daily surfing without the distraction of seeing a page you've seen a thousand times before. Read on to find out how to choose any of these options.

Changing Your Start-Up Home Page

For new users and experienced users whose purposes are fairly general, the Welcome to Netscape page or another of those we describe in this chapter might be best. For example, you might find it handy to make your start-up home page a page that's deeper in the Netscape site, like the Net Search page, with its listings of comprehensive directories and search tools. Or you might want to use search.com (described later in this chapter), a compendium of search gizmos from the broad to the special interest. That'll give you a good launch pad that's more general and comprehensive than the Welcome to Netscape page, which is devoted primarily to Netscape and Netscape users. For those with specific interests, a home page geared to those interests might be better.

 To speed Web access, you might want to choose as your start-up home page one residing on a server that's near you—the closer the better. This is getting easier to do, with the Web's rate of growth. Or perhaps you work for a company that has its own home page. You can even construct your own custom home page using Netscape's nifty bookmark features, as described in Chapter 4, or using HTML, as you'll see in Chapter 9.

To change your start-up home page, you'll use Netscape's Preferences dialog box—this handy dialog box is your entrance way to changing many facets of Netscape's behavior on your machine.

Here are the steps for changing your home page:

1. Start Netscape by clicking on its icon, without bothering to start your Internet connection. (What we're doing here is strictly a local operation.)

2. From the menu bar, choose Options ➤ General Preferences. The Preferences dialog box will appear.

3. From the tabs along the top of the Preferences dialog box, select Appearance. The dialog box will change to reflect your choice.

4. Roughly in the middle of the dialog box, find the Browser Starts With option. Next to it are two choices: Blank Page and Home Page Location. Click on Home Page Location to make it active. In the text box below this, you'll find the URL for the home page currently slated for display at start-up (see Figure 8.1).

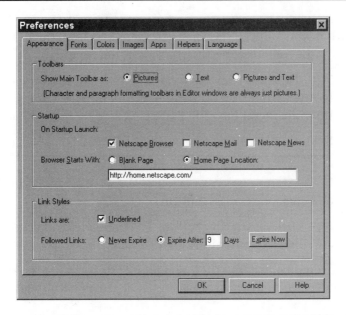

Figure 8.1: Enter the URL for the home page you want to appear at start-up. The URL shown here is the default Welcome to Netscape page.

5. Highlight that URL and type in its place the URL for the home page you want.

6. Click on the OK button. The Preferences dialog box will close, and the Netscape window will reappear.

If you do happen to have been connected to the Internet when you performed this procedure, you can check to make sure you typed the URL correctly by pressing the Home button on Netscape's tool bar.

When next you start Netscape, you'll see the page you just designated as your start-up page rather than the original default start-up home page. And from now on, every time you press the Home button on Netscape's tool bar, your new home page of choice will appear. You can change this page as often as you like.

Let's say you have some reason for not wanting to see any home page at all when you launch Netscape. The steps you'll follow to do this are similar to those for changing the start-up home page:

1. With Netscape running (you don't have to be connected to the Internet while you do this), select Options ➤ General Preferences from the menu bar. The Preferences dialog box will appear.

2. From the tabs along the top of the Preferences dialog box, select Appearance.

3. In the Startup box area labeled *Browser Starts With*, find Blank Page and click on its radio button.

4. Now click on the OK button. The Preferences dialog box will close, and the Netscape window will appear.

What could be easier? When you launch Netscape again, you should see absolutely no home page. Instead you'll see an empty document window.

If you've elected to have no home page appear but you want to return to a home page you've designated in the Home Page Location box (as described in the preceding procedure), click on Home on Netscape's tool bar, and *voilà!* You return to your chosen home page in a flash. And even though you've changed your start-up home page or arranged for none to appear at start-up, you can always access the Welcome to Netscape page whenever you want. Simply click on the N icon in the upper-right corner of your screen.

What's Out There

You can always go home again. The URL for the Welcome to Netscape page is `http://home.netscape.com/`. You can bookmark it, as described in Chapter 4, or you can click on the N icon for even easier access.

Now let's look at some alternative choices for your start-up page, including a few all-purpose directories, but starting with the default start-up home page you've heard so much about—Netscape's own wildly popular and very useful site.

The Netscape Web Site

As might be expected, Netscape has one of the most frequently visited Web sites on the Internet. (Figure 3.1 in Chapter 3 shows the Netscape home page.) From the Netscape Web site you can always get the scoop on the company and its upcoming products. You can download the latest version of their software, get information about other software that enhances Netscape, and get general information about the Web and the Internet. Because the Netscape Web site includes so much important information, we talk about different aspects of it throughout the book. Here we'll talk about the resources on the Netscape site that are best suited as jumping off points for the rest of the Internet.

Destinations Courtesy of Netscape

Netscape offers a jumping-off point for your Web travels called Netscape Destinations, which is an index of Web sites hand-picked by the good people at Netscape. You can get to Netscape Destinations in a number of ways, including:

◆ Click on the Destinations button on Netscape's Directory button bar.

◆ Click on the <u>Netscape Destinations</u> link on the Welcome to Netscape page.

◆ Open the URL `http://home.netscape.com/escapes/`.

Registering Netscape

The first time you start Netscape, take the time to read the licensing agreement that appears on screen and register the program. It's the honest, right thing to do, and it couldn't be easier. You can check out the licensing agreement and register via links on the Netscape site.

The agreement says that Netscape is free for the use of students, faculty members, staff of educational organizations, employees of nonprofit corporations, and *individuals evaluating the program*. If you fall into the last group, you must pay a license fee once your evaluation period is up.

Filling out the registration form is terrifically simple; really it's just like filling out a paper registration card, except that you're doing it on screen.

Follow links on the Netscape home page or open the URL `http://home.netscape.com/misc/quick_purchase` to get to the Netscape Quick Purchase page. Here you can fill out the simple forms to order and pay for a copy of the latest version of Netscape Navigator (a.k.a. "Netscape") or any number of other software products Netscape offers.

Regardless of which method you choose, you'll see the Netscape Destinations page on screen. Each of the icons that appear in the Netscape Destinations site links to a page listing more specific Web sites. For example, to see links to sites about Finance, just click on the Finance icon. When we clicked on the Finance icon, we got the page shown in Figure 8.2.

Search Gizmos and More

The Netscape site also offers easy access to many search engines that are scattered throughout the Web. You can access the Netscape Search page in any one of many ways, including:

◆ Clicking on the Net Search button on the button bar

◆ Selecting from Netscape's menu bar, Directory ➤ Internet Search

◆ Clicking on the Net Search link at the bottom of the Welcome to Netscape page

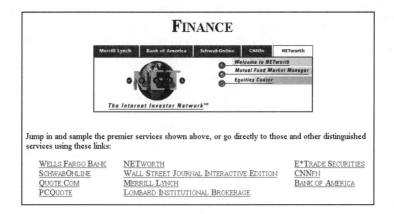

Figure 8.2: We clicked on the Finance icon and found all sorts of personal finance resources that appear on the Net.

Other Points of Departure

Many Internet service providers and online services are creating their own starting points for the Internet. If you have a version of Netscape that you got from your provider, it may be configured to load up their home page (instead of the Netscape home page) whenever your start it. You should take a look around at the page and see what they have to say. Many providers put important announcements on the default home page that their version of Netscape loads.

Regardless of how you bring up the Netscape Search page, you'll see something like what we saw, which is shown in Figure 8.3. Some of the premiere directories and search engines appear one at a time in a graphic at the top of the page—there are tabs labeled with the names of those directories and search engines at the top of the graphic. To select any of these featured search gadgets, click on the tab for the one that interests you.

Some other directories and search engines, including specialized sites about the environment and Java, are listed below the graphic and don't actually appear in the graphic. This is not because they are lesser options; it is because they did not pay for the privilege of appearing in the more eye-catching graphic at the top of the page. To use any of the non-featured search tools, click on the link (below the graphic) for the one that interests you, and either its home page or its search page will appear. You'll find directions later in this chapter for using many of these search tools. Turn to the *About Search Tools* section of this chapter for general information, then to the section about the particular directory or search engine that interests you.

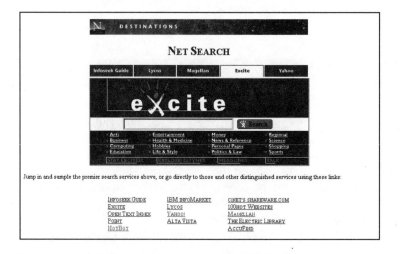

Figure 8.3: Net Search offers you quick access to a gaggle of Internet directories and search engines. When we visited, Excite popped up first.

To actually use Net Search, just follow the bouncing ball:

1. Open the Netscape Search page by any of the methods listed above.

2. Click on the tab for the search engine of interest and the graphic will change to present that one. (Or you can use whichever one popped

up first.) Note that each search tool will organize and display the information in the graphic according to its own wisdom, but in general they'll all have a text box into which you can type a word or phrase for what you seek, and a button labeled Search, Find, or some such, that you'll click on to conduct the search. (Some will also cram in the list of categories they cover in their browsable index, but that's another story).

3. In the text area, type a word or phrase for what you seek.

 Later in this chapter we cover the major directories and search engines in more detail, including tips for how to conduct a more exact search. Read on for more information.

4. Click on the Search button (or Find, or whatever this particular search tool calls it). In a few seconds you'll see the results of your search.

What actually appears on the results page varies from one search engine to another, but it will generally be some sort of a list, with links from which you can now jump to any of many resources that match your interest.

 Once you've searched for an item of interest using one of the search engines, you can use the Back button or the Go menu to return to Netscape's Net Search.

◆ About Search Tools

Let's say you work in the planning department of a large corporation, and you need to write a business report about "reengineering." Say you want to pepper your report with statistical data—productivity levels in American business over the past 10 years, unemployment levels, inflation rates, and so on. You also want to describe the viewpoints of financial, economic, and business experts and address forecasts for the future of business.

The Web is gigantic, webby, and *growing*. (We've said this before.) You just can't expect everything on the Web to be contained in any one place or to be searchable with any one tool. To do your Web research—on our example topic or on any other topic—you'll use a number of tools. You may use Alta Vista, Lycos, or InfoSeek to find a comprehensive listing of pages that contain some reference to your topic, then you may use Excite to find hand-selected, top-rate sites on some specific aspect of your topic.

 Just as each Web page you encounter bears the mark of its publisher (in the form of what's included and excluded and how information is presented), each search tool also has been affected by its publishers' knowledge and interest. For example, if you search for material on a specific topic in Yahoo and don't find anything, that doesn't mean your topic is not represented on the Net. Search again, using Alta Vista, search.com, or one of the other tools, and see what comes up there.

When you conduct your search, you'll have to describe the information that you want. In general, you will enter one or more words into a text box on screen. The search *engine* (the program or search tool that actually does the search) you're using will compare this text (called a search *string*) with some part of or all the text associated with all the Web pages this search engine knows. (Most search engines also employ what's called a *Web crawler* to find out in an automated way what's on the Net. That's how they learn of the pages they then "know" about. See *What Web Crawlers Do*.)

As we describe various search engines in upcoming sections, we'll show you through the use of examples how they compare. This should give you an idea of how best to use each search tool.

 A lot of sites and pages are known to any given search engine, but not every single one can be. Only those that have been discovered by the search engine's Web crawler will appear in that database. This is true of all search tools—the Web grows faster than they can catalog it, though all the search tools are expanding all the time.

Types of Searches

As mentioned, each search engine focuses on some part of or all the pages; sometimes you'll even be able to specify whether what you are searching for will appear in the Web page's:

◆ Title

◆ URL

◆ Text

or

◆ In a description, abstract, or review of the Web page

or

◆ All of the above

The search engine will sift through the pages it knows of, looking for the text you specified, and it will return a list of all the pages that contain the text you specified. If you specified that the search engine look only in titles, URLs, or text, it will look *only* in those parts of the document(s). Thus, the exact way the search engine matches up what you

Using Logical Operators in More Complicated Searches

To make your searches more specific, you can use *logical operators*—AND and OR, for example—which work kind of like conjunctions in English grammar. The way you use logical operators varies a bit from one search tool to another, but the ideas remain the same. In general, if you want to find documents that contain *all* the words in a search string, you can join the words with AND. If you want to find *any* of the words in a search string, you can join the words with OR.

Here's an example: If you want to find documents that discuss American business, simply entering *American business* as your search string will often result in a list of documents that contain either the word *American* or the word *business*. That would be an awful lot of documents, only a few of which would discuss American business per se. If you join the two words with AND, as in *American AND business*, the search tool will look for documents that contain both words rather than either word. If you joined them with OR, as in American OR business, you'd get all the documents that contain either word and all the documents with both words.

...Logical, eh?

are searching for with its database is partly controllable by you and partly dependent on the particular search gizmo you are using. Obviously, the searches that are most useful are those that search the text of the page along with the page's title and URL, turning up a list of the most relevant pages. Even then, some search engines search smaller portions of the text than others do.

When a search engine offers you a list of pages it has to put them in some type of order. It usually decides this order based on *relevancy*, which can include many different criteria. One of the most common is *frequency*, or the number of times a particular phrase is mentioned. For example, if you search on the word *widget*, the Web page that has the most frequent mentions of the word *widget* will appear first. The search engine—which, after all, is only so bright—has found what it thinks to be the most relevant page. Now, whether that page actually has any substantial information about widgets is another story....

What Web Crawlers Do

At the heart of most Internet search tools is a *Web crawler*, a program that "crawls" around the Web looking at page after page and site after site, bringing the address, the titles, and in some cases descriptive pieces of the pages' contents into a gigantic searchable database. The speed and efficiency of these Web crawlers is what makes legendary the databases compiled using them. In Chapter 2 you can find out more about Web crawlers in a section titled *Wanderers, Spiders, and Robots*.

When you encounter those text boxes into which you type the stuff you want the search engine to go looking for, it's important to know how much or how little text you are allowed to type and whether the search engine can make some basic distinctions. For example, the smartest search engines "know" enough so that you can type a phrase such as *pigeons for sale* and they will not bother matching the word *for* or will skip over words that include *for*. Other search engines will return everything that matches at all, without much discrimination; so you'd get not just all the sites that include the words *pigeons* and *sale* (the important words in this case) but also *for*mat, *for*tune, be*for*e, and every other instance of the combination of the letters *f*, *o*, and *r*.

This is all pretty basic stuff—very quickly, in fact, search engines are growing more and more sophisticated. All the search gizmos we discuss in this chapter include advanced settings so that you can control how they look for documents and the scope of their searches, and they'll all undoubtedly add features to their already impressive capabilities as time goes on.

There are all kinds of search tools. Let's look at some of the big names in searching, and let's take a look at a terrific all-in-one search page that pulls in lots of options for searching the biggies and the more-specialized.

Okey dokey, now let's take a closer look at some of these directories and search engines.

◆ Yahoo: A Subject-Oriented Index

Yahoo, the big, beautiful index begun at Stanford University by a couple of (presumed) yahoos, has since gone commercial, with not only a bunch of Web sites, but books and magazines bearing its name, and TV commercials blaring its existence. Yahoo the index is very easy to use; it consists of a hierarchical list of a whopping number of sites on the Web, organized by subject (see Figure 8.4). (The number's growing at a phenomenal rate.) All you do is click your way from here to there along a logical path to find what you seek.

What's Out There

You can mosey on over to Yahoo with the URL `http://www.yahoo.com/`.

Some categories we found when we looked were Art, Business and Economy, Computers and Internet, Education, Entertainment, Government, Health, Sports, and so on. (There are plenty more.)

Yahoo doesn't employ any crawlers or spiders to find Web sites. Instead, it relies on human beings—both Yahoo employees and users of Yahoo—to find links worth including and submit them for consideration. That means that Yahoo is limited by human bandwidth, but it also means that it indexes only those pages with some modicum of actual content. You won't find Aunt Sally's Web site filled with snapshots of cousin Sue here—unless it's a work of art.

Figure 8.4: Yahoo's subject-oriented list allows you to click around until you find what you seek.

If you know of a page that is not in the Yahoo lists, click on the Add link on any Yahoo page. A form will appear into which you can type the URL of the page you want included in Yahoo. The people who run Yahoo will review your submission, and, if they like the page, it will become part of Yahoo's list.

Searching through Yahoo

Like many Internet directories, Yahoo is not just clickable—it's searchable. To do a simple search of Yahoo from its home page, follow these steps:

1. At the top of the Yahoo home page, you will find a text box followed by a Search button. In the text box, type one or more words (separated by spaces) that describe what you seek (Yahoo will find only entries that contain all the words you enter in the text box; so be careful about what you enter).

2. Click on the Search button. A page will appear showing a listing of pages (all appearing as links) that contain all the words you set out for the search.

You are not limited to searching Yahoo based on a few simple words. Yahoo also has a search page that gives you much more control over how it locates the information you want. To use this alternative Yahoo searching method:

1. Click on the <u>Options</u> link (it's to the right of the Search button, which you'll find either at the top or bottom of any Yahoo page). The Yahoo Search page will appear (see Figure 8.5).

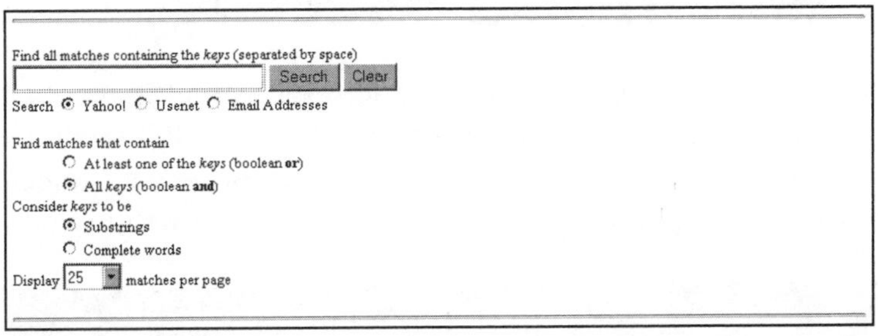

Find all matches containing the *keys* (separated by space)

[   ] Search | Clear

Search ⦿ Yahoo! ○ Usenet ○ Email Addresses

Find matches that contain
  ○ At least one of the *keys* (boolean **or**)
  ⦿ All *keys* (boolean **and**)
Consider *keys* to be
  ⦿ Substrings
  ○ Complete words
Display [25 ▾] matches per page

Figure 8.5: Yahoo is searchable!

2. In the text box, type one or more words (separated by spaces) describing what you seek.

3. Make selections to indicate whether you want:

- ◆ To search in Yahoo (the main database), Usenet (the DejaNews Usenet archives), or Email Addresses (the Four11 e-mail directory)

- ◆ To find pages that include *all* the words you entered (the *and* button) or *any* of them (the *or* button)

- ◆ The search to look for whole words (complete words) or pieces of the words (*substrings*)

- ◆ To see the maximum number of documents as the result of your search

4. Click on the Search button. A page will appear showing a listing of pages (all appearing as links) that match the criteria you set out for the search.

To check out the pages that appeared in the listing as the result of your search, simply click on their links. If you click around a while and get away from the page listing the result of your search, you can always go back to that page by selecting Go from the menu bar and then selecting Yahoo Search from the list that appears.

◆ Excite: More Than a Directory

Excite offers a number of features and services that make it an ideal starting point for your Internet exploration. From Excite, you'll be able to search a large database of Internet resources, browse a subject-oriented catalog of Web pages, or read current news articles and columns.

What's Out There

You can access Excite at `http://www.excite.com/`.

You can access all of the different areas of Excite right from its home page. Along the top of the page you'll see a number of different tabs. Click on one of the tabs and a new page related to the subject of the tab will appear (Figure 8.6).

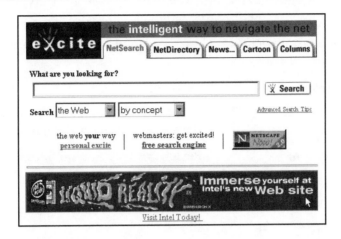

Figure 8.6: The many editorial and navigational features of Excite are a single click away from its home page.

Among the features that you can access from Excite's home page are:

Net Search	A search engine that lets you pinpoint Web sites of interest
NetDirectory	A subject-oriented directory of what's on the Web
News	The latest news, updated throughout the day
Cartoon	A weekly hypertext cartoon
Columns	Columns written by Excite personalities and editors

Searching Using Excite

One of Excite's most powerful features is its search capabilities—Excite will search through its database of Web sites and give you a brief description of those that might interest you based on the topic of your search. To use this feature:

1. With the Excite home page open, click on the Net Search tab along the top of the window. A search page will appear.

2. In the text box labeled *What are you looking for?* type a word or phrase to describe what you seek.

3. You can specify which parts of the Internet you want to search. Your options are:

Select	To Search
The Web	The entire Web (or at least the part of the Web that Excite's Web crawler has encountered)
Reviews	Reviews of Web sites produced by Excite's staff
Usenet	Usenet news articles
Classifieds	Classified ads posted in various Usenet newsgroups

4. Now specify whether you want to search "by keyword," or "by concept." If you elect to search by keyword, only those sites that include one or more of the exact words you entered in step 2 will appear. If you elect to search by concept, sites that include related words (but that may not include the exacts words you entered) will appear.

5. Click on the Search button. In a few seconds, a page will appear listing sites that correspond to the criteria you set.

6. To fine-tune your search, click on the Refine Search button.

To view any of the pages that appeared in the listing as the result of your search, simply click on their links. If you click around a while and get away from the listing of your search results, you can always go back to that page by using the Back button in the Netscape tool bar.

As Excite's crawlers and human surfers find sites and categorize them, they work into their database a list of "concepts" for each site. This list is used in a way that echoes a thesaurus and that enables you to find a site based on what it's about as much as by the words or phrases it contains. Let's say a site is about coffee but the word coffee is never used in the site—maybe it's always called java or joe in this site. If you search Excite for coffee sites, you'll find this one, because someone was smart enough to apply the concept coffee to it. That's what concept searching is.

◆ c|net: On the Air and Online

Is it a Web site, a TV show, or more? c|net is an unique venture that encompasses both television (in the form of a TV show about the online world) and the Web (in the form of a Web site that covers the same topic). Because this is a book about Netscape and not TV, we'll talk about the Web site, which is a good starting point for your general investigation of what's on the Internet. The c|net site offers constantly updated news (with a slant towards computers and the Internet), feature articles, reviews, and other special features. This (perhaps along with Wired's HotWired site) is the place to look for the latest about the Web.

In addition to the primary c|net site, the folks who bring you c|net run a number of other Web sites, including shareware.com (a great place to find shareware) and search.com (a wonderful source for search tools—not just the biggies, but specialized ones that run the gamut from art to wines).

What's Out There

For Web news, reviews, and starting points, tune in to c|net at `http://www.cnet.com/`.

Downloading Shareware, Helpers, and Plug-Ins

From c|net's shareware.com you can easily search many repositories of shareware, freeware, and public domain software scattered throughout the Internet. Whatever you're looking for—from that handy little address book program to video players, you'll find it quickly via shareware.com. What's more, you'll find a short review of the software, a list of new and popular releases, and tips on downloading. And, of course, you'll be able to download the stuff that interests you.

Using shareware.com is a snap. All you have to do is:

1. From Netscape's menu bar, select File ➤ Open Location. The Open Location dialog box will appear.

2. In the text box, type `http://www.shareware.com/` and press ↵. The Open dialog box will close and, in a few seconds, the shareware.com home page will appear, as shown in Figure 8.7.

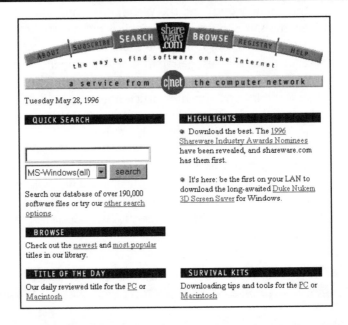

Figure 8.7: The shareware.com home page is your starting point for quickly finding and getting that shareware, freeware, or public domain file you've been seeking.

What's Out There

Your convenient source for shareware, freeware, and public domain software is shareware.com, at `http://www.shareware.com/`.

3. Enter what you are searching for in the text box along the top of the page and click on the Search button. (For example, to search for a program to play MPEG video files—MPEG is a compressed video format commonly used on the Internet—type **MPEG** and click on the Search button.) In a few seconds, the results of your search will appear (Figure 8.8), in a list with descriptions.

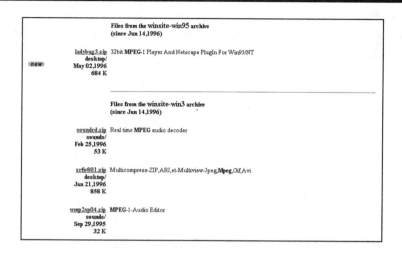

Figure 8.8: We found a number of files related to MPEG video.

4. Look through the descriptions until you find something that appeals to you. Click on the link (the file name) next to the description of interest. (In our example, the file is LADYBUG2.ZIP.) A page will appear listing links to the FTP sites that contain the file. (You may have to scroll down the page a bit to find the list.) The FTP sites will be listed based on reliability, with the most reliable at the top.

5. To download the file of interest, click on the link at the top of the list. The old familiar Save As dialog box will appear, allowing you to save the file to your local machine in the usual way. Just accept the filename as is, and click on Save. (That's when the file is actually downloaded.)

 If you don't experience success in downloading the file from the first site that appears in the list, try another site—search.com usually displays a dozen or so FTP sites that contain the file of interest, and one of them is bound to work.

That's about all there is to using shareware.com. As you can see, this is a gemlike way to get software for your computer quickly and conveniently.

 Somebody releases some new plug-in or helper app that you can use with Netscape just about weekly. Each of these plug-ins or helper apps makes Netscape do something new or better than before, but keeping up with all the new stuff can become overwhelming. Luckily, those thoughtful people at Netscape maintain two pages about plug-ins and helper apps. *Plug-ins* are special programs written especially for Netscape. *Helper apps* are not written solely for Netscape—they are general Windows programs that Netscape can use to display some type of data it receives over the Net that's beyond its own capabilities. You can find out all about plug-ins and helper apps in Chapter 12.

Dealing with Compressed Files

Often you'll find that the software files you download from shareware.com (or from the Web in general) are *zipped*—they've been compressed with a utility such as PKZip or Lharc, which you'll know because the filename ends in either ZIP (for PKZip) or LZH (for LHarc). Files are zipped (*compressed, shrunk,* or *compacted*) to make them smaller, so that they can be transmitted more quickly. Compressed files often can be half the size of the original file; some files can be compressed to as little as $\frac{1}{20}$ their original size. If a file has been compressed, you'll need a companion program to uncompress the file. PKZip/PKUnzip is available commercially; WinZip is downloadable shareware (which you must pay a fee for if you like it and want to keep using it); and LHarc is downloadable freeware (meaning you can use it without paying for it). Other compression/decompression programs are also available—some emulate or are compatible with their commercially available cousins (WinZip, for example, will compress and uncompress PKZip files). Of course, you can find all the compression utilities you need by using shareware.com.

What's Out There

WinZip is a very good Zip/Unzip program for Windows. You can find out all about it—and even download it—from `http://www.winzip.com/`.

◆ One-Stop Searching with search.com

For a starting point from which to launch a comprehensive search, try search.com (Figure 8.9), which was created by the folks at clnet. They composed this page by compiling what seems like every search gizmo around, ranging from the big whoppers such as Alta Vista, Lycos, Inktomi, and Infoseek, to smaller, more specialized search tools that cover specific topics. This wonderful resource provides you with the opportunity to go to a one-stop location and search a bunch of databases quickly and conveniently. Best yet, the folks at clnet describe each and every site included in their list of sites to search; their favorites are marked *top pick*.

Once you have search.com's home page on screen, you are ready to search any one of many different search engines. On the search.com home page you'll see text boxes and buttons for many of the popular search engines on the Web.

What's Out There

You can access search.com at http://www.search.com/.

There are a bunch of specialized search tools listed by topic along the left side of the search.com page. Click on a topic and the search.com page will display a list of search engines related to your chosen category. You can then select one and work with it as you like. (The listings on the left will still appear.) To return to the search.com page, click on the Start Here icon in the top-left corner of the portion of the page containing the listing.

1. Open search.com's home page, and you'll see the names of many of the general purpose search engines available on the Net, along with a search box for each of them. To use one of the engines listed, find the text box below the search engine of interest, and type into it a word or phrase that describes the subject of your search. (The options you have in your search vary from one search

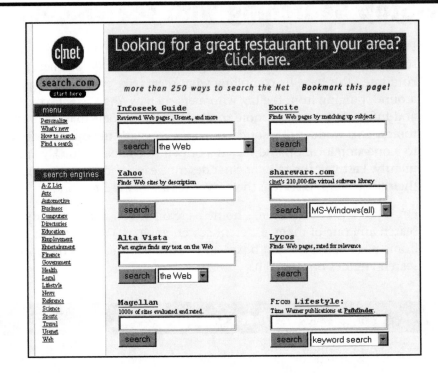

Figure 8.9: For a place to start any kind of search, the extraordinarily comprehensive search.com can't be beat.

tool to the next—we talk about many of them in detail in other sections of this chapter, though, so you can find out more by turning to the appropriate section.)

2. Click on the Search button for the search engine you wish to search. (It may be labeled *Find* or something else instead of *Search*.)

In a few seconds, the search.com page will be replaced by your chosen search tool's listing of the sites that match your criteria.

 Of course there are specific tips and tricks for each search engine that appears on search.com. We cover the biggies in this chapter; read on to find out more about them.

Clnet's search.com is just exquisite—a wonderful starting point for your Web travels no matter what your topic of interest, because it rounds up a lot of options and offers you convenient access to all of them. Be sure at least to add it to your Bookmark list; it may even be a good choice for a start-up home page.

What's Out There

William Cross created the "original" All-in-One Search page (`http://www.albany.net/allinone/`) by compiling every search gizmo of merit, ranging from the big whoppers to smaller, more specialized search tools. This wonderful resource provides you with the noncommercial opportunity to go to a one-stop location and search a bunch of databases quickly and conveniently.

Now, with Netscape starting-point basics under your belt, let's take a wider look at the big, powerful search engines available to you on the World Wide Web.

◆ Searching with Alta Vista

Alta Vista is well known as a very *fast* search engine, with an incredible number of Web pages documented in its database. If it's on the Web, you'll probably find it in Alta Vista, and the list Alta Vista returns when you search will appear at lightning speed. The trouble is, when you search for something in Alta Vista, you don't get a list of *sites* that have something to do with the subject of your search, you get a list of *pages*. Thus, a hundred Web pages in a single site might appear in the list of stuff Alta Vista finds matching your search string. Some of them will even be repeats—the same Web page might be listed several times with slightly different URLs.

The advantage of Alta Vista then is that it excludes nothing; the disadvantage, similarly, is that Alta Vista does not engage in any selection or ranking process. Alta Vista is your best choice if you're trying to find some relatively obscure piece of information, but if you want to find all the "best" sites on your topic, Alta Vista is going to leave you with lots of hand sifting to do.

What's Out There

You'd think it would be easy to find Alta Vista because the URL would include something like `altavista.com`, but it ain't so. The URL for Alta Vista is `http://www.altavista.digital.com/`, but the nice people at `http://altavista.com/` do include a link to Alta Vista.

To perform a search using Alta Vista, follow these steps:

1. Start up your Internet connection, launch Netscape, and open up Alta Vista's home page.

2. In the Search text box of the Alta Vista home page, type a word or a phrase that describes what you want to find. Alta Vista works best when you give it a number of words.

 You may have to try a number of variations on the words you use to describe what interests you before you find the exact resource you need (auto, vehicle, and car will all turn up different pages). Try to be specific, but not too specific. Using the plural books, for example, will omit instances of the singular book. A good technique often is to search first for a more general word, like software, then, if the results of your search are too overwhelming, search for a more specific word, like Photoshop. Also note that Alta Vista is partially case-sensitive. If you search for Photoshop, Alta Vista will ignore any records in which photoshop is not initial-capped.

3. Click on the Submit button to begin the actual search. The Netscape N icon will become animated. In a few seconds, a new page will appear, listing everything matching your search criteria that was found in the database. (Figure 8.10 shows some of the results of a search for *personal finance*.)

Alta Vista lists only the first 10 records that meet your criteria, ranking them by relevancy. You can click on the links along the bottom of the page to get any additional records or start again by entering new search criteria and clicking on the Submit button.

If you're using the simple (regular) search option, the words AND, OR, and NOT in your search string will be ignored. Instead, you can use plus (+) and minus (–) signs to accomplish something similar. If you search for *Charlie+Brown*, for example, your results will find only those pages that include both *Charlie* and *Brown*. Alternately, if you search for *Dylan Thomas–Bob*, any pages that feature the word *Bob* will be excluded from your search for pages that do contain *Dylan* and *Thomas*. (Thus, you'll get the *Dylan Thomas* pages and not the *Bob* Dylan pages, but here's a quiz: will you get some *Thomas* Jefferson pages?)

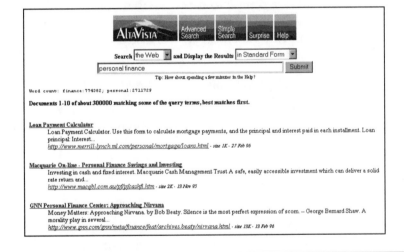

Figure 8.10: Here you see some of the results of searching Alta Vista for personal finance.

If you have a home page or some sort of Web presence, try typing your own name into the Alta Vista search box sometime and see what comes up. You may be surprised.

Performing More Complicated Searches with Alta Vista

You don't have to limit yourself to entering simple text such as we've described as your search criteria. You can use the Advanced Search page to do more sophisticated, complex searches.

To use the Advanced Search page, follow these steps:

1. From the Alta Vista home page click on the words Advanced Search in the Alta Vista banner graphic along the top of the page. A page will appear that has a number of new searching options (see Figure 8.11).

2. In the text box labeled Selection Criteria near the top of the page, type a word or a phrase to describe what you want to find, just as you did in the simpler search. You can type multiple words into the Selection Criteria text box, and also special words that describe how the words relate to what you are searching for.

Use	Like This Example	And It Will
AND	Adobe AND Photoshop	Find all records that contain both the word *Adobe,* and the word *Photoshop*.
OR	Photoshop OR CorelPaint	Find all records that contain either *Photoshop*, or *CorelPaint*, or both.
NOT	NOT Macintosh	Find all records that do not contain the word *Macintosh*.
NEAR	Macintosh NEAR Clone	Find all the records that include the word *Clone*, within 10 words of the word *Macintosh*.
" "	"Image Pals"	Find all the records that include the phrase *Image Pals*.

To get a lot of very helpful advice about using these search options, click on the <u>Selection Criteria</u> and <u>Results Ranking Criteria</u> links in the Alta Vista Advanced Query page.

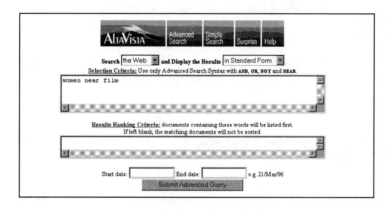

Figure 8.11: Click on Alta Vista's <u>Advanced Search</u> link, and a number of more sophisticated search options will be yours. Here we are searching for *women near film*.

3. In the Results Ranking Criteria area of the page, you can control the order in which documents that meet the criteria you specified in step 2 will appear when they are listed. Enter words that are in the documents that you wish to appear at the top of the list. If you leave this area blank, the results of the search will appear unordered.

4. If you're searching Usenet, you can specify start and end dates for the posting of Usenet articles. Only articles that were posted between these two dates will appear in the search results. In the Start date and End date text boxes, type the earliest and/or latest dates you want to search between.

5. Once you've entered the text you want to search for and have filled in any of the other options described in the preceding steps, click on the Submit Advanced Query button. The famous N will become animated, and in a few seconds a new page will appear, listing everything matching your criteria that Alta Vista's search engine found in the Alta Vista database.

The listing that appears will follow Alta Vista's policy of providing those sites that most closely match your criteria at the top of the list.

You might notice that one or another handy search tip appears under the Alta Vista search box. (The tips appear in rotation.) You can find a whole bunch of these tips (for tasks like searching within certain domains and finding links to your own home page) by clicking on <u>Tips</u> at the bottom of any Alta Vista page.

◆ Searching with Lycos

Lycos was developed by a group at Carnegie Mellon University as a tool for cataloging enormous amounts of Internet material. Currently operated by a private company, Lycos has (as of this writing) more than 10 million pages listed in its database. Like other search tools, Lycos is actually composed of two pieces:

◆ A Web crawler that seeks out and catalogs pages on the Web, logging everything it finds into a database

◆ A set of Lycos Web pages with which you can access and search the database

Unlike some others, the Lycos Web crawler records a site's URL and title in the database, *and it records the first 20 lines of the page.*

What's Out There

You can call on Lycos using the URL `http://www.lycos.com/`.

Lycos' great strength is that its database is so huge you're bound to find something about your topic listed there. Let's take a look at how to search Lycos.

1. In the Query text box of the Lycos home page, type a word or phrase that describes what you want to find.

2. Right below the Query text box, you'll see three radio buttons labeled Lycos Catalog, A2Z Directory, and Point Reviews. Select the radio button next to Lycos Catalog because that is the database we are searching.

3. Click on the Go Get It button. Lycos will start searching, the Netscape N icon will become animated, and in a few seconds a page will appear with a detailed list describing the stuff Lycos found that matched your criteria.

In this list you'll get the title and URL of each Web page that matched your criteria. You'll also get an excerpt of the page (generated automatically) showing the beginning of the document. Figure 8.12 shows the results of a search for *Fela Anikulapo Kuti*, a popular Nigerian musician.

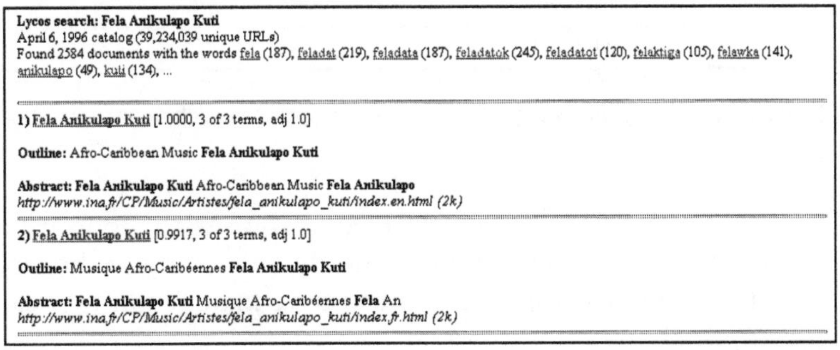

```
Lycos search: Fela Anikulapo Kuti
April 6, 1996 catalog (39,234,039 unique URLs)
Found 2584 documents with the words fela (187), feladat (219), feladata (187), feladatok (245), feladatot (120), felaktige (105), felawka (141),
anikulapo (49), kuti (134), ...

1) Fela Anikulapo Kuti [1.0000, 3 of 3 terms, adj 1.0]

Outline: Afro-Caribbean Music Fela Anikulapo Kuti

Abstract: Fela Anikulapo Kuti Afro-Caribbean Music Fela Anikulapo
http://www.ina.fr/CP/Music/Artistes/fela_anikulapo_kuti/index.en.html (2k)

2) Fela Anikulapo Kuti [0.9917, 3 of 3 terms, adj 1.0]

Outline: Musique Afro-Caribéennes Fela Anikulapo Kuti

Abstract: Fela Anikulapo Kuti Musique Afro-Caribéennes Fela An
http://www.ina.fr/CP/Music/Artistes/fela_anikulapo_kuti/index.fr.html (2k)
```

Figure 8.12: Lycos found a whole bunch of information on the Web about Fela Anikulapo Kuti, a popular but not entirely famous Nigerian musician.

Performing More Complicated Searches with Lycos

The Lycos database is so big that even a search for a little-known topic is likely to turn up scads of pages. You'll often want to perform more focused searches so as to find only the stuff that's most relevant. You can use the Customize Your Search link to do so.

Follow these steps:

1. From the Lycos home page, click on the Customize Your Search link. The Lycos Search Form page will appear, as shown in Figure 8.13.

2. In the Query field of the Lycos Search page, type a word or a phrase that describes what you want to find.

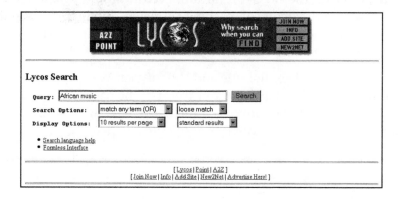

Figure 8.13: You'll have great control over your search when you use the Lycos Search page.

3. Two pull-down lists appear next to the Search Options label. In the first pull-down list, you can specify how many of the words you typed into the box you want to have matched in the search. The options are:

To Match	Select the Option
All the words	Match all terms (AND)
Any one word	Match any term (OR)
Any *n* number of words (where *n* is replaced by a number from 2 to 7)	Match *n* terms

In the second pull-down list, you specify how closely the search engine must match your criteria. The options are fairly self-explanatory:

◆ Loose match

◆ Fair match

◆ Good match

◆ Close match

◆ Strong match

Selecting loose match will retrieve the most documents; selecting strong match will retrieve the least number of documents.

What's Out There

You can further investigate the search options Lycos presents by looking into `http://www.lycos.com/reference/search-help.html`.

4. Two more pull-down lists appear next to the Display Options label. In one of them, you can specify how many of the pages that the search engine finds you want to see. You can choose anywhere from 10 to 40.

Don't worry that you aren't seeing every single page that matches your search criteria. You can simply click on the Next n hits link at the bottom of the page of results to get even more.

In the second pull-down list, you can specify what is to be displayed for each site that matches your search criteria.

If You Select	You'll Get
Summary results	Just the titles of the matching pages
Standard results	The title and the excerpt (called an abstract)
Detailed results	The title, the outline (just a short summary—usually just the first few words of the excerpt), and a longer excerpt

5. When you've completed all the settings and your search criteria are fully specified, click on the Search button. The Netscape N icon will become animated. In a few seconds, a page will appear listing the sites that match the criteria you specified.

The A2Z Directory

Lycos is a big whopping giant of a database, and it's accessed many, many times a day by a lot of people. Wouldn't it be dandy to know which of the sites cataloged by Lycos are most popular—the most sought after sites? The A2Z directory tells you just that. It's a browsable, indexed list of reviews of the most popular entries in the Lycos database. The A2Z directory is organized into general categories, much like other indexes, and like other indexes, it offers a search function. The A2Z database of reviews is nowhere near as large as the main Lycos database, however, so you might not find anything in A2Z that satisfies your search.

What's Out There

You can go straight to A2Z via the URL `http://a2z.lycos.com/`.

◆ Searching with HotBot

HotBot is a zippy new search tool developed by Wired Ventures using the Inktomi search engine. Inktomi, which debuted in late 1995 amidst great fanfare, was an experimental Web searching tool developed by Eric A. Brewer and Paul Gauthier at the University of California at Berkeley. They developed it as a sample application for *parallel computing*—which just means it runs on more than one computer at a time. This is good, because if one machine fails or slows down, another takes over and keeps the work going. (You may recall that this is the same principle on which the Internet was founded.) What started as the parallel computing experiment of a group of CS (Computer Science) students became a wonderfully useful (and *fast*) tool for finding information on the Web, which was then developed by the folks who bring you HotWired into a slick, user-friendly search tool (Figure 8.14).

What's Out There

HotBot is there for all the world to work with, at `http://www.hotbot.com/`. Inktomi's special qualities are apparent at `http://www.inktomi.com/`.

HotBot is very simple to use. In fact, it's pretty much the most user-friendly search tool going. Basically you just type in some text that

Figure 8.14: HotBot: The new kid on the block

describes what you want to find and click on the Search graphic. Let's go over the steps in detail, however. Here they are:

1. Open the HotBot home page. In the text box, type a word or phrase that describes what you seek.

2. Using the handy pull-down menu, you can specify whether to look for:

- ◆ All of the words
- ◆ Any of the words
- ◆ The phrase
- ◆ The person
- ◆ The URL

3. Click on the Search Button. The Netscape N icon will become animated as HotBot searches its database for matching documents, and in a few seconds a new page will appear listing the results (see Figure 8.15).

The results will be shown in the order of relevancy. In other words, if you type three words as your search criteria, the site that contains the largest number of references to all three of those words will appear first in the list of results.

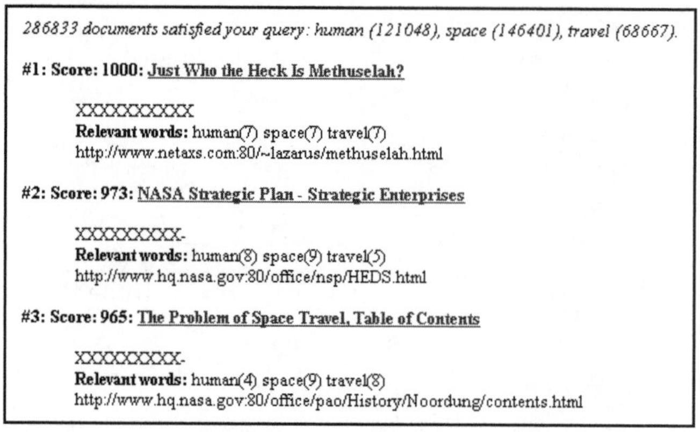

286833 documents satisfied your query: human (121048), space (146401), travel (68667).

#1: Score: 1000: Just Who the Heck Is Methuselah?

XXXXXXXXXX
Relevant words: human(7) space(7) travel(7)
http://www.netaxs.com:80/~lazarus/methuselah.html

#2: Score: 973: NASA Strategic Plan - Strategic Enterprises

XXXXXXXXX-
Relevant words: human(8) space(9) travel(5)
http://www.hq.nasa.gov:80/office/nsp/HEDS.html

#3: Score: 965: The Problem of Space Travel, Table of Contents

XXXXXXXXX-
Relevant words: human(4) space(9) travel(8)
http://www.hq.nasa.gov:80/office/pao/History/Noordung/contents.html

Figure 8.15: When you search HotBot, you'll get a page like this one that lists documents.

HotBot typically displays only 10 documents at a time on its results page. If your search resulted in more than 10 matching documents, a Return Next 10 hits link will appear at the bottom of the results page. Clicking on that link will display the next set of matches.

Performing More Complicated Searches with HotBot

HotBot includes right there on the initial search page some very easy-to-use features that let you control which documents it returns. This is where HotBot excels—the advanced search options are terrifically easy to use.

To perform more complex searches with HotBot, proceed as described here:

1. On the HotBot search page, click on the Modify link to display advanced search options. A new HotBot page will appear, where you can focus your search.

2. Pull-down lists and text boxes appear in the page. Use them to specify whether you want pages that must not, must, or should contain the word, phrase, person, or URL you then type into a text box.

 You can set up as many of these focused criteria as you like by clicking on the button with the plus sign (+) in it. To delete the bottom one, click on the button with the minus sign (–).

 HotBot offers even more advanced search options. To get to them, just click on the <u>Expert</u> link. A bunch of pull-down lists and text boxes will appear, allowing you to search the Web based on a page's modification data, media type (HTML vs. Java for example), or physical location.

3. To actually accomplish the search, click on the Search button. The Netscape N icon will become animated, and in a few seconds the results of your search will appear.

HotBot is a promising new search tool; keep an eye on how its features affect the capabilities of other search tools over time.

◆ Searching with InfoSeek

InfoSeek is yet another combination Web-crawler/database search engine. This one differs from others in that the company that brings you InfoSeek allows you to glean *some* results of a search without compensation to them, but charges a fee for full access. For example, you can search the Web and Usenet archives for free, but you must pay for access to Infoseek Professional, which includes computer industry newspapers and magazines, newspaper newswire services, company profiles, movie reviews, book reviews, video reviews, and so on in its available databases.

In this section, we'll show you what you can do using the free parts of InfoSeek.

Searching via InfoSeek is a breeze. Simply follow these steps:

1. In the text box of the InfoSeek home page, type a word or a phrase that describes what you seek.

What's Out There

Seek InfoSeek, and you'll find it at `http://www.infoseek.com/`. Infoseek Professional is ensconced at `http://professional.infoseek.com/`.

---

2. Click on the Seek Now button. The Netscape N icon will become animated, and in a few seconds, the InfoSeek Net Search Results page will appear, showing the results of your search. Figure 8.16 shows an example.

InfoSeek displays only 10 matches at first; if your search produced more than these initial 10 matches, you can see the additional ones by clicking on the <u>Next</u> link that appears at the bottom of the page.

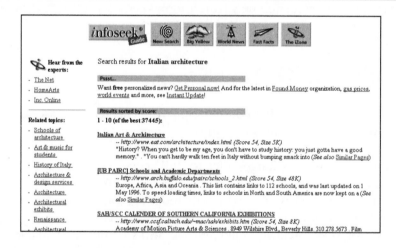

Figure 8.16: Get a gander at these results of an Infoseek search for *Italian architecture*.

Performing More Complicated Searches with InfoSeek

Like Inktomi, InfoSeek does not provide a separate page for advanced searching—instead, you conduct more advanced InfoSeek searches simply by entering special characters into the same text box you originally used to do a basic search in InfoSeek.

To perform a more complicated search of InfoSeek, follow these procedures:

1. In the text box where you enter the words that describe what you want to search for, you can add special characters before each word to control its meaning. Here are your options:

Use This	And That Will Mean
	Entering nothing special with a word means that the word may appear or may not appear in the document for the document to be considered a match.
+	Prefixing a word with a + means that the word must be in the document for the document to be considered a match.
−	Prefixing a word with a − means that the word must not appear in the document for the document to be considered a match.
[ ]	Surrounding words with square brackets means that the words should appear near each other in the document for the document to be considered a match. (InfoSeek considers 2 words within 100 words of each other to be near each other.)
" "	Surrounding words with quotation marks means that the words should appear next to each other in the document for the document to be considered a match.
—	Separating words with a dash has the same meaning as surrounding them with quotation marks. The specified words must appear next to each other in a document for the document to be considered a match.

As an example, to search for documents that are about Netscape Navigator, but not about version 2.0, you can type +**"Netscape Navigator"** −**"2.0"** in the search box.

2. With the search criteria entered, click on the Search button. The Netscape N icon will become animated, and in a few seconds the results of your search will appear.

Infoseek's search functions are case-sensitive. This is actually handy when you're searching for proper names. If you search on a couple of words that start with uppercase letters, Infoseek assumes you are searching for someone (or thing) with a name. If, for example, you search for *Bill Gates*, Infoseek will seek the words *Bill* and *Gates* near each other, and will ignore all references to "paying your *bill*s" and "*gate* crashing." You can find more handy Infoseek search tips by clicking on the Help link on any Infoseek page.

Now You Know

Having read this far, you now know everything you need to know to check out what's on the Web. Maybe at this point you'd like to find out how to publish your own Web pages, including how to make your own home page. In the next chapter we'll look at HTML, the great enabler of Web publishing, and how to use it. We'll also explore including HTML in your e-mail messages, effectively making them into Web documents.

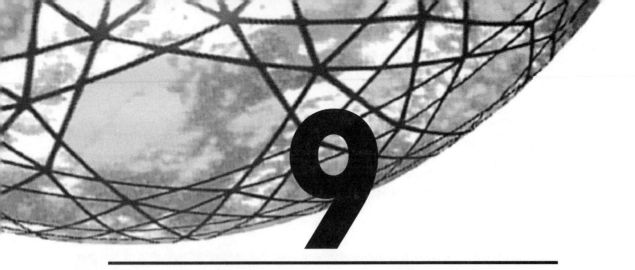

You Too Can Be a Web Publisher

By now, having used Netscape to roam the World Wide Web, you've seen the power of hypertext firsthand. You've seen that hypertext acts as both the Web's glue and its strands—binding it together yet hiding the complexities of Internet cruising. HTML (the Hypertext Markup Language) is the *standard* (the agreed-upon system of marking up text to create pages and links) that makes the Web possible. Maybe now you want to get into the act. This chapter will tell you how to get started as a Web publisher.

There are five basic steps to creating your own Web page:

◆ Organizing your concepts and materials

◆ *Storyboarding* (sketching out) the page(s) you intend to create

◆ Building a prototype

◆ Testing the prototype and making adjustments

◆ Putting your page on a server

This stuff isn't difficult—it helps to have a little experience, but, hey, everybody's got to start somewhere. Let's look at how HTML works and how you too can write HTML documents.

Don't expect to publish on the Net via your PC with a dial-up connection to the Internet. To actually publish a document for public viewing on the Web, you'll need access to an HTTP or FTP server. Most Internet service providers now provide access to an HTTP or FTP server at little or no additional cost. (We'll go over this in more detail at the end of this chapter.)

What's Out There

A great Beginner's Guide to HTML is available to all at
`http://www.ncsa.uiuc.edu/General/Internet/WWW/HTMLPrimer.html`.
The Composing Good HTML page is at
`http://www.cs.cmu.edu/~tilt/cgh/`.

◆ About HTML: The Hypertext Markup Language

There is plenty to know about HTML and creating and publishing Web documents. Sadly, we'll have to leave the finer points to the bigger books, but let's go over the basics: how to use formatting effects to make your page look attractive; how to make the heads in your documents appear in big, bold letters; how to link your documents to other documents; and how to embed pictures in your document.

The documents you see on the World Wide Web via Netscape look nice, but quite a bit of minor technological magic is going on. In actuality, the files for these documents are stored on a machine somewhere as plain ASCII text files—unlike word processing files, these ASCII text files include no formatting, and they employ no fancy fonts or attributes such as **bold** or *italics*. They are plain as plain can be (see Figure 9.1). All the special effects that you see in a Web document—**bold**, *italic*, <u>links</u> to other documents—are represented in the ASCII text files with special codes that also are made up of plain text characters.

10 PM
by Brenda Kienan

How many women lie in darkness in Quakertown, Lansdale, Perkasie; considering their pasts, with the undusted rifle rack hanging over the bed and the green afghan heaped and dragging from the arm of a chair onto the carpet where the kids pulled it down and went on. Through the drawn shades the sound of a thousand crickets and wind sweeping between this trailer and the next. These are the elements of redemption: the wind rising,

```
10 PM
by Brenda Kienan

     How many women lie in darkness in Quakertown, Lansdale, Perkasie;
considering their pasts, with the undusted rifle rack hanging over the
bed and the green afghan heaped and dragging from the arm of a chair
onto the carpet where the kids pulled it down and went on. Through the
drawn shades the sound of a thousand crickets and wind sweeping between
```

Figure 9.1: The document shown on the top was created in a word-processing program; shown on the bottom is the same document in ASCII format. Notice that all the attributes (bold type) and all the formatting (different font sizes, for example) are lost in the translation.

This means, luckily, that you can use any word processor (Word for Windows 95, WordPerfect, whatever) or text editor (DOS Edit, Windows NotePad) to create your HTML documents. We use Microsoft Word for Windows 95 to create our HTML documents; you can use any word processor or text editor you like. The only inflexible condition is that you must save the file as plain ASCII text before Netscape—or any other Web browser—can display it. So be sure your word processor can do that (most can).

Turn off the smart quotes (or curly quotes) when you're using your word processor to create HTML; if you don't, those nifty curly quote marks will trip things up and your links and images won't work.

What's Out There

You'll find loads of resources for creating Web pages at the WWW & HTML Developer's JumpStation—the URL is `http://rampages.onramp.net/~babel/dev-page.html`. MIT, that wonderland of technology, offers a page called Publishing on the Web and Tech Info at `http://web.mit.edu/publishing.html`.

Okay, so we just made the big point that you don't need a special HTML editor, yet HTML editors are available. Though unnecessary for writing basic HTML documents, an HTML editor certainly would prove beneficial when you're dealing with hundreds of pages of text. A good HTML editor can help you enter HTML tags and verify that you have all the details correct, making it easier to ensure that your Web documents will be displayed correctly in a Web browser.

What's Out There

A number of freely available programs exist to help you write HTML documents. These can be of great use when you are writing longer documents or complex Web pages. HotDog, a powerful yet friendly HTML editor, is available at `http://www.sausage.com`. Another good editor, WebEdit, is available at `http://www.nesbitt.com`. HoTMetaL PRO for Windows (a favorite) from SoftQuad is available at `http://www.sq.com/products/hotmetal/hmp-org.htm`.

◆ The Elements of Web Page Design

Your Web home page will be accessed by anywhere from dozens to hundreds of thousands of people a day. You'll want it to convey clearly and concisely the message you intend to promote (whether that's your resume, your company's policy on hiring technical professionals, or an account of what's happening at the local soda pop machine). In this section, we'll cover some basic guidelines for successful Web page design, tossing out for your consideration all the big-hitting tips we've picked up in our Internet travels.

Get Organized

The best way to get started in the design of your home page is to organize your assets: the existing documents and images you want to work with, for example. Think about the message you want to convey and which types of images or text might be appropriate. (Is it fun and lighthearted or seriously corporate?)

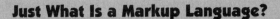

Just What Is a Markup Language?

Traditionally, a markup language uses defined sequences of control characters or commands embedded within a document. These commands control what the document looks like when it is output to, say, a printer. When you print the document, the control character sequences or commands format the document, displaying such elements as bold headlines, subheads, bulleted items, and the like.

HTML is unlike typical markup languages in that it is not so much concerned with typefaces and character attributes, but rather with the internal document markup itself. In a traditional markup language, you use commands to indicate the typeface, font size, and style of text *in a document*. In HTML, the commands indicate the headings, normal paragraphs, lists, and even links *to other Web pages*.

HTML is derived from the Standard Generalized Markup Language (SGML), which has come into increasingly common use in word-processing and other programs for creating print documents. HTML follows the SGML paradigm in that it uses *tags* to do its formatting. Tags are pieces of coding that usually, but not always, come in pairs consisting of a start-tag and an end-tag marking off *elements*.

When you create HTML documents, bear in mind that not all Web browsers support all HTML extensions, or they may support other aspects of the HTML language differently. In fact, some of the HTML tags we illustrate in this book are understood *only* by Netscape. Be this as it may, the basic HTML structure presented in this chapter works well in most instances.

Create a Storyboard

With the stuff you want to work with in hand, sit down with paper and pencil (or some nifty drawing software) and plot the thing out. *Storyboard* (sketch) your home page and each page it will link to; include all the elements you're considering (text, images, buttons, hyperlinks), and don't be afraid to make adjustments. If your original concept doesn't flow nicely, can it and start again. *You can't do too much advance planning.*

What's Out There

A U.S. copyright law page published by Cornell University is at `http://www.law.cornell.edu/topics/copyright.html`, and an FAQ (frequently asked question) list published by Ohio State is at `http://www.cis.ohio-state.edu/hypertext/faq/usenet/ Copyright-FAQ/top.html`.

Build a Prototype and Test It

When you've got your pages planned, go ahead and build a prototype. Then test it, test it, and *test it again*. Ask friends and colleagues to try it out and comment, and do all the fine-tuning you can. You want to make your best work public, not some funky work-in-progress.

 You can test your prototype without making it public. At the end of this chapter you'll find a section titled *Using Netscape to Check Your HTML Document* that tells you how.

◆ A Quick Look at Successful Web Page Designs

The best way to get ideas and to explore creating a winning Web page is to study examples. We've been showing you Web pages throughout this book; here we're going to take a look at a few especially well-designed pages, pointing out what makes them so terrific. Most of the pages we've selected use fairly basic HTML to achieve stunning results. We've also included a few pages that use tables, frames, or forms to show you what you might one day aspire to—after you've learned the basics, you can move on to more complex and challenging effects as you see fit.

Top Tips for Pages That Eat Like a Meal

You have two seconds to grab your reader's attention. That's common knowledge in advertising and publishing circles. You can't go wrong if you follow these basic tips for designing an eye-catching page with links that work.

- Start with an idea, and watch your concept turn into content as you sketch out your ideas on a storyboard.
- Make the title short, catchy, descriptive, and accurate. And whatever you do, fulfill its promise. If you call your page "Thousands of Yummy Recipes," it had better be that.
- Provide clues about what you have to offer at the top of the page; don't expect anyone to scroll down.
- If your page is longer than three "screenfuls," break it up into more than one page.
- A sense of balance is key; don't let your page design get lopsided. But do balance white space, large and small images, and blocks of text to give your page interest and variety.
- It isn't "cool" to overload your page with extraneous doo-dads.
- Use text and link colors that complement rather than clash with the background.
- Be sure that anything that looks like a button behaves like one.
- Don't create two links with the same name that go two different places or two links with different names that go to one place.
- Make your links descriptive; avoid the generic. "Click Here!" isn't all that intriguing.
- Use well-compressed images that contain fewer than 50 colors.
- Use thumbnails as links to larger images.
- Remember that people will access your pages using different browsers that have different capabilities.
- Keep filenames short and make them consistent.
- Tell people the size of any downloadable files you include.
- Get permission to use text or images created by someone else.
- Make a link to the e-mail address of the Webmaster (that's you).
- Build a prototype and test it. Make sure you test every link on all of your pages before you announce your site to the world.

If you want to see exactly what a Web designer did to create a specific page, launch Netscape, load the page of interest, and from the menu bar, select View ➤ Document Source. The HTML code for the page you're looking at will appear in a separate window, baring any secret techniques to you.

What's Out There

A great way to explore successful Web page design is to look at the sites of successful Web designers. You may find it useful to keep an eye on what's up with Organic at `http://www.organic.com`, Mann Consulting at `http:www.mann.com`, and Design/Systems of New York at `http://www.designsys.com`. Be sure to check out the pages of the clients, which are often given more attention than the designers' own home pages.

Another great way to get a grip on what works is to look at what *not* to do. Look as long as you're able at Clay Shirky's Worst Page on the World Wide Web at `http://www.panix.com/~clays/biff/`. For some more finger-pointing fun, check out Mirsky's Worst of the Web, at `http://mirsky.com/wow/`, or Yecch, a great parody of Yahoo, at `http://www.yeeeoww.com/yecch/yecchhome.html`.

Simple, Friendly, and Clear

Larry Rodrigues' U.S. Navy Airship Online Electronic Picture Book (Figure 9.2) documents his time spent around and aboard blimps while he was in the U.S. Navy in the 1950s. This picture book is an excellent example of how to combine pictures and text to make a page that's both easy to read and easy on the eye—even more so than many "real" photo albums that sit on coffee tables. The secret to this is that he kept things simple, using text wrapped around art in some of the site, and while he does use tables (which are beyond the scope of this chapter) for attractive page headers, Larry created the main body of the picture book using simple HTML.

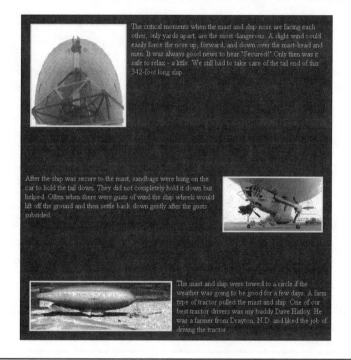

Figure 9.2: This page of the U.S. Navy Airship Online Electronic Picture Book is from the section called *Refueling at Sea.*

What's Out There

Fly by Larry Rodrigues' U.S. Navy Airship Online Electronic Picture Book at `http://www.GeoCities.com/CapeCanaveral/1022/`.

Terrifically Clickable

The Exploratorium's online exhibits are consistently well-designed—they're both beautiful to see and fun to navigate. The page shown in Figure 9.3 is from the section of the site called *Learning Studio*. The red bar running down the left side of the page is a background GIF—this popular technique

Figure 9.3: The Exploratorium's Learning Studio is fun, engaging, and no slouch when it comes to eye appeal.

can be highly effective. The buttons also have plenty of eye appeal, and you can tell at a glance what lies behind them.

What's Out There

Perhaps you've seen the Exploratorium's home page at `http://www.exploratorium.edu`. You should also check out the Learning Studio section of the site, located at `http://www.exploratorium.edu/learning_studio/`.

A Selective Color Palette

The Place of General Happiness (Figure 9.4) is not a run-of-the-mill personal home page, and Mark Thomas, its creator, doesn't use run-of-the-mill page design. Part electronic art exhibit, part creative writing journal, and part just plain weirdness, this site is a gem. Everything in these pages

Figure 9.4: The Place of General Happiness uses unconventional design for unconventional content.

is kept simple, which is part of what makes the site look so good. A selective color palette helps pull together the visuals, and an icon at the bottom of every page to send you home helps pull together navigation.

What's Out There

Make your way to the Place of General Happiness at `http://www.panix.com/~sorabji/`. For a look at another unique navigation scheme, try the Hole, at `http://www.panix.com/~sorabji/index2.html`.

Clever Use of Fonts

Addicted to Stuff is a stylish, funny, and downright amazing home page produced by Linda Abrams. She doesn't do it for money, but it looks just as good as many big-budget commercial sites we know. Her front page (Figure 9.5) is primarily made up of text, with different font types cleverly used to give the page visual interest. The columns are achieved through the use of tables with the borders turned off. Although most of this site is worth perusing, you might be particularly interested in her HTML tips for beginners, called *Addicted to HTML* or *So You Want a Home Page*.

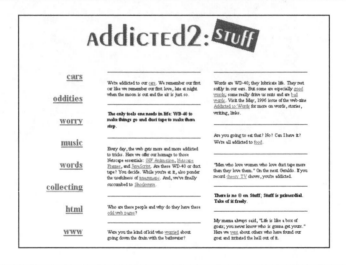

Figure 9.5: Addicted to Stuff uses borderless tables in this clever site that collects everything but dust.

What's Out There

Addicted to Stuff can be found at `http://www.morestuff.com/`. To jump right to Addicted to HTML, try `http://www.morestuff.com/htmlpage/a2html.htm`. For insight into using tables to create visual effects, scope out Netscape's guide to tables at `http://home.netscape.com/assist/net_sites/tables.html`.

Frames at Their Best

HotWired's Cocktail (Figure 9.6) is a hiply snooty site that talks about the culture and recipes of the mixed drink. It's also a fine example of successful use of frames—just about the best on the Web. Click on something in Cocktail's left frame, and stuff about that something shows up in the right frame. (Now *this* is useful.)

Figure 9.6: The frames-enhanced menu at HotWired's Cocktail is almost as slick as the recipes for drinks served up here.

What's Out There

Sip Cocktail at `http://www.hotwired.com/cocktail/`. When you're ready to tackle frames yourself, visit Netscape's guide at `http://home.netscape.com/assist/net_sites/frames.html`.

Button, Button, Who's Got the Button?

Using a button bar may well be one of the best ways to provide your site's users a clear navigation scheme. The one we show in Figure 9.7 is from the IRS's daily newsletter, a surprisingly non-stodgy piece of publishing from everybody's favorite government agency.

What's Out There

There's nothing taxing about the design at the IRS site (`http://www.irs.ustreas.gov/prod/cover.html`).

Figure 9.7: The button bar at the bottom of the IRS's pages is clearly clickable.

What's Out There

David Siegel is a master Web designer whose site is jam-packed with tips, solid information, examples, and links to other sites you may find helpful in your Web designing adventures. David Siegel has his own domain name, and his home page, at `http://www.dsiegel.com/`, is in itself an example of good design. Be sure to follow the <u>Web Wonk</u> and <u>Typography</u> links for great advice on Web page design, and go to the <u>Nine Act Structure</u> for wonderful information on structuring content. Siegel bestows the High Five Awards for excellence in Web design and presentation every week; take a look at `http://www.highfive.com/` to see winners of this selective award.

◆ Using HTML to Mark Up a Document

Now let's take a look at how all this is done. Marking up a document is a pretty simple matter of identifying what you want any given element to be and then literally *marking* it as that type of element (see Figure 9.8).

The markup, or *tag*, in HTML documents is surrounded by angle brackets, like this:

```
<title>
```

These tags usually come in pairs and affect everything between them. For example, surrounding a heading you'll see <h1> at the beginning, matching the </h1> at the end. ...More on this as we go along.

There are a few exceptions to the pairing of HTML tags, which we'll point out during the course of this chapter.

HTML tags can be written using upper- or lowercase letters—it doesn't matter.

In Figure 9.9 you can see all the elements of a basic HTML document. Take note of:

◆ The entire document enclosed between <html> and </html>

◆ The title of the document enclosed between <title> and </title>

◆ The header of the document enclosed between <h1> and </h1>

◆ The body of the document enclosed between <body> and </body>

```
<html>
<head>
<title>10 PM</title>
</head>
<body>
<h1>10 PM</h1>
<h2>by Brenda Kienan</h2>
<p>
        How many women lie in darkness in Quakertown, Lansdale, Perkasie;
considering their pasts, with the undusted rifle rack hanging over the bed and the
green afghan heaped and dragging from the arm of a chair onto the carpet where the
kids pulled it down and went on. Through the drawn shades the sounds of a thousand
crickets and wind sweeping between this trailer and the next. These are the elements
of redemption: the wind rising, rattling the corrugated plastic roof of the neighbor's
carport, the husband coughing over the droning tv news, the washer clicking and
getting louder as the clothes inside it spin out of balance. This is an ordering of events
that carries one day to the next.<p>
        How many women, each in her own separate darkness, surveying what might
have happened, while the rushing wind finds its way into heating ducts and whistles
through tin.<p>
        <i>Papa, it is vanishing.</i> The blue June evenings and the scent of dusty
pavement as a long-awaited rain falls. <i>I thought I'd still know, but I'm
drifting.</i> White tulips. Gold star confetti sprayed across starched tablecloths.
The priest's thick fingers holding a book.<p>
        How many women making a list, of the ways they might have gone, of the
friends they see in markets, marriages lost, pushing carts full of children, sugary
cereals, cheap meats. How many mornings of driving: her own child to another's care,
her husband (who's lost his license) to work, herds of teenagers in a yellow bus to
school. How many times the red-haired boy pushing his way to the seat behind her,
bringing her gifts of novelty pencils, a sandwich, cloisonn&eacute; earrings.<p>
        How many women wondering, each in her cool separate darkness, if the news
is yet over, if the wind will grow still.<p>
<h3>Copyright 1995 Brenda Kienan</h3>
</body>
</html>
```

10 PM

by Brenda Kienan

How many women lie in darkness in Quakertown, Lansdale, Perkasie; considering their pasts, with the undusted rifle rack hanging over the bed and the green afghan heaped and dragging from the arm of a chair onto the carpet where the kids pulled it down and went on. Through the drawn shades the sounds of a thousand crickets and wind sweeping between this trailer and the next. These are the elements of redemption: the wind rising, rattling the corrugated plastic roof of the neighbor's carport, the husband coughing over the droning tv news, the washer clicking and getting louder as the clothes inside it spin out of balance. This is an ordering of events that carries one day to the next.

How many women, each in her own separate darkness, surveying what might have happened, while the rushing wind finds its way into heating ducts and whistles through tin.

Papa, it is vanishing. The blue June evenings and the scent of dusty pavement as a long-awaited rain falls. *I thought I'd still know, but I'm drifting.* White tulips. Gold star confetti sprayed across starched tablecloths. The priest's thick fingers holding a book.

How many women making a list, of the ways they might have gone, of the friends they see in markets, marriages lost, pushing carts full of children, sugary cereals, cheap meats. How many mornings of driving: her own child to another's care, her husband (who's lost his license) to work, herds of teenagers in a yellow bus to school. How many times the red-haired boy pushing his way to the seat behind her, bringing her gifts of novelty pencils, a sandwich, cloisonné earrings.

How many women wondering, each in her cool separate darkness, if the news is yet over, if the wind will grow still.

Copyright 1995 Brenda Kienan

Figure 9.8: In an HTML-coded document (above) you see tags (within angle brackets) surrounding the element to which they refer. In the resulting Web document (below), you do not see the tags—you see only the effect they have on the document displayed.

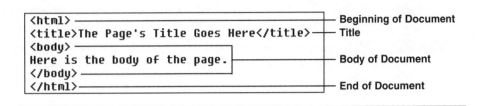

Figure 9.9: Here you can see the HTML coding for the basic elements of a Web document.

In the sections that follow, we'll look at the basic HTML tags you can use in your documents. Remember as we go along that these tags are the same whether you are marking up a document in a word processor or in an HTML editor.

If you're using a word processor to create an original document you intend for Web publication, you can, of course, simply write in the HTML coding as you go along; you don't have to write the document first and enter the tags afterward. Turn off the smart quotes (or curly quotes), however, because they'll confound your links and images.

Every Document Must Have the "Required" Tags

Every HTML document must include certain tags, which essentially identify the document as an HTML document and, as such, show its beginning and end. Note that even these fundamental HTML tags come in pairs—the `<html>` at the beginning of the document matches the `</html>` at the end of the document.

Marking Up Heads

HTML supports six levels of heads. Each level of head will look different when it's displayed in a Web browser such as Netscape. The highest level (let's call this the "1" head) will be larger and more obvious; the lowest level (the "6" head) will be smallest and most discreet.

 The actual way each head looks is different from one browser to the next. In other words, HTML allows you to say what text is a head, but not what the head will look like when User A accesses it with Netscape, User B with Spyglass Mosaic, and User C with Internet Explorer.

The text of the head should appear between two head tags **<h***n***>** and **</h***n***>**, where *n* can be any number between 1 and 6. It is customary to start your document with a head of level 1, to indicate the important topic that comes first. You can follow a level 1 head with heads of lower levels; you can also place new level 1 heads farther down in your document, as you please.

Beginning New Paragraphs

You must explicitly code each and every new paragraph of text by placing the **<p>** tag at its beginning. You needn't close a paragraph with any coding, however. This new paragraph business is one of the major exceptions to the "opening and closing" paired tags that are the general rule in HTML.

 Web browsers will not start a new paragraph if you do not include the <p> tag, regardless of how your document looks in your word processor.

Changing the Justification of Paragraphs

When you use the **<p>** tag, what you'll get is the regular, left-justified paragraphs you're used to seeing most often in print. You can change the alignment of a paragraph—to make it either centered or right-justified—by embedding the **align** command in the **<p>** tag in that paragraph. Embedding the **align** command is a simple matter of inserting a space and a bit of text into the **<p>** tag between the **p** and the **>**.

For example, let's say you want the opening text of your home page centered on the screen. The coding would look like this:

```
<p align=center>Welcome to Lori s Home Page!
```

You'll have to mark the next paragraph with another **<p>** tag, of course, as you always have to do; unless you specify otherwise, that next paragraph will appear left-justified, as usual. Here are the commands you can embed to change any paragraph's justification:

The Command	Will Produce
align=center	Centered paragraphs
align=right	Right-justified paragraphs

Be sure to include a space before the **align** command.

Inserting Ruled Lines

Rules, or ruled lines, are horizontal lines that you can use to separate parts of your document. To place a rule in your document, use the **<hr>** tag. (See Figure 9.10.) Again, it's not necessary to indicate the end of the rule with a closing tag.

```
Send e-mail to <a href="mailto:info@sybex.com">info@sybex.com</a> for more information
<hr>
Thanks for visiting!
```

Send e-mail to info@sybex.com for more information.

Thanks for visiting!

Figure 9.10: The coding you see in the HTML document above results in the rule you see in the Web document below.

The **<hr>** tag inserts a shaded, engraved line that crosses your Web page (no matter what size the page appears to be on screen) from the left margin to the right.

Netscape also allows you to vary the look of ruled lines by embedding commands in the `<hr>` tag (just like you can embed the `align` command in the `<p>` tag). You can embed as many commands as you like to achieve the effect you want. For example, if you would like the ruled line to be exactly 250 pixels wide and to be centered on the page, you can use the following code:

```
<hr width=250 align=center>
```

You can use these commands with the `<hr>` tag to change the look of ruled lines:

The Command	Will Produce a Ruled Line That Is...
`size=n`	*n* pixels thick
`width=n`	*n* pixels wide
`width=n%`	*n* percentage of the width of the page
`align=left`	Pushed up against the left margin (left-justified)
`align=center`	Centered on the page
`align=right`	Pushed up against the right margin (right-justified)
`noshade`	A solid bar with no engraving or shading

Go ahead and play around with all these options to see what kind of ruled lines are most effective in your document.

Creating Lists

You can have two types of lists in a Web document: numbered and bulleted. In HTML lingo, numbered lists are called *ordered* lists, and bulleted lists are called *unordered* lists.

Ordered Lists

Ordered (numbered) lists result from text nested between the `<ol>` and `</ol>` tags. Each new item in the ordered list must start with the `<li>`

tag. Unlike most other HTML tags, the `<li>` tag need not end with the `</li>` tag. For example, a numbered list of types of fruit would look like:

```
<ol>
<li>Apple
<li>Orange
<li>Cherry
</ol>
```

A Web browser would display the list like this:

1. Apple
2. Orange
3. Cherry

When you're coding an ordered list, you need not enter the numbers. The HTML coding tells the Web browser to number the items sequentially in the order in which they appear.

Netscape also lets you control the type of numbering in an ordered list. To specify the type of numbering you want, you can embed the type command in the first `<ol>` tag. For example, if we modify our fruit list like this:

```
<ol TYPE=I>
<li>Apple
<li>Orange
<li>Cherry
</ol>
```

Netscape will display it with roman numerals, like this:

I. Apple
II. Orange
III. Cherry

You can use the following commands to specify the type of numbering you want:

The Command	Will Produce
type=A	Uppercase letters, starting with A
type=a	Lowercase letters, starting with a
type=I	Uppercase roman numerals, starting with I
type=i	Lowercase roman numerals, starting with i
type=1	Arabic numerals, starting with 1

 Not all Web browsers "understand" the type options for numbers as Netscape does. If you create a page using these options and someone loads the page using a Web browser that doesn't allow for this, he or she will see the items listed using arabic numerals.

Unordered Lists

Unordered (bulleted) lists result from text nested between the `<ul>` and `</ul>` tags. This, of course, is similar to what you do to create an ordered list. Each new item in the bulleted list must begin with the `<li>` tag. This is exactly like what you do with each item in an ordered list; it is the **o** or **u** in the opening and closing tags that "tells" Netscape whether the list is to be numbered or bulleted—and, again, you need not bother with placing any type of bullets. They will appear when the document is viewed on screen wherever you have placed the `<li>` tag in your unordered list.

 Remember that the bullets will look different and will be of different sizes in the various Web browsers.

By default, Netscape uses solid discs as bullets, and it does not indent bulleted lists. You can change bullets to squares instead of discs. Doing so is a simple matter of embedding the `type=square` command in your opening `<ul>` tag, like this:

```
<ul type=square>
```

Other than that one little change, you create your bulleted list as described above. If you use the `type=square` command in this way, all bullets in your list will be neat, stolid squares.

Creating Links

Now we get to the heart of things. As you know well by now, the beauty of the Web is the way documents are interrelated through being linked—that's what makes the Web so wonderfully webby. Let's take a look behind the scenes at the HTML underpinnings of a link.

In HTML lingo, a link is really what's called an *anchor*, the opening code for which is `<a`. What the anchor looks like when it appears as a link in a Web document will differ depending on the Web browser being used, but usually it'll show up as underlined text in a special color. When you click on the link (the underlined text in some special color), the anchor is activated, and the file with which it is associated (the other end of the link, if you will) is loaded and displayed on screen.

Here's an example of how this works in HTML: If you wanted the word *Internet* to appear in a document as a link, you'd code the word like this:

```
<a href= http://www.sybex.com/internet.html >Internet</a>
```

Then, when the document is viewed with any Web browser, such as Netscape, the word Internet will appear as a link. When a user clicks on it, the file INTERNET.HTML will automatically be transferred from the HTTP server, and a list of Internet-related books will appear on screen.

 Remember, you must indicate the type of file to which you are linking; this will "tell" the Web browser employed by any given user how to deal with the file. When it comes to images, some Web browsers "out of the box" can deal only with GIF and JPG files. Users who have those browsers will need special viewers and players to view images or play sounds in other file formats.

What's Behind That Sound, Graphic, or Video Link

In your Web roamings, you've probably found links that go not to HTML documents but perhaps instead to graphics, sounds, and videos. The URL in a link doesn't have to point to another HTML document; it can point to any type of file. For example, the anchor

```
<a href= http://www.iuma.com/IUMA/ftp/music/Madonna/
Secet.mpg >Madonna</a>
```

creates a link to the machine where a video clip from Madonna's Secret video is stored. When you click on the link, the video will be transferred to your computer, and a player for MEPG files will start up so that you can see the video—the trigger for that action is in the HTML coding shown above. You can create links to any type of file in this manner—just include the full path to the file in the URL.

Creating Glossaries

A *glossary* in a Web document is a special element designed to let you place definitions in your documents. Glossaries look a bit like lists when they are coded with HTML; the list of items this time must be surrounded by the tags <dl> and </dl>. Each defined term in the glossary starts with the tag <dt>. The definitions themselves follow the term to which they apply and begin with the tag <dd>. Neither <dt> nor <dd> tags need closing tags.

Here is a sample of coding for a glossary:

```
<dl>
<dt>Apple
<dd>A round fruit, often red in color when ripe but sometimes
green or yellow
<dt>Orange
<dd>A round, orange fruit
<dt>Cherry
<dd>A small, round, red fruit
</dl>
```

The result of this sample coding will look like this:

> Apple
> A round fruit, often red in color when ripe but sometimes green or yellow
> Orange
> A round, orange fruit
> Cherry
> A small, round, red fruit

Inserting Addresses

Address is a special HTML element that was originally designed to hold the address of the author of the page (the snail-mail address, the e-mail address, or both). Most Web browsers display this element in an italic font, smaller than body text. For example,

```
<address>
Daniel A. Tauber and Brenda Kienan
<br>Sybex
<br>2021 Challenger Drive
<br>Alameda, CA 94501
</address>
```

will appear as shown here:

> *Daniel A. Tauber and Brenda Kienan*
> *Sybex*
> *2021 Challenger Drive*
> *Alameda, CA 94501*

We've used the **
** tag in the preceding example instead of the **<p>** tag. The **
** tag inserts a line break without adding extra space between lines, as the **<p>** does.

Assigning Text Attributes

You are probably familiar with *text attributes* from word processors. Things such as bold, italic, and font color, which differentiate some text from the usual, are all known as *attributes* in a word processor. You can specify attributes such as these using HTML.

Remember that none of the formatting or text attributes you might have in your word-processed document will carry over to your Web document—you must specify what you want using HTML coding.

The types of attributes you can specify using HTML are broken down into two classes:

◆ Physical

◆ Logical

The *physical* attributes specify how text characters will look: italic or bold, for example. They will be italic or bold no matter which Web browser is used for viewing (as long as the browser understands that particular type of formatting). The *logical* attributes specify the amount of emphasis you want to give to important text; you can choose to make text *big, small, emphasized,* or *strongly emphasized.* Different Web browsers will have different ways of displaying logical attributes (some may show strongly emphasized text as bold, others may show it as red or in a slightly larger size, for example). The choice of using logical or physical attributes is yours. Some people prefer to use physical attributes because they want to control the way the text finally looks. Other people prefer to use logical attributes because they convey "meaning" without specifying what the text should look like.

Physical Attributes

You can use physical attributes to make text appear bold, italic, superscript, or subscript.

The tags used to apply these attributes are summarized here:

To Get This Attribute	Use the Starting Tag	And the Ending Tag
Bold	`<b>`	`</b>`
Italic	`<i>`	`</i>`
Superscript	`<sup>`	`</sup>`
Subscript	`<sub>`	`</sub>`

 You can use several attributes together simply by embedding them. Just be sure the opening tag that's first-in corresponds to the closing tag that's last-out. For example, to make the phrase *Bungee Jumping* both bold and italic, use the coding `<b><i>Bungee Jumping</i></b>`.

Logical Attributes

You can use logical attributes to give emphasis to text you feel is important. The way the text actually appears when viewed in a browser depends on the browser's individual way of handling these attributes. The logical attributes that you can use are:

To Get This Attribute	Use the Starting Tag	And the Ending Tag
Emphasis	`<em>`	`</em>`
Strong Emphasis	`<strong>`	`</strong>`
Big Typeface	`<big>`	`</big>`
Small Typeface	`<small>`	`</small>`

Here you can see the result of making text emphasized and strongly emphasized and viewing the text with Netscape:

Emphasis and **Strong Emphasis**

This is what big and small typefaces look like compared with the default, regular-sized font:

Big type and Small type

Changing Font Size

Netscape allows you to change the size of the font in your document. You can use this feature to vary text size, down to the letter. Changing the font size allows you to use effects such as large initial capital letters (an elegant way to display important text).

The font size in an HTML document has a base value of 3 (this doesn't mean 3 point sizes; it's an arbitrary number set by Netscape). To change the font size, you insert the `<font size=`*n*`>` tag wherever you would like it to apply, and you insert the closing tag `</font>` wherever you would like it to end. *N* is the new size of the font. You can express the new font size in one of two ways:

◆ You can set it as a value between 1 and 7

◆ You can set it relative to the size of the base font, by using a + or a - sign

For example, to create large initial capital letters, you would use the following HTML coding:

```
<font size=+2>I</font>NITIAL <font size=+2>C</font>APS
```

You're telling Netscape to make the first letter of each word two sizes larger than the base font. Here is the result once you view the text with Netscape:

INITIAL CAPS

You can also change the value of the base font using the `<basefont=`*n*`>` tag. For example, if you would like all the text in your document to appear larger (say, size 4 instead of the default size 3), you would place the following HTML tag wherever you would like the base font size to change:

```
<basefont size=4>
```

Changing Font Color

Not only can you vary text size, you can specify colors for regular text, hyperlink text, *active* hyperlinks (ones that are in the process of being clicked), and *visited* hyperlinks (hyperlinks you have already activated). You set these colors by embedding commands in the **<body>** tag at the beginning of your HTML document.

As for the colors themselves, Netscape recognizes the *hexadecimal* color system. This system uses a six-digit code to specify the red, green, and blue balance of the color. This may seem like a bit of esoteric information, but you can use it to create beautiful effects on your page.

 Not all browsers "understand" the use of custom colors in an HTML document. Even those of your readers who are using Netscape may have monitors with limited or no color capability. Keep these caveats in mind when using color in your Web pages.

What's Out There

You don't have to memorize hex codes to be able to add color to your Web page. InfiNet's Color page lists about 100 colors you can choose from, along with their hexadecimal equivalents. Visit `http://www.infi.net/wwwimages/colorindex.html` to open this big box of color.

To specify colors, just embed the following commands in the **<body>** tag, where *n* is the hexadecimal code for the color you choose:

Use This Command	To Change the Color Of
`text= ` *n*	Regular body text
`link= ` *n*	Hyperlink text
`alink= ` *n*	Active hyperlink
`vlink= ` *n*	Visited hyperlink

For example, if you would like to create a Web page with black text, green hyperlink text, hyperlinks that turn yellow while you click on them, and magenta after you've visited them (wow! what a color scheme), your **<body>** tag would look like this:

```
<body text= 000000  link= 00FF00  alink= FFFF00
vlink= FF00FF >
```

 Because the text color commands are embedded in the **<body>** tag, they can be set only once for each Web page. You cannot change text color halfway through your document, for example.

Using Special Characters

Some special characters are readily available in HTML. For example, you'll often want to use the special character for the copyright symbol (©), and that one's no problem—there's a code you can use for it. But HTML files are really plain text files, so you don't have access to some other special characters. The symbol that's used to indicate copyright for digital audio, a letter P enclosed in a circle, is one unfortunate example.

Some "special" characters you'd use fairly regularly in word-processed text, such as angle brackets and even the ampersand, have special meanings in HTML, which you already know if you've read earlier sections of this chapter. To include characters such as these in your HTML document, you'll have to insert special escape codes in your file. Here are some examples:

For the Symbol	Which Means	Use the Code
&	Ampersand	&amp;
>	Greater-Than	&gt;
<	Less-Than	&lt;
®	Registered Trademark	&reg;
©	Copyright	&copy;

What's Out There

You can get a complete list of special characters and how to code for them at
`http://hyperg.tu-graz.ac.at/T0x811b9908_0x00058490`.

Embedding Images

Images that appear as part of a Web page are called *inline images*. Although it is possible to place many, many inline images in your document, remember that including them will greatly increase the time required to load and view the document.

It's best in some circumstances to place thumbnails of images in your page—thumbnails load a lot faster than larger images—and link the thumbnail to the larger image, allowing users to download the bigger image if they want to and have time to wait for it. See *Mixing Elements*, the next section in this chapter.

Any image that you want to include as an inline image in a Web document must be in one of two graphics file formats: GIF or JPG. Let's look more closely at the ever-popular GIF format in this section.

Some Web browsers (including Netscape) can display inline images in JPG format. JPG files are much smaller in size than other image files, so they appear on screen much more quickly—a real advantage. The drawback for the publisher, however, is that not all Web browsers can display them. If you use JPG and a user tries viewing your document with a browser that can't handle JPG, all he or she will see is a little error message where the image should be.

You can use the `<img>` tag to place an inline image into your HTML document. For example,

```
<img src= http://www.sybex.com/sybexlogo2.gif >
```

will cause the image stored in the file SYBEXLOGO2.GIF on the machine to be displayed as part of the Web document.

A couple of other nifty things you can do with Netscape involve text wrapping around images on screen. To cause an image to appear to the left of text with the text wrapping around the image, use the **align=left** command, like this:

```
<img src= http://www.sybex.com/sybexlogo2.gif  align=left>
```

To cause an image to appear to the right of text with the text wrapping around the image, use the **align=right** command, like this:

```
<img src= http://www.sybex.com/sybexlogo2.gif  align=right>
```

What's Out There

You can scope out a helpful FAQ file for extensive tips on scanning images to use in your Web documents. To find the Scanning FAQ, use the URL `http://www.infomedia.net/scan`. Transparent GIFs are GIFs in which one of the colors is invisible. (You might want to do this if you'd like the background color the user's Netscape is using to be one of the colors in the image.) To find out how you can make your GIFs transparent, look into the URL `http://members.aol.com/htmlguru/transparent_images.html`.

Changing the Background

We've talked about how you can use font colors and inline images to brighten up your pages. You can also change the way the background of your document looks by specifying a color or using an image as the backdrop for the document text (as opposed to the browser's default background color of gray or white).

 The color and/or image you choose for your background should harmonize with the color of your text. We've seen quite a few examples of enthusiastic Web authors who pick flamboyant colors for their documents, only to render them unreadable.

Like changing text color, you change the way the document background looks by embedding commands into the **<body>** tag.

 Not all Web browsers can display custom colors or images as backgrounds. For this reason, be sure your document depends on the overall design of text and graphics—not on the background—to look good.

Setting the Background Color

Changing the background color of your document from the default background to something more interesting is an easy way to lend drama and allure to your page. To specify a background color, use the **bgcolor=***n* command, like this:

```
<body bgcolor= 000000 >
```

 More and more Web browsers recognize Netscape-specific design features such as nifty background colors, but some older or less capable browsers can't interpret the **bgcolor** command. When a page that uses this command is accessed by a browser that doesn't recognize background color, the browser will just ignore the command and use whatever its default background color is—probably gray or white. No harm done.

Using an Image for Your Background

Another way to spice up your document is to use an image for its background. You can use any GIF or JPG graphic file as your background image (any browser that recognizes custom backgrounds can also display JPG images). For example, many companies like to use dimmed versions of their logos as background graphics—kind of like a watermark in expensive stationery (see Figure 9.11).

 Netscape *tiles* the graphic you specify as a background to make it fill up the entire window. That is, it will repeat the graphic in its original size until it covers the page's viewing area.

To specify a GIF or JPG file as your background image, use the **<body background=>** command, like this:

```
<body background= clouds.gif >
```

Figure 9.11: Microsoft uses its logo here as a background graphic.

What's Out There

Asha Dornfest, who designed the What's Out There page on the CD that comes with this book, maintains a solid site full of resources for designers, at `http://www.dnai.com/webpub/`. Check out her HTML page, Software Library page, and the *Image Maps Made Easy* article especially.

◆ Mixing Elements

Just as you can create ***bold-italic*** text by embedding the italic tag within the bold tag, you can embed one type of HTML element within another element. For example, you might want to create an unordered (bulleted) list in which each element is a link to another Web page. In fact, if you think about it, your entire HTML file is embedded between the `<html>` and `</html>` tags; so everything in your document is already embedded between two standard HTML tags.

Another practical use for embedded HTML tags is a link that leads to an image. In that case, the inline image tag is embedded inside the link tag. (And this, dear reader, takes us to the next section.)

Using Pictures As Links

To make an image act as a link to another document, you can use the link tag, **<a**, followed by indicators of what you're linking to, followed by **</a>**. In a nutshell, here's what you do: Where you'd normally place the text the user would click on to activate the link, you can instead place the tag to display an inline image. For example, if you have an image called TOCATALOG.GIF, you could place

```
<a href= http://www.sybex.com/catalog.html ><img
src= http://www.sybex.com/tocatalog.gif ></img></a>
```

in your Web document to create a link to the page stored in the file CATALOG.HTML. This causes a Web browser to display the image TOCATALOG.GIF with a border around it. When a user clicks anywhere in the picture, the link will become activated, and, in this case, the catalog page indicated will appear.

 You can remove the border that appears around images used as links by adding the **border=0** command to the **img** command.

Creating Lists of Links

Let's say you want a list of links. To do this, create an ordered or unordered list, placing a link as each item in the list. For example,

```
<ul>
<li><a href= http://www.sybex.com/index.html >Sybex s Home
Page</a>
<li><a href= http://www.sybex.com/catalog/catalog.pl >Sybex s
Catalog</a>
<li><a href= http://www.sybex.com/internet.html >Sybex s List
of Internet Books</a>
</ul>
```

produces a bulleted list with three items, each of which is a link to another page:

- Sybex's Home Page
- Sybex's Catalog
- Sybex's List of Internet Books

Java: The Hot Ticket to Live Action

If you've been out Websurfing of late, you've probably come across sites that include "live action." These are often examples of Netscape's support for *Java,* a programming language developed by Sun Microsystems that enables a vast new frontier of interactivity. Using Java, developers can create little applications, called *applets,* which, when they're embedded in HTML documents, create dazzling effects such as animation that might be used in games or for illustrations; ticker tape feeds for news, sports, and stock data; real-time interactivity that can be used for anything from crossword puzzles to the sharing of medical data; and handy gadgets such as mouse pointers that change shape when you drag them over something. Creating Java applets requires a fairly high level of programming knowledge and, as such, is beyond the scope of this book. Still, you should know that it is an option should you decide to become a Web-publishing guru.

◆ Creating a Simple Home Page

Great. Now, having read this chapter, you know all the HTML tags that go into creating a simple page. Let's go step by step through creating a home page. We'll use Word for Windows 95 to do this, and when we're done, we'll save the file as a plain text file.

To follow along, start up Word and open a new, empty document window.

Just about everything we do here you can do in any word processor. If you use a different word processor—WordPerfect, for example—you can follow along, substituting as necessary the functions and commands your word processor uses.

1. In your blank, new document window, type **<html>** and press ↵ to start your page. (Remember that all HTML documents should be surrounded by the <html> and </html> tags. We'll put in the </html> later, at the end of these steps.)

2. Now type **<title>Herkimer Uglyface's Home Page</title>** and press ↵. (You can replace Herkimer Uglyface with your own name, which is probably more attractive anyway.) This will make the title of your home page appear in the title bar when your page is viewed by a user.

3. Now type **<h1>Herkimer Uglyface's Home Page</h1>** and press ↵. This will make the title of your home page appear at the top of your home page. (Although it's customary to use the same text for the title and the first head, you can actually enter whatever you want in place of "Herkimer Uglyface's Home Page" here.)

4. Now we are ready to enter some body text, so type **<body>** and press ↵. This will tell the Web browser that what follows is the body text of the document.

5. Type in a few paragraphs of body text. Remember as you do this to use the **<p>** tag at the beginning of every new paragraph.

6. If you want people viewing your page to reach you by e-mail, you can add a link to your e-mail address. Type **<a href="mailto:** followed immediately by your e-mail address (with no space after). After your e-mail address (again no space should follow the address), type **>**. (Don't type that last period. It's only there to make our editor happy.) Press ↵.

7. Once you have typed the body text for your page, and added your e-mail link if you chose to, type **</body>** to end the body text and **</html>** to end the document. These two HTML tags match their counterparts at the beginning of the document. You can press ↵ after each of these tags if you're a stickler for aesthetic consistency, but it's not necessary.

Now it's time to save the document. (Remember, we're using Word for Windows 95 for this demo.)

1. From the Word menu bar, select File ➤ Save As. The Save As dialog box will appear.

2. In the Save As dialog box, click on the down arrow next to the text box labeled Save As Type. A list of file types recognized by Word will appear. From this list, select Text Only (see Figure 9.12).

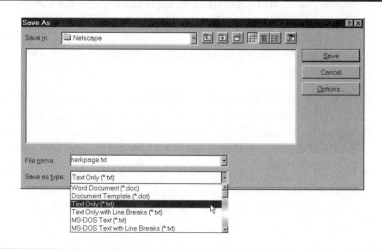

Figure 9.12: In the list of file types, select Text Only.

3. Type a path and a filename for the file in the File Name text box. If you're saving the file to your hard disk and placing it in your Netscape directory, the path will probably be C:\PROGRAM FILES\NETSCAPE. Our hero, Herkimer Uglyface, named his file HERKPAGE.HTM—you can name yours what you like, but you'll have to end the file with the extension .HTM, because this is an HTML file you are saving.

4. Click on the OK button to save the file.

When Word is finished saving the file, the Save As dialog box will close automatically. You can now exit Word. Don't be alarmed if it asks if you want to save changes to your file when you exit even though you just saved the file as a text file. Just answer No and continue to exit Word for Windows.

 Don't answer Yes when Word asks if you want to save changes to your file when you exit after having saved the file as a text file; if you do, Word will overwrite your text file with a Word file.

Good work. We're ready to look at the file with Netscape to see how it turned out.

Using Netscape to Check Your HTML Document

You've created an HTML document and saved it as a text file on your hard disk. Before you make your page public, you'll want to test it. You can use Netscape to see what your finely crafted page will look like when it's viewed with a Web browser. To load a file from your hard disk into Netscape, follow these steps:

1. Start Netscape and select File ➤ Open File from the menu bar. The Open dialog box will appear.

2. In the Open dialog box, highlight the filename you gave your page. (The Open dialog box works here just as it does in any Windows application.)

3. Click on the OK button. The dialog box will close, and in a few seconds your home page will appear on screen, in the form of a beautiful Web document!

If an old version of your HTML document appears by some chance, select View ➤ Reload from the menu bar to load the latest version of your HTML into memory.

What's Out There

For help in checking your page for typos, errors in grammar, and consistency in style and usage, stop by the Crusty Old Slot Man's Copy-Editing Peeve Page at `http://www.access.digex.net/~bwalsh/editing.html`. Look into the archive for some real gems of wisdom.

You won't be able to fix typos or other errors or add things to your HTML document while you are viewing it with Netscape. If you want to make changes, close Netscape, open up your word processor, and make the changes there. Then, you can save the modified file, and reopen it in Netscape to see the changes you just made.

After Your Page Is Rich and Famous

You say your page is up and running? *Great*, but…you're not finished yet! You need to *maintain* the thing. Here's how to make sure your Web page is as good in a month as it is now:

◆ *Check your links.* Make sure they haven't eroded over time. If you rename a file, you have to rename all the links to it. If you're linked to the outside world, make sure those links are live.

◆ *Respond to feedback.* If someone e-mails you about a problem with your page, they are not criticizing you as a person, only the parts of your page that don't work. Thank your helpful fan for caring enough to point out what concerns him or her, and make a decision on your own about what to do with the feedback.

◆ *Keep your content fresh.* If you promise to add more content, people will hold you to it. Telling visitors that you'll post a new joke every day and then following up once a month instead is bad form.

◆ Making Your HTML Document Available to the World

Having created a wonderful HTML document on your own computer, you'll want to make it available to the world. As a Web publisher, you can, if you have a big pile of money, buy a machine and set it up as a Web server. This is simply not practical for most people; so we're going to skip it. You can also, if you have access to a Web server at a university or elsewhere, sneak your page onto that server (but don't say we said so). A third option, more practical for a lot of people, might be to publish your page with the help of your Internet service provider.

Many Internet service providers (and even some commercial online services) offer you the option of publishing your Web page on their server as a perk for your use of their service. Unfortunately, however, this is sometimes not free—check with your service provider about costs, and if there is an unreasonable charge, switch providers.

The technical specifics of making your Web pages available to the world vary from one Internet service provider to another; so we cannot go into great detail in this book. Contact your service provider to see how it recommends that you make your documents available to the Internet public.

◆ When Your Page Is Ready, Publicize It

If there are no links to your page, you will get no hits. This is a law of physics on the Web. You want many entry points to your site, and lots for people to do and see once they get there. You want *backlinks* (links from other sites to yours), and listings in directories and search engine databases. You want to get your site the attention it deserves.

 The best way to get publicity for your site is to make it such a whiz-bang piece of genius that no one can ignore it. Make sure your site includes outstandingly well developed content presented in an appropriate style, with great design, easy navigation, a dash of wit, and a pinch of originality. That will make it easier for visitors to your site to recommend it to friends and colleagues, and will make your site appealing to those in the know who see so many and recommend so few. That's your best bet.

Get Listed with Directories and Search Engines   You can get your page listed in many big directories such as Yahoo or Excite quite easily by submitting your URL via a handy form that you'll find at the directory's site. Or you can go to a central location (like Pointers to Pointers or Submit It!) that lists a lot of these places, select as many or as few directories as you'd like your site to appear in, click on an oh-so-easy-to-use

Submit button, and—wham-o!—an announcement of your site's birth is blasted off to all the appropriate places in cyberspace in no time flat.

What's Out There

Pointers to Pointers is at `http://www.homecom.com/global/pointers.html`; Submit It! is at `http://www.submit-it.com/`. To check out other places to promote your page, visit Yahoo's list of Announcement Services at `http://www.yahoo.com/Computers_and_Internet/Internet/World_Wide_Web/Announcement_Services`.

If your site is a personal home page, submit it to GNN's Netizen directory at `http://gnn.com/gnn/netizens/addform.html`. If it is commercial, try Open Market's Commercial Sites Index, found at `http://www.directory.net`, or the LinkStar commercial directory, at `http://www.linkstar.com`.

Get Webmasters to Backlink to You   Surely you're not the only person on the planet who collects lunchboxes, goes spelunking, or conducts genetic programming experiments with marmosets. Find like-minded Webmasters and trade links.

Get Listed with "What's New"   Your page is *new*—and some special pages post links to other pages that have just launched. The criteria for acceptance varies; some are choosy, like NCSA's What's New, while others, like What's New Too, list anybody who's new.

What's Out There

Give NCSA's choosy What's New page a go at `http://www.ncsa.uiuc.edu/SDG/Software/Mosaic/Docs/whats-new.html`. Anything goes at Internet Magazine's What's New page (`http://www.emap.com/whatsnew/`). What's New Too is at `http://newtoo.manifest.com/WhatsNewToo/`.

Pay for Premium Listings   If you've got a big-ticket budget for promoting your page, you may want to invest in premium listings. You can spend upwards of $1000 to have your site appear in Yahoo's Web Launch or Lycos' New2Net for one week. Getting listed on Netscape's What's New page may be even more pricey.

What's Out There

Yahoo's Web Launch (`http://www.yahoo.com/docs/pr/launchform.html`), Lycos' New2Net (`http://www.lycos.com/new2net.html`), and commercial announcement services like WebPromote (`http://www.webpromote.com/` or PostMaster `http://www.netcreations.com/postmaster/`) are not for low-budget amateurs.

Announce Your Site in Selected Newsgroups   You can announce your site in various newsgroups and mailing lists via announcement services; just be sure to choose appropriate venues based on whether their topics are related to the topic of your page. Be discreet—no one wants to get junk mail in newsgroups any more than in "real" life. Make sure your announcement is timely, relevant, to the point, and respectful of a particular newsgroup's culture.

Take Advantage of E-Mail Publicity   Place your site address in a very brief signature file that appears at the conclusion of all your e-mail messages. This will get the word out to those with whom you correspond on any topic. Also, create an e-mail mailing list so you can send out announcements to interested parties when you launch or update your page. You can embed your URL into an e-mail message and send that out (see *HTML in Netscape's Electrifying E-Mail*).

Don't send e-mail to every e-mail address you see. It's important to avoid the very rude practice known as *spamming*—the unnecessary junking up of newsgroups or people's e-mail in boxes with messages of no interest to them.

You can also announce your page via Internet mailing lists such as Net-Happenings. NetHappenings, by the way, is a wonderful way to stay current on what's happening on the Internet. To subscribe to NetHappenings, send e-mail to `majordomo@lists.internic.net`; in the body of your message, type **subscribe <net-happenings>**.

Use Print Media   Print your site's URL on your business card (if that's appropriate), your stationery, or in ads (if yours is a commercial venture). Some magazines list the addresses of Web sites, sometimes for a small fee.

◆ HTML in Netscape's Electrifying E-Mail

You can embed hyperlinks, inline images, and other HTML tags right into the body of your e-mail messages, effectively transforming them into working HTML documents. This is remarkably easy. Figure 9.13 shows an e-mail message with an image embedded in it.

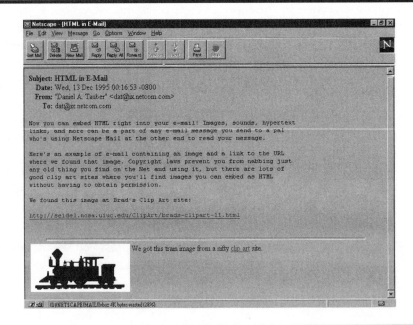

Figure 9.13: You can embed links, images, and other HTML right into your e-mail message.

Make sure that anyone to whom you send HTML marked-up e-mail is using Netscape Mail. Remember that if you embed HTML into your e-mail message and send it to a friend that is not using Netscape Mail, all that lucky person will see is a bunch of gibberish-like HTML coding.

With this handy integrated e-mail capability, readers of your e-mail messages can, for example, jump directly to a Web page without a second thought. No more cutting and pasting URLs from your e-mail into the Open Location dialog box; it's as if your e-mail messages were mini Web pages in and of themselves!

You can incorporate links to Web pages into your e-mail most easily by typing URLs directly into regular e-mail messages. (Whenever a URL appears in a Netscape Mail or Netscape News message, the URL automatically becomes an actual link to the page it specifies.)

You might want to delve into using HTML itself in an e-mail message if you've got something more complicated than a couple of URLs you want to send off. Here are the details:

1. Follow the steps and guidelines throughout earlier sections in this chapter to create a file with any of the HTML trappings you want. You can use any of the tags we discuss in this chapter in HTML e-mail. As an example, to embed a URL in your e-mail, open your word processor and type **<html>Take a look at this <a href="http:// www .dnai.com/~vox/netscape">Netscape</a> page</html>**. (Not the period at the end; it's just there to stop the sentence.) This will become a brief HTML file that will be the body of your e-mail message. Note that the word *Netscape* is linked to a URL. Give this document a descriptive name with the extension HTM (NETMSG.HTM, for example) and save it as a text file. Close your word processor.

2. Start Netscape and create a new e-mail message as described in Chapter 5's quick and easy instructions.

3. After you enter the recipient's name and address and the subject of the message in the Message Composition window as usual, click on the Attachment button. The Attachments dialog box will appear.

4. In the Attachments dialog box, click on the Attach File button. The Enter File to Attach dialog box will appear.

5. In the dialog box's list of files, highlight the name of the file you just created and click on the Open button. The Enter File to Attach dialog box will close, and the Attachments dialog box will reappear, this time with the file you just selected listed in its large list box.

6. Click on the Attachments dialog box's OK button. The dialog box will close, and the Message Composition window will be visible. The name of the HTML file you created will appear in the Message Composition window's Attachments text box.

7. Now send off your HTML file, just as you would any other e-mail message, by clicking on the Message Composition window's Send Message button.

When your message arrives, the HTML file you created will look just like any other e-mail message, but it will contain whatever HTML functionality you built into it—in our example, the word *Netscape* will actually be a link to a Web page. The pal we sent it to will be able to click on the Netscape link and will be zapped right over to a page about this book.

That's all there is to using HTML tags in your e-mail. You can experiment with using the different HTML options discussed in this chapter in your e-mail messages.

What's Next?

Well. Now you know all you need to know to browse the Web, search for what you find intriguing or useful, create your own home page, and include HTML in your Netscape e-mail messages. In Chapters 10 and 11, we're going to cover the nitty-gritty technical details: how to get connected and install Netscape. Then, in Chapter 12, we'll show you how to get some nifty plug-ins and helper apps from the Internet itself.

Part Three:

Getting Started with Netscape

10

Laying the Groundwork for Installing Netscape

Roll up your sleeves—this is the part where we get down and dirty and put things together. In this chapter, we're going to get you on the Net, set up your Internet connection, and *go get Netscape* from the Internet itself.

Before you can start cruising the Internet with Netscape Navigator—or even download the program to your computer—you have to have your Internet connection ready to go. Until recently, connecting your stand-alone home computer to the Internet meant installing complicated software on your computer—called SLIP/PPP software—and configuring it with information about your Internet service provider. Two developments have made connecting to the Internet much easier:

◆ Windows 95 includes the software you need to access the Internet via any Internet service provider (you don't need separate, special SLIP/PPP software any more, though you do need a SLIP/PPP account).

◆ Many commercial online services (such as America Online and CompuServe) now offer Internet access to their subscribers as part of their services.

Internet Service Providers and Commercial Online Services: The Big Difference

Believe it or not, commercial online services such as America Online and CompuServe are not part of the Internet. They do provide Internet access these days, but in actuality, commercial online services are separate, distinct entities—what's the difference? Well, a commercial online service provides content, such as online magazines, consumer reports, and reference material; forums in which people discuss their interests; contests; and online access to celebrities—whatever's deemed commercially viable and of interest—to subscribers who pay a (usually monthly) fee for that service. As part of all this, the commercial online services have begun to provide access to the Internet as well. An Internet service provider gives you access to the Internet for a (usually monthly) fee, but does not usually provide any content whatsoever—all the content, in this case, comes from the Internet itself. Commercial online services often charge extra for some "premium" aspect of their services; they may also charge for receipt of e-mail. Internet service providers generally charge only for access time, not for any kind of premium stuff.... Now you know.

In this chapter we'll cover the major ways to get connected and get Netscape:

◆ Using Windows 95 Dial-Up Networking to access the Internet via any of a lot of Internet service providers

◆ Using Netcom's Netcomplete software to access the Internet

◆ Using software provided by some of the major commercial online services—America Online, CompuServe, or Microsoft Network—to access the Internet

If you're just getting started using the Internet, you may want to read this entire chapter before you decide which method of connecting is best for you. If you already have an account with an Internet service provider, turn to the section titled *Getting Connected via Windows 95 Dial-Up Networking*; if you have an account with Netcom's Netcomplete, turn to the section titled *Getting Connected via Netcom's Netcomplete*; if you have an account with America Online, turn to the section titled *Getting Connected via America Online*; if you have an account with CompuServe, turn to the section titled *Getting Connected via CompuServe WinCIM*; and if you have an account with the Microsoft Network, turn to the section titled *Getting Connected via the Microsoft Network*.

Depending on the type of Internet connection you use (Windows 95 Dial-Up Networking, AOL, Netcomplete, WinCIM, and so on) you'll get and use either the 32-bit or 16-bit version of Netscape. Turn to *A Tale of Two Versions* in Chapter 11 for a description of these two versions.

◆ Getting Connected via Windows 95 Dial-Up Networking

When it comes to using an Internet service provider and your Windows PC to access the Internet, there are two eras: before Windows 95, and after Windows 95. Before Windows 95, setting up your Netscape connection with an Internet service provider was a big drag. You had to install several separate pieces of software (including special SLIP/PPP software that "introduced" your Internet service provider to Netscape at the beginning of every session). Then you had to configure your machine and all this software to work neatly together—it might have taken a whole day!

You still need an account with an Internet service provider, but you're saved all that other hassle, because Windows 95 includes all the software you need to get connected to the Internet. You do still need a SLIP/PPP account, but you *don't* need special SLIP/PPP software. You can use Windows 95 Dial-Up Networking with just about any Internet service provider that offers SLIP or PPP, and these days, they pretty much all do.

What's Out There

You can get the latest news about Dial-Up Networking on Windows95.com's TCP/IP set-up page at `http://www.windows95.com/connect/tcp.html`.

What You Need

To run Netscape on your Windows PC using an Internet service provider, you need:

◆ An account with an Internet service provider

◆ Netscape itself

◆ Windows 95 Dial-Up Networking Software (which comes with Windows 95)

Setting up an account with an Internet service provider is up to you. Suffice it to say, the most important considerations in selecting an Internet service provider are

◆ Whether it provides a local access phone number so that you can avoid long distance charges

◆ Whether it offers SLIP/PPP accounts (most do, but verify anyway)

You also need a Windows PC with at least 8MB of RAM (12MB or more is a lot better), 10MB of available hard disk space, and a fast modem (at the very least 9600 bps, although 14,400 bps or 28,800 bps is much better). Except for the modem, this is the same stuff you need to run most Windows programs, so you're probably set.

In the section that follows this one, we'll talk a bit more about choosing an appropriate Internet service provider. Appendix A lists some reputable Internet service providers you can contact if you like; but read on first so that you'll know what you need.

By the way, getting Netscape is usually a matter of going out on the Internet and downloading an evaluation copy of the software; we'll go over that in an upcoming section of this chapter. You can also get Netscape in a box from any of many retail outlets, but we're going to leave it to the documentation in that box to tell you how to install Netscape if you go that route. The thing to remember is that, no matter how you got your copy of Netscape and how you connect to the Internet, the software itself runs the same.

Okey dokey, let's get cracking. Before we do, however, a few words of caution: This section is going to deal with material that's a little more technically demanding than what we've done so far in this book. Setting up Windows 95 Dial-Up Networking involves a lot of making little "pieces" work together. Don't let this discourage you—take your time, have patience, read carefully, and ask your Internet service provider for help if you get stuck.

 Take into consideration the willingness of an Internet service provider to help you get your Windows 95 Dial-Up Networking when you choose whether to set up an account with that service provider—it's an indication of that company's overall attitude toward customer service.

In the end you'll have Netscape running, and it'll be well worth your effort.

Selecting an Internet Service Provider

You need to think about some things as you select an Internet service provider to work with Netscape. Let's go over the important points.

Ask about SLIP/PPP

If you're going to run Netscape on a home computer equipped with a modem (that's what we're here for, isn't it?), you're going to need a SLIP account *or* a PPP account. Most Internet service providers offer SLIP/PPP now as their primary service, and commercial online service accounts such as America Online and CompuServe include it, too.

SLIP stands for *Serial Line Internet Protocol,* and PPP stands for *Point-to-Point Protocol.* Some Internet service providers offer one, some offer the other, some offer both. For your purposes at home, they are equivalent; either kind of account will allow you to run Netscape just fine (that's why we talk about them as a unit, using "SLIP/PPP" for shorthand).

In telecommunications jargon, SLIP/PPP allows you to send TCP/IP packets (see Chapters 1 and 2) over a serial communications device—a *modem.* Remember, while you are logged on to your SLIP/PPP account, your machine at home *is actually part of the Internet.* Your machine becomes part of the network of millions of computers that make up the Internet, and you can communicate with any one of them by sending and receiving e-mail, files, or whatever.

Consider the Costs

A major consideration in selecting a service provider is cost. Essentially two costs are involved: a monthly or hourly fee you pay the service provider for access, and the fee you pay (or do not pay if you are clever and find a service provider with local access) to the phone company for long distance charges. *Shop around for a good deal*, and when you ask about the deal, remember to ask about a local access number.

Ask about technical support too. Is it available by telephone seven days a week or only through e-mail? Is the provider's technical support group fully staffed? Are people available at the time you'll call? If you have pals you can consult, ask them about the quality of support and the provider's reputation for reliability.

In this chapter we concentrate on using Dial-Up Networking with a modem to attach to the Internet over a standard telephone line. You can also use Dial-Up Networking, and other similar pieces of software, to connect to the Internet at much faster speeds with new technologies. Some of these technologies include ISDN and cable modems, which promise connection speeds from 4 to over 350 times as fast as the fastest modem.

What's Out There

Two good sources of information about cable modems are @Home (a company that is building the physical network on which they'll work) at `http://www.home.net` and the Cable Modem Resources on the Web page at `http://rpcp.mit.edu/~gingold/cable/`. For a good list of ISDN resources, load up Yahoo's Computers and Internet: Communications and Networking: ISDN page at `http://www.yahoo.com/Computers_and_Internet/ Communications_and_Networking/ISDN/`.

Make Note of Some Technical Details

Once you choose a provider, you can usually set up your account over the telephone. It should take only a few days (if that) for your service provider to get you going.

But let's back up a minute. While you've got them on the line, find out some technical information you'll need to set up Windows 95 Dial-Up Networking for use with Netscape. Make note of the answers as you go—we'll use this information later in this chapter. Specifically, ask for the following information:

◆ The IP Address assigned to your machine at home (unless your provider "dynamically assigns" an IP address)

◆ The IP Address of the provider's primary domain name server

◆ The IP Address of the provider's secondary domain name server, if any

If you're already familiar with addresses in the **domain.names.separated .by.periods** format, you'll know that **violet.berkeley.edu** is a machine at the University of California, Berkeley. This is *not* what you want here, however. In our discussion in Chapters 1 and 2, we described how an address such as **violet.berkeley.edu** is the easier-to-remember version of what's really a numeric address. You want the IP address in a *numeric* format—numbers separated by periods—such as **126.54.32.1**.

Ask for the four-number address the provider is assigning to your computer. *Every* computer on the Internet has such an address, called an *IP (Internet Protocol) address*. Note that some providers assign your machine a permanent IP address; others assign an IP address "dynamically," meaning that each time you log on to your SLIP/PPP account, the provider's server automatically assigns your computer an address for use in that session only.

If your provider assigns your machine a permanent IP address, write it here:

_____._____._____._____

If your provider assigns an IP address dynamically, just leave these blanks empty.

Last, you will need to know the IP address of your service provider's primary and, if it has one, secondary domain name servers. Write these addresses here:

_____._____._____._____

_____._____._____._____

In addition to the IP addresses above, you also need the names of a few servers that your Internet service provider maintains:

◆ News (also know as NNTP) server.

◆ Mail (also know as the POP3 and SMTP) servers. This may be a single server, or it may be two different servers.

Write the name of the news server here:

_____

 You'll use these server names in the next chapter when you get Netscape running. You don't need the numeric IP addresses here. Simply entering the servers' names, such as `news.abc.com`, is fine.

Now write down the name of the POP3 and SMTP servers here (if the same server is used for both, simply write down the name twice).

_____

_____

There is one teensy caveat here: If you want to connect via a SLIP account (rather than PPP), you'll need the CD-ROM version of Windows 95. The CD-ROM version includes both SLIP and PPP capability; the diskette version does not include the Windows 95 SLIP driver. PPP is more commonly offered than SLIP, however, and PPP has some performance advantages over SLIP. So unless you have some special reason to want SLIP, the PPP driver that comes with Windows 95 will probably fit your needs.

Installing Windows 95 Dial-Up Networking

Now that you have an account with an Internet service provider, you are ready to install and set up Dial-Up Networking. (Actually, you can go ahead and install Dial-Up Networking before you have your Internet service provider account; you just can't finish installing and using it until you get the account information from your provider.) You must (obviously) *install* Dial-Up Networking before you can use it to connect to your Internet service provider. If, during your installation of Windows 95, you indicated that you wanted Dial-Up Networking installed, it'll be there, but the Windows 95 installation process does not automatically assume that you want Dial-Up Networking. You can install Dial-Up Networking now if you need to, using the Add/Remove Software Component Control Panel. To do so, follow these steps:

1. From the Start menu, select Settings ➤ Control Panel. The Control Panel window will appear.

2. In the Control Panel window, double-click on the Add/Remove Programs icon.

Add/Remove
Programs

The Add/Remove Programs Properties dialog box will appear (see Figure 10.1).

Click here to display installed Windows 95 components.

Click here to display Communications components.

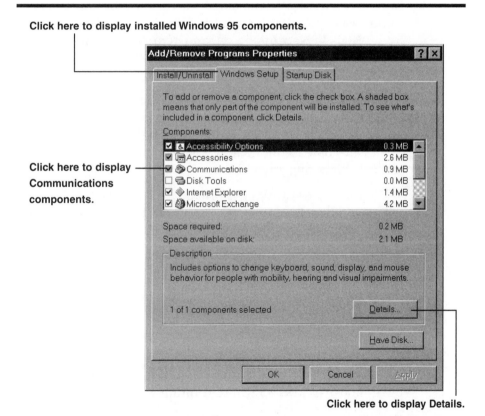

Click here to display Details.

Figure 10.1: You can use the Add/Remove Programs Properties dialog box to add Windows 95 Dial-Up Networking components to your computer if you don't have this gem installed already.

3. Along the top of the dialog box, you'll see a number of tabs. Click on the Windows Setup tab, and the window's contents change to show which portions of Windows 95 have been installed on your computer.

4. Because Dial-Up Networking is all about communicating, it is grouped with other communications options in Windows 95. Click on the Communications entry in the Components list along the left side of the dialog box, and then click on the Details button. The Communications dialog box will appear, showing the Windows 95 communications options you can install.

5. In the Communications dialog box, click on the checkbox next to the Dial-Up Networking entry. (This indicates that you want to install Dial-Up Networking on your computer.) Now, click on the OK button to continue. The Add/Remove Programs Properties dialog box will reappear.

6. In the Add/Remove Programs Properties dialog box, click on the OK button to start installing Dial-Up Networking. Windows will ask you to insert either the Windows 95 diskettes or the CD-ROM as files are copied from them to your computer. Insert the diskettes or CD-ROM as requested.

7. When Dial-Up Networking is installed, a dialog box will appear telling you that you must restart your machine before Dial-Up Networking will actually work.

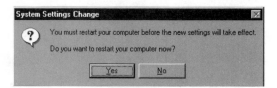

Click on the Yes button to finish installing. Your computer will restart and Windows 95 will start running again.

When your machine restarts, Dial-Up Networking is installed. You will not see any obvious changes as a result of the installation (except that you will have a new icon in your My Computer window called

Dial-Up Networking). Even though you now have the software required to access your Internet service provider, you still need to:

◆ Create a new connection for your Internet service provider.

◆ Enter information about your Internet service provider.

Once you complete these two steps, you'll be ready to start using the Internet.

Introducing Dial-Up Networking to Your Internet Service Provider

Now you're going to set up Dial-Up Networking to work with your Internet service provider. In particular, you'll:

◆ Create the connection that tells Dial-Up Networking the telephone number to dial for your Internet service provider.

◆ Configure the connection so that Dial-Up Networking knows how to access the Internet via your Internet service provider.

We are now ready to start creating the connection you'll use to hook up with your Internet service provider.

 If your PC is on a LAN (a Local Area Network), you must contact your network administrator before you configure Dial-Up Networking—otherwise you can make a real mess of things and cause that person a lot of grief.

1. From the Start menu, select Settings ➤ Control Panel. The Control Panel window will appear.

2. In the window, double-click on the Network icon.

Network

The Network dialog box will appear.

3. In the Network dialog box, click on the Add button. The Select Network Component Type dialog box will appear (see Figure 10.2).

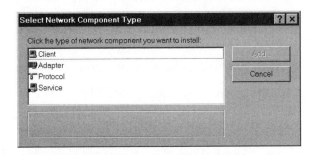

Figure 10.2: The Select Network Component Type dialog box

4. Now, in the Select Network Component Type dialog box's list box, double-click on the word Protocol. The Select Network Protocol dialog box will appear (see Figure 10.3).

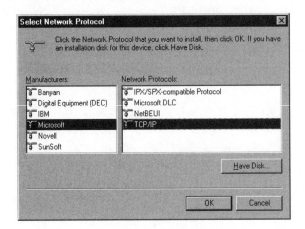

Figure 10.3: The Select Network Protocol dialog box with Microsoft and TCP/IP highlighted

5. Along the left side of the Select Network Protocol dialog box, you will see a list box labeled *Manufacturers*. In the list, highlight Microsoft, and you will see a list of network drivers—the software that Windows uses to communicate over a network such as the Internet.

6. In the list of network drivers (which you can see in Figure 10.3),
   click on the entry titled TCP/IP (remember, TCP/IP is the Internet
   protocol we discussed in Chapter 2).

7. With the TCP/IP entry highlighted, click on the OK button. The
   Network dialog box will reappear, with TCP/IP now listed in
   the Network Components list as shown in Figure 10.4.

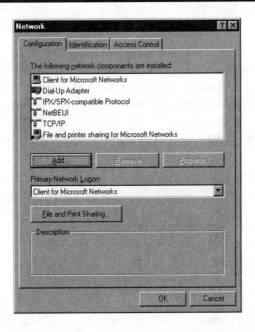

Figure 10.4: TCP/IP is now listed under Network Components.

8. When you installed Dial-Up Networking, Windows set it up to
   access a bunch of networks, such as Microsoft NT and Novell
   Netware, in addition to the Internet. In this step, we'll remove
   the pieces that are used to access these other networks, just leaving
   what is required to access the Internet. In the Network dialog box's
   Network Components list, highlight IPX/SPX Compatible Protocol,
   and click on the Remove button, and then highlight NetBEUI, and
   click again on the Remove button. Finally, highlight File and
   Printer Sharing for Microsoft Networks and click once more on
   the Remove button.

 If your machine is on a LAN, messing around too much with this list can really wreak havoc. Please, please talk to your network administrator first.

9. At this point, only Client for Microsoft Networks, Dial-Up Adapter, and TCP/IP should appear in the Network Components list. If this is so, click on the OK button to continue. The Network dialog box will close, leaving you with your familiar Desktop.

You've established all the network settings required to access the Internet using Dial-Up Networking. Now you have to create the actual Dial-Up Networking connection, which means in essence that you must provide Windows with detailed information about your Internet service provider.

Creating a New Dial-Up Networking Connection

To actually use Dial-Up Networking, you create something called a *connection*. According to Microsoft, a connection holds information about your Internet service provider—for example, its telephone number. Once you have created the connection, you can use Dial-Up Networking by double-clicking on the Connections icon on the Desktop.

 You need to have a modem installed in your computer and configured for Windows 95 in order to use Dial-Up Networking. If you don't have this stuff all together, you'll be prompted to rectify matters during this set-up procedure.

To create a connection, follow these steps:

1. When you installed Dial-Up Networking, Windows created a new icon in the My Computer window called Dial-Up Networking. Open the My Computer window by double-clicking on the My Computer icon on the Desktop. Now double-click on the Dial-Up Networking icon.

Dial-Up
Networking

The Dial-Up Networking window will appear. As you create Dial-Up Networking connections, they will appear in the Dial-Up Networking window as icons.

2. In the Dial-Up Networking window, double-click on the Make New Connection icon. You double-click on this icon whenever you want to create a new connection for Dial-Up Networking. The Make New Connection dialog box will appear, as shown in Figure 10.5.

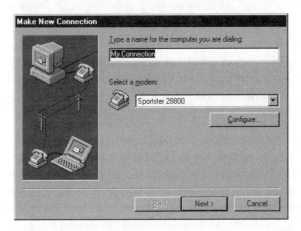

Figure 10.5: In the Make New Connection dialog box, you'll provide detailed information about your Internet service provider.

3. In the Make New Connection dialog box, type a name for the connection—the name of your Internet service provider is a logical choice—in the Type a Name for the Computer You Are Dialing text box. Don't press the ↵ key after you enter the name; we still need to enter some additional information in this dialog box before moving along.

4. In the Select a Modem pull-down list, select the modem you plan to use. Odds are that you have only a single modem installed on your computer, so this should be simple—you probably won't have to make any changes to this item.

5. Now click on the Next button to move to the next Make New Connection dialog box (don't get confused—all the dialog boxes used to create the connection have the same title). In this dialog box, enter the phone number you will use to dial up your Internet service provider.

6. First, type the area code in the Area Code text box, and then type the telephone number in the Telephone Number text box.

Do not enter a 1 or any other special access numbers before the area code. Windows treats all those special access digits specially— you specify them when you set up your modem.

7. Now in the Country Code pull-down list, select the country where your Internet access provider is located. (Odds are this already indicates the correct country, unless you are calling internationally for your Internet access.) Click on the Next button to continue. The last Make New Connection dialog box will appear.

8. The last Make New Connection dialog box informs you that you have successfully created the connection. Click on the Finish button to finish creating the connection, or if you see a boo-bette, click on the Back button to return to the previous Make New Connection dialog box so that you can fix it. (You can travel back and forth through the Make New Connection dialog boxes by clicking on the Next and Back buttons. When you're done making corrections, simply click on the Next button until you get to the last Make New Connection dialog box and then click on the Finish button.) The Dial-Up Networking window will appear on the Desktop (as shown in Figure 10.6) listing the new connection that you just created.

Now it's time to actually introduce your Internet service provider to your machine and to Windows.

Configuring Your Dial-Up Networking Connection

You've created the connection for your Internet service provider, and in the process of that you specified your Internet service provider's name and telephone number. Now you must specify all that other information you got from your Internet service provider when you set up your account (remember that from the earlier section?). That's all part of *configuring* (setting up) your connection.

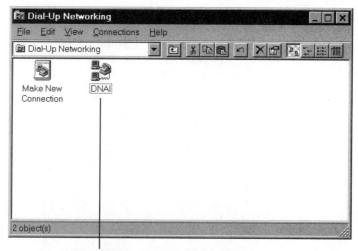

Here is the connection you just created.

Figure 10.6: The new connection you just made appears in the Dial-Up Networking window.

Follow these steps:

1. In the Dial-Up Networking window, which should still appear on your Desktop, right-click on the icon for the connection you just created.

A menu will appear.

Note that the name of the icon will depend on the name you entered in the first Make New Connection dialog box in the last section. It is probably the same name as your Internet service provider. In the menu, select Properties. The Properties dialog box will appear, as shown in Figure 10.7.

2. In the Properties dialog box (again, see Figure 10.7), click on the Server Type button. The Server Types dialog box will appear (see Figure 10.8).

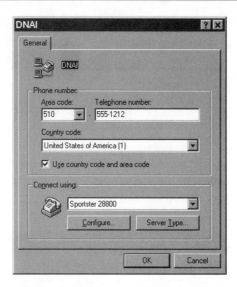

Figure 10.7: Here is the Properties dialog box. The name of your Internet service provider will appear in the title bar.

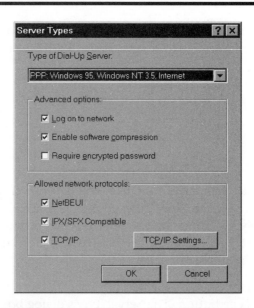

Figure 10.8: In the Server Types dialog box, you'll verify that PPP is selected as the service type.

3. In the Server Types dialog box, you'll specify a number of things about your Internet service provider. In the Type of Dial-Up Server drop-down list, the phrase *PPP: Windows 95, Windows NT 3.5, Internet* should appear. If you don't see this phrase, pull down the Type of Dial-Up Server list and select the entry *PPP: Windows 95, Windows NT 3.5, Internet.*

 You can also use Dial-Up Networking to make a SLIP connection, though we're just describing the more common PPP connection here. To use SLIP to connect to the Internet, you need to install the SLIP driver that comes only on the Windows 95 CD-ROM (not on the diskettes). Refer to the Windows 95 Resource Kit, also on the Windows 95 CD-ROM, for details.

4. Now, in the Server Types dialog box, click on the TCP/IP Settings button, and the TCP/IP Settings dialog box will appear (see Figure 10.9).

5. In the TCP/IP Settings dialog box's Specify an IP Address text box, enter the IP address assigned to you by your Internet service provider. If your provider uses dynamic IP—in other words, if it gives you a new IP address each time you connect—simply select the Server Assigned IP Address button.

6. In the Primary DNS (Domain Name Server) box, enter the IP address of your Internet service provider's Primary Domain Name Server. Again, if your Internet Service Provider assigns you a DNS server every time you connect, select the Server Assigned Name Server Addresses button.

7. If your Internet service provider gave you the IP address of a Secondary Domain Name Server, enter its address in the Secondary DNS text box. A Secondary Domain Name Server is not required, however; so if you don't happen to know it, leave this field blank.

8. You're finished with this bit; so click on the OK button. The Server Types dialog box will reappear.

9. In the Server Types dialog box, click on the OK button, and the Properties dialog box will reappear.

10. Finally, in the Properties dialog box, click on the OK button to save the information you just entered. The Dial-Up Networking window will appear on the Desktop again.

Click here if a new IP address is assigned
each time you call.

Enter your IP address here.

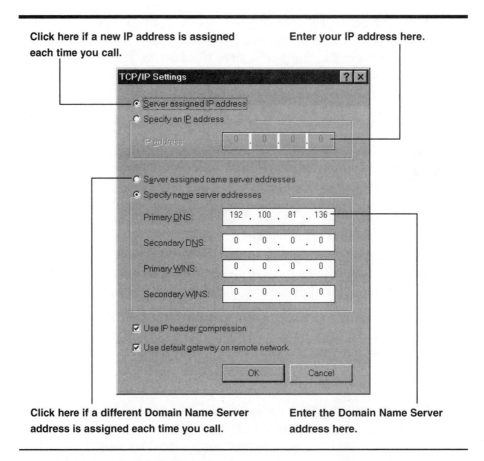

Click here if a different Domain Name Server
address is assigned each time you call.

Enter the Domain Name Server
address here.

Figure 10.9: In the TCP/IP Settings dialog box, you'll enter all that pertinent information you got from your Internet service provider.

You have entered all the information necessary to access the Internet via your Internet service provider and Dial-Up Networking. You are now ready to connect to the Internet.

Actually Connecting!

Now that you've created and configured your connection you are ready to actually connect to the Internet. Remember, you must start up the connection before you use Netscape. This connection is what allows

Netscape or any other Internet application on your computer to talk to the world. To connect, follow these steps:

1. The Dial-Up Networking window should still be displayed on your screen. In the Dial-Up Networking window, double-click on the icon for the connection you created. The Connect To dialog box will appear.

2. In the Connect To dialog box, click on the Connect button. Windows dials the phone number you specified and then waits for your Internet service provider to answer. Leave the User Name and Password fields blank—they are used only when connecting to other types of networks, not when connecting via Dial-Up Networking.

3. You'll hear your modem dialing your Internet service provider. When you're actually connected, a dialog box will appear to let you log in to your account. What this dialog box looks like depends on your Internet service provider's preferred look and feel; Figure 10.10 shows one that is more or less typical.

Figure 10.10: A dialog box that looks something like this one will let you log in to your account.

4. Log in to your account according to the instructions your provider has given you—the actual procedure varies from one provider to another.

5. Once you are logged in, click on the Continue button. A small dialog box will appear showing how long you've been connected.

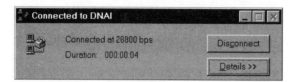

This dialog box remains in view until you disconnect from the Internet. You can minimize this dialog box by clicking on its Minimize button in the upper-right corner of your screen. That will get it out of your way.

Now—once you get Netscape—you can start it up. Netscape will use Dial-Up Networking as its go-between to make the vital connection to your Internet service provider.

Getting Netscape from the Internet via Dial-Up Networking

Now we can go on to our bigger purpose—getting a copy of Netscape so that we can install and use it. As we mentioned earlier, you can get Netscape from the Internet itself or, more specifically, from the FTP site of Netscape's manufacturer. An FTP site is basically a public archive of files accessible to anyone on the Internet who has an FTP program (like you, now that you've got Dial-Up Networking all set up).

 The FTP program that comes with Windows 95 is character-based, meaning that it does not appear in the nifty way that Windows programs do; you'll have to type text-based commands to get it to work.

Here's what you do to get Netscape:

1. If you are not still connected to the Internet, connect now, using the instructions in the preceding section.

2. From the Start menu, select Run. The Run dialog box will appear.

3. In the Run dialog box, type **ftp ftp.netscape.com** in the Open text box and press the ↵ key. An FTP window will appear.

> Only so many people can use Netscape's FTP server at once. You may have to try several times or at odd hours (like at 2 AM) before you can connect successfully. The absolute worst time to do this, in fact, is noon. It seems like every soul on the face of the earth is on the Net at lunchtime; so it's better not to do your FTPing over a ham sandwich.

4. Near the top of the FTP window, you should see a line that says User, followed by the name of a computer on the Internet. Netscape has things set up so that when you access `ftp.netscape.com`, you are actually accessing any of a number of identical FTP servers. Don't worry—each server contains the same set of files. The Netscape folks do it this way so that the thousands of simultaneous FTP connections they get when they release a new version of Netscape won't bring the house down. We are using anonymous FTP to get Netscape; so at the User prompt mentioned earlier in this step, type **anonymous** and press ↵. A request for a password will appear.

5. It is customary to enter your e-mail address as a password when using anonymous FTP. This gives the people who run the FTP site some information about who is using their site. Go ahead and type your e-mail address and press the ↵ key. A welcome message will appear.

> Steps 4 and 5 describe the standard conventions for using anonymous FTP.

6. Netscape is in the directory /NETSCAPE/WINDOWS on Netscape's FTP server. Type **cd/pub/navigator/3.0/windows/standard** and press ↵ to change to the directory that holds Netscape for Windows. (Note that those are forward slashes instead of the familiar backslashes used by DOS.) A message describing Netscape and its licensing terms will appear.

7. Now type **bin** and press the ↵ key. The **bin** command tells FTP that you are transferring binary files instead of ASCII text files.

8. You must now specify where on your local computer the file you transfer should be stored. Type **lcd c:** and press the ↵ key. This tells FTP to store files that you transfer in the root directory of your C: drive.

9. Now type **ls** and press the ↵ key. You will see a list of files like those shown in Figure 10.11. In the list of files, you'll see one called N3230S.EXE. This is the one that contains the 32-bit version of Netscape Navigator for Windows 95.

Figure 10.11: In this list of files you'll see one called N3230S.EXE. That's the one you want.

10. We are now ready to copy Netscape from Netscape's FTP server to your machine. Type **get n3230s.exe** and press the ↵ key. This file is more than 6MB in size; it may take 30 minutes or so to arrive. The FTP prompt will return on screen when the transfer is finished.

Make a note of the size of the file before you actually begin downloading, then check that number against the size of the file you finally receive. If your file transfer ends before the complete file arrives (which you'll know has happened when you check the size of the file), you'll have to repeat the process until you successfully receive the whole file.

11. When the transfer is finished and the files are on your machine, type **quit** and press the ⏎ key to quit FTP. The Windows 95 Desktop will appear again.

Now Netscape is on your machine; let's disconnect from the Internet, just for practice. This is something you'll have to do pretty much every time you shut down Netscape; it's the technique for closing down your Dial-Up Networking Internet connection.

12. Earlier, you minimized the Connected To dialog box to get it out of your way. Now you need to see it again. Click on the Connect To button on the task bar, and the dialog box will reappear.

13. In the Connected To dialog box, click on the Disconnect button. The Connected To dialog box will close, and your connection to the Internet will be snapped.

You made it! You've got a copy of Netscape, just waiting to be installed and configured on your machine. So, when you're ready, turn to Chapter 11 and let's install it already.

◆ Getting Connected via Netcom's Netcomplete

Netcomplete is a popular all-in-one Internet access package from Netcom that provides not only Internet access, but a really nifty point-and-click interface. That's great for beginners and powerful enough to grow into once you've got some experience under your belt. Netcomplete is like Netcom's former service, NetCruiser, except that it's updated and includes some content, too. Like a commercial online service such as AOL, Netcomplete software works only with Netcom's Internet service, not with other Internet service providers. Netcomplete includes access to all the popular features of the Internet—including the World Wide Web—but its Web browser is notoriously weak, lacking many of the more advanced features found in Netscape and loved by millions. Because of this combination of factors, many people enjoy running Netscape on top of Netcomplete, which is in many ways the best of both worlds.

Netcom's new Netcomplete package is very similar to their old NetCruiser access software. You can follow all the directions we give here for getting going with Netcomplete and Netscape even if you are using NetCruiser. The one exception is that you should download and install the 16-bit version of Netscape Navigator to use with NetCruiser instead of the 32-bit version. (You can and should use the 32-bit version with Netcomplete.) See *A Tale of Two Versions* in Chapter 11 for more on the two versions of Netscape.

What's Out There

You can find out more about Netcom and Netcomplete from Netcom's home page at `http://www.netcom.com`.

What You Need

To run Netcomplete, you need a Windows 95 PC with 8MB of memory and about 8MB of free disk space. A 9600 bps modem is the bare minimum; a 14,400 or preferably even 28,800 bps is better. You also need Netcomplete itself. You can often pick up the disk for free at trade shows or computer stores, but it will come without documentation. Perhaps the best way to get Netcomplete is along with a terrific book, *Access the Internet!*, written by David Peal and Jennifer Kirby, and published by Sybex, that will tell you all about using Netcomplete.

Netcomplete and NetCruiser are included among the connectivity options on the CD that comes with this book.

Installing Netcomplete is an incredibly simple matter that is described in a phrase on the disk and in detail in the book. Here, we're going to focus on getting Netscape by using Netcomplete, and then on making a Netscape connection via your Netcomplete account.

Getting Ready to Run Netscape with Netcomplete

You don't really have to do anything to get ready to run Netscape along with your Netcomplete software. Netcomplete is ready to run Netscape—as well as any other Internet application you wish to run—without any fussing.

Getting Netscape from the Internet via Netcomplete

Although you have Netcomplete and it is ready to run Netscape, you're still missing one crucial piece of stuff: Netscape. In this section you'll learn to download Netscape to your computer using Netcomplete. In the next chapter you will learn how to install Netscape. To get Netscape, follow these steps:

1. Start up Netcomplete and get connected as you usually do.

2. From the Netcomplete menu bar, select Internet ➤ FTP Download. The FTP To: dialog box will appear, as shown in Figure 10.12.

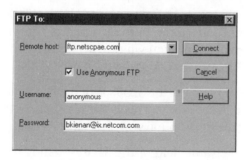

Figure 10.12: The FTP To: dialog box after we entered the address of Netscape's FTP server

3. In the Remote host text box, type **ftp.netscape.com**. Then, select the Use Anonymous FTP checkbox.

4. Now click on the Connect button to accept the default entries. You should now see a window titled ftp.netscape.com:/, as shown in Figure 10.13.

5. The ftp.netscape.com window is split into two sections—the left part of the window contains directory names, and the right part of the window contains filenames. Scroll the list until you see the PUB directory, and then double-click on it. The contents of the right part of the window will change to show the directories in the PUB directory.

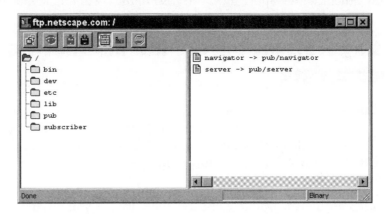

Figure 10.13: You'll use the ftp.netscape.com window to transfer Netscape from Netscape's FTP server to your computer using Netcomplete.

6. Now double-click, in order, on the NAVIGATOR, 3.0, WINDOWS, and STANDARD directories in the left part of the window. The right part of the ftp.netscape.com window will change to list the files located in the /PUB/NAVIGATOR/3.0/WINDOWS/STANDARD directory.

7. Locate the file named N3230S.EXE in the lower part of the window, and double-click on it. This is the file that contains the 32-bit version of Netscape for Windows 95. The Save As dialog box will appear.

8. In the File Name field of the Save As dialog box, type **c:\n3230s.exe** and press ↵. Netscape will transfer the file you need to your local computer. You can see the progress of the file transfer in the status bar along the bottom of the FTP To: dialog box.

9. When the transfer is finished, close the ftp.netscape.com window by clicking on its close box in the upper-right corner.

You now have a copy of Netscape Navigator on your computer, and you are totally ready to install it. Chapter 11 covers installing Netscape on your computer.

◆ Getting Connected via America Online

AOL is at the moment America's most popular commercial online service; its Web browser, however, is very disappointing compared to Netscape. So— what's a Net surfer to do? Happily, you can now use Netscape with AOL.

Getting and installing the America Online software is plenty easy, because the America Online software is often bundled with magazines and new modems, as well as sent in the mail, and the installation process is simple as pie.

What You Need

To get and use Netscape with America Online, you'll need version 2.5 or newer of the America Online software for Windows, along with a 14,400 bps or preferably 28,800 bps modem. In addition to the America Online software, you'll also need a special program called WINSOCK.DLL, which, luckily, you can download from America Online.

With AOL 3.0 you do not need to do anything special to run the 16-bit version of Netscape. If you are using AOL 3.0, skip directly to *Getting Netscape from the Internet via America Online.*

Getting Ready to Run Netscape with America Online

Before you can run Netscape with the America Online software, you'll have to replace the file WINSOCK.DLL in your C:\Windows directory with a version downloaded from America Online's Internet Connection section. To download this file:

1. Start up your America Online software and connect to America Online.

2. From the America Online menu bar, select Go To ➤ Keyword. The Keyword dialog box will appear.

3. In the dialog box's Enter Word text box, type **winsock** and press the ↵ key. The Winsock Central window will appear.

4. In the Winsock Central window, click on the Click Here to Download Winsock label as shown in Figure 10.14. The Winsock for America Online 2.5 window will appear.

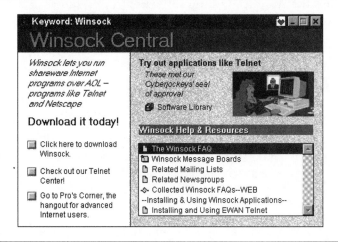

Figure 10.14: From the AOL's Winsock Central window you can download the software you need to run Netscape with AOL 2.5.

5. Read the important information in the window and then click on the Download Now button to continue. The Download Manager dialog box will appear.

6. The Download Manager dialog box is a standard Windows Save As dialog box. Select the C:\WINDOWS directory as the one you want to save the file you are downloading (WINSOCK.DLL) into, and click on the OK button to continue. A dialog box will appear showing the progress of the download.

7. Once downloading is completed, a dialog box will appear saying that the file has been downloaded. Click on the OK button to continue and you'll be returned to the America Online window.

That's all there is to making your copy of America Online Netscape-savvy. You're all set to move along to downloading and installing Netscape.

 You must exit AOL and restart Windows before the new WINSOCK.DLL file will work.

Getting Netscape from the Internet via America Online

You have two options for getting Netscape via America Online. You can use America Online's FTP tool to download it straight from Netscape's site, or you can download it from America Online's own area. We're going to show you how to download it straight from the Netscape site, because the Netscape site always has the most up-to-date version of Netscape available. (And you wouldn't want to be using an old version of Netscape, would you?)

1. From AOL's menu bar, select Go To ➤ Internet Connection to go to the Internet Connection section.

2. In the Internet Connection window, click on the FTP icon. The File Transfer Protocol window will appear, as shown in Figure 10.15.

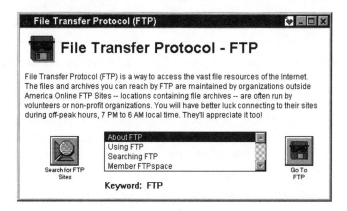

Figure 10.15: The File Transfer Protocol window is your doorway into FTP sites on the Internet.

3. In the File Transfer Protocol window, click on the Go to FTP button. The Anonymous FTP window will appear.

4. In the Anonymous FTP window, click on the Other Site button. The Other Site dialog box will appear.

5. In the Other Site dialog box's Site Address text box, type **ftp.netscape.com** and click on the Connect button. The Connected dialog box will appear.

6. The Connected dialog box contains some information about the Netscape FTP server. It's not a bad idea to read this stuff. Click on the OK button to continue. The ftp.netscape.com:/ dialog box will appear, as shown in Figure 10.16.

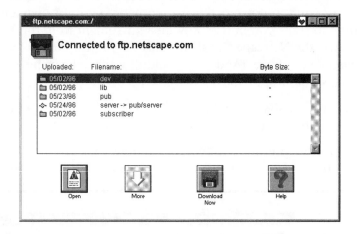

Figure 10.16: You can use America Online's ftp.netscape.com dialog box to download software from Netscape's FTP server.

7. Now we need to go to the directory on Netscape's server that holds Netscape. In turn, double-click on the following: pub, navigator, 3.0, windows, and standard. The dialog box should now show a list of files that includes the file N1630s.EXE, the 16-bit version of Netscape.

8. Double-click on N1630S.EXE. The ftp.netscape.com dialog box shown in Figure 10.17 will appear.

9. In the dialog box, click on the Download Now button to start downloading Netscape. The Download Manager dialog box will appear.

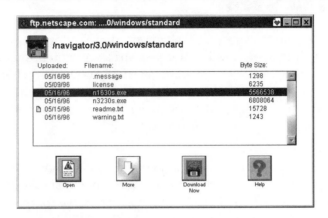

Figure 10.17: In this ftp.netscape.com dialog box, you see information about the file you are about to download.

10. The Download Manager dialog box is actually a standard Windows Save As dialog box. Select the C:\ directory as the one you want to save the file you are downloading into and click on the OK button. The Download Manager dialog box will close and a dialog box showing the status of your download will appear.

11. Once downloading is completed, a dialog box will appear saying that the file has been downloaded. Click on the OK button to continue.

When the download is done, you'll have Netscape on your computer and be ready to start installing it. Turn to the next chapter for the full scoop on installing Netscape.

◆ Getting Connected via CompuServe's WinCIM

CompuServe's services have grown in the recent past to include quite credible Internet access right from within WinCIM version 2.0 or later. WinCIM comes with a Web browser, but many people enjoy running Netscape instead because of Netscape's many state-of-the-art features and popularity.

What You Need

To run CompuServe's WinCIM you need a Windows PC with 8MB of memory and about 8MB of free disk space. A 9600 bps modem is the bare minimum; a 14,400 or preferably even 28,800 bps is better. You also need a CompuServe account. Disks that will get you going are frequently bundled with magazines and modems for free and are also often available at trade shows or in computer stores.

 WinCIM is included among the connectivity options on the CD that comes with this book. You can also always download the latest version of WinCIM from CompuServe (once you have a CompuServe account)—just GO WINCIM.

Installing WinCIM and setting up a CompuServe account is very easy; you'll be walked through that process on screen when you pop the disk into your machine. For a good, detailed description in print, refer to the book *Your First Modem*, written by Sharon Crawford and published by Sybex. Here, we'll focus on getting Netscape by using CompuServe's WinCIM.

What's Out There

You can get information about CompuServe from its home page at `http://www.compuserve.com`.

Getting Ready to Run Netscape with WinCIM

WinCIM 2 comes all ready to run Internet applications like Netscape. All you need to do is start up WinCIM and connect to CompuServe as you usually do. Once you are connected, just minimize the WinCIM window and start up the Internet application, like Netscape, you want to run.

Getting Netscape via WinCIM

You're all set to download Netscape to your computer using your CompuServe connection to the Internet. CompuServe Mosaic will still be running; you'll use it to download Netscape.

To download Netscape, follow these steps:

1. From the CompuServe Mosaic menu bar, select File ➤ Open. The Open Web Page dialog box will appear.

2. In the text box of the Open Web Page dialog box, type **ftp://ftp.netscape.com/pub/navigator/3.0/windows/ standard** and press ↵. The contents of the directory on Netscape's FTP server will appear in the CompuServe Mosaic window as shown in Figure 10.18.

/pub/navigator/3.0/windows/standard

<u>Up to Parent Directory</u>

- .
- ..
- <u>.message (1298 bytes)</u>
- <u>license (6235 bytes)</u>
- <u>n1630s.exe (5566538 bytes)</u>
- <u>n3230s.exe (6808064 bytes)</u>
- <u>readme.txt (15728 bytes)</u>
- <u>warning.txt (1243 bytes)</u>

Figure 10.18: The contents of Netscape's FTP server as displayed by CompuServe Mosaic.

Netscape's FTP servers are so popular that they're often over-worked, and sometimes they just plain don't respond to anonymous FTP requests. The worst time to do something like this is lunchtime, when everybody seems to be on the Net and many procedures slow to a crawl—and it gets *really* bad the week after Netscape announces the availability of new software. You may have to try several times or at odd hours (like at 2 AM) before you can connect successfully.

3. You'll have to indicate which of the listed files you want to download; click on the link <u>n1630s.exe</u>. That's the one for the 16-bit, Windows 3.1 version of Netscape. A dialog box will appear asking if you want to save the file to disk. Click on the Yes button.

4. The Save As dialog box will now appear. In the Save As dialog box, type **c:\n1630s.exe** in the File Name text box and press ↵. The Save As dialog box will close as the file transfer begins.

5. As the file is transferred from Netscape's FTP server to your computer, the status bar along the bottom of the CompuServe Mosaic window will show the procedure's progress. When the status bar has moved all the way to the right side, the file transfer is complete.

It's time now to install Netscape. Turn to Chapter 11 for detailed directions.

◆ Getting Connected via the Microsoft Network

The Microsoft Network is Microsoft's very own online service, designed to work in tandem with Windows 95. Starting with version 1.05 of the Microsoft Network software, you have full access to the Internet from your computer—you won't even need Windows 95 Dial-Up Networking. If you have an earlier version of Microsoft Network, however, (which you very well may, because early copies of Windows 95, of course, included earlier versions of Microsoft Network), you'll have to download an update from the Microsoft Network's Internet Center. (You'll also find directions and support for doing this at the Internet Center.)

What You Need

You can run Microsoft Network on any computer that runs Windows 95 and is equipped with a modem. For best performance, you should have at least 8MB of RAM. The Microsoft Network software takes up an additional 10MB of disk space. You also need a 9600 bps or faster modem—14,400 or even 28,800 bps is much better.

Getting Ready to Run Netscape with Microsoft Network

There isn't much to this; the Windows 95 installation process installs the Microsoft Network. If you have Windows 95 installed on your machine,

you're set. So why doesn't everyone go this route? Well, it's easy—
Microsoft made it no trouble at all—but it's certainly not as fast as it
could be. Nonetheless, it's the most no-brain method of getting connected. So let's move along to the part where you *do* something....

Getting Netscape from the Internet via Microsoft Network

Microsoft Network comes with the Microsoft Internet Explorer—yet
another Web browser similar to Netscape but lacking its popularity. We're
going to use the Internet Explorer to download Netscape Navigator to
your computer. To download Netscape using Microsoft Network's Internet
Explorer, follow these steps:

1. In the Windows 95 Desktop, double-click on The Internet icon.

The Internet

The Microsoft Internet Explorer will start.

2. From the Microsoft Internet Explorer menu bar, select File ➤ Open.
The Open Internet Address dialog box will appear.

3. In the Open Internet Address dialog box's Address text box, type
**ftp://ftp.netscape.com/pub/navigator/3.0/windows/
standard**. Press ↵. In a few seconds, the contents of Netscape's
FTP server will appear, as shown in Figure 10.19.

4. Click on the link n3230s.exe. This is the 32-bit version of Netscape
for Windows 95. The Confirm File Open dialog box will appear, as
shown here.

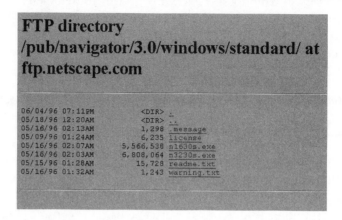

FTP directory /pub/navigator/3.0/windows/standard/ at ftp.netscape.com

```
06/04/96 07:11PM      <DIR> .
05/18/96 12:20AM      <DIR> ..
05/16/96 02:13AM      1,298 .message
05/09/96 01:24AM      6,235 license
05/16/96 02:07AM  5,566,538 n1630s.exe
05/16/96 02:03AM  6,808,064 n3230s.exe
05/15/96 01:28AM     15,728 readme.txt
05/16/96 01:32AM      1,243 warning.txt
```

Figure 10.19: The Netscape FTP server as seen from the Microsoft Internet Explorer.

5. In the dialog box, click on the Save As button. The Save As dialog box will appear.

6. In the Save As dialog box's File Name text box, type **c:\n3230s.exe**. Press ↵. The file will transfer from Netscape's FTP server to your machine. You can monitor the transfer progress by looking at the bar that appears along the right side of the status bar at the bottom of the Internet Explorer window.

When the transfer is done, quit the Internet Explorer by selecting File ≻ Exit. The now familiar Windows 95 Desktop will reappear. You'll have a copy of Netscape on your machine, and you're ready to start installing it. Turn to the next chapter for the scoop on installing Netscape.

Forging Ahead

Whether your preferred connectivity option is Windows 95 Dial-Up Networking, Netcom's Netcomplete or NetCruiser, America Online, CompuServe, or the Microsoft Network, you now have a connection to the Internet going and a copy of Netscape sitting on your hard drive. In the next chapter you'll actually install Netscape, which is a simple enough process. Then, with Netscape installed, you'll be fully equipped to start cruising and using the very wonderful World Wide Web.

Getting Netscape Navigator Going

In Chapter 10 we walked you through actually getting Netscape by downloading the appropriate version from the Internet. In this chapter, we're going to make the software work. First, we'll install it (a simple, largely automatic process), then we'll make it run, and finally we'll show you how to make some minor changes to enhance operations.

◆ Installing Netscape Navigator

Installation varies slightly between the 32- and 16-bit versions of the program. If you are using Windows 95 Dial-Up Networking, Netcomplete, or the Microsoft Network to connect to the Internet, you downloaded the 32-bit version of Netscape and should follow the directions in the *Installing the 32-Bit Version* section. If you are using NetCruiser, America Online, or CompuServe WinCIM, follow the directions in the *Installing the 16-Bit Version* section.

A Tale of Two Versions

There are two versions of Netscape Navigator 3. One, the 32-bit version, works with Windows 95 Dial-Up Networking, the Microsoft Network, and Netcomplete. It offers full Java capability and faster, more reliable response than the 16-bit version. The 16-bit version works with CompuServe WinCIM, America Online, and with many other types of Internet access software. The real difference between these versions is that the 32-bit version only works with 32-bit operating systems—Windows 95, in other words. If you're still using Windows 3.1 or Internet access software that's based on Windows 3.1, you need the 16-bit version of Netscape Navigator 3.

Thus, the file you downloaded in Chapter 10 would have been one of two versions, depending on whether you needed the 32-bit version or the 16-bit version. If you are using Windows 95 Dial-Up Networking, Microsoft Network, or Netcomplete to connect to the Internet, you downloaded N3230S.EXE—the 32-bit version. If you are connecting with CompuServe WinCIM or America Online, you downloaded N1630S.EXE—the 16-bit version.

Installing the 32-Bit Version

The 32-bit version of Netscape Navigator works with 32-bit Internet connection software, such as Windows 95 Dial-Up Networking or the Microsoft Network.

Here's how to install it:

1. Click on the Windows 95 Start button to display the Start menu, and select Run. The Run dialog box will appear.

2. In the Open field of the Run dialog box, type **c:\n3230s** and press ↵. A dialog box will appear with a message confirming that you are about to install Netscape Navigator.

3. Click on the Yes button. A dialog box titled Extracting will appear, followed by another welcoming you to Netscape's own Setup program.

4. Click on the Next button to proceed. The Choose Destination Location dialog box will appear, as shown in Figure 11.1. Netscape's Setup program will put Netscape in a folder called C:\Program Files\Netscape\Navigator unless you tell it to do otherwise.

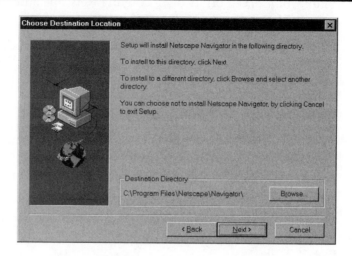

Figure 11.1: In the Choose Destination Location dialog box, choose the folder in which you want to store the Netscape files.

It's best to let this happen, but if you really, really want to, you can specify another folder by clicking on the Browse button to display the Choose Directory dialog box. In the Path field of the Choose Directory dialog box, enter the name of the folder in which you want to install Netscape and click on the OK button.

 Perhaps you've noticed a slight switch in terminology here—suddenly in the middle of talking about Windows 95 *folders*, we're using a dialog box called Choose *Directory*....This is just a holdover from the past. Nothing to worry about.

Back to business...

5. Click on the Choose Destination Location dialog box's Next button to proceed. A dialog box will appear asking if you want to install CoolTalk.

6. In the dialog box, click on the Yes button to install CoolTalk (you can find out more about CoolTalk in Chapter 6). Or you can click on the No button if you do not want to install CoolTalk.

Now Setup will proceed on its own, copying Netscape and all its affiliated files to the folder you chose in step 3.

7. After all of the copying is done, a dialog box will appear asking if you want to install the CoolTalk Watchdog program. This program is useful only if you have a dedicated connection to the Internet, so if you are using a dial-up connection (through an Internet service provider), you should select No.

8. Now that all of the Netscape components are installed, a dialog box will appear asking if you want to connect Netscape's Setup site. There's no need to do so—click on the No button. Another dialog box will appear, this time saying that installation is complete.

9. Click on the dialog box's OK button to continue. A second dialog box will now appear, giving you the option of reading Netscape's README file.

10. Click on the dialog box's Yes button to read the file in Windows Notepad. You can then exit Notepad by selecting File ➤ Exit from the menu bar. (If you prefer not to read the file, you can click on the No button instead of Yes; this will end the installation program.) The ol' familiar Windows Desktop will appear.

The Netscape program archive N3230S.EXE is still in your Temp folder (or wherever you put it). It's always a good idea to have backups in case something unfortunate happens; so move N3230S.EXE to another folder on your hard disk, just in case.

You've got Netscape installed on your machine now, but you still have to do a thing or two (or three or four) to set everything up to work properly. Skip to the section titled *Making a Netscape Navigator Connection* to find out about configuring Netscape to work on your machine.

Installing the 16-Bit Version

Until such time as CompuServe and America Online create 32-bit versions of their Internet connection software, you'll need the 16-bit version of Netscape Navigator to work with CompuServe WinCIM and America Online.

The art in this book shows the 32-bit version of Netscape, which was designed for use with Windows 95, but the 16-bit version behaves pretty much identically. You can use this book as a guide to either version.

The installation procedure for the 16-bit Netscape occurs in two parts, neither of which is very complicated. In the first part, you'll "unpack" and move the file you downloaded in Chapter 10 (N1630S.EXE) to a temporary folder in preparation for installation. In the second part, you'll actually install the software.

Unpacking the Files

The file you downloaded in the last chapter, N1630S.EXE, is what is known as a *self-extracting archive* file. An archive file is one that contains one or more (often *many* more) files that are shrunk to some fraction of their original size. This is much like the *zipping* of files we talked about when we described zipped files and compression technology in Chapter 8. We'll talk more about it in Chapter 12. Archive files and zipped files are a great convenience on the Internet; instead of downloading many large files, you can download one smaller one, which will save you scads of connect time and, therefore, money.

The compressed file that contains Netscape, N1630S.EXE, contains several files, including:

◆ The Netscape program itself

◆ Associated files that are necessary to make it run

◆ Files that contain information about the license you need to use the program

The big difference between this file and the zipped files we've already discussed is that this one is *self-extracting*, which simply means that you don't need any particular unzipping software to restore the file to its original, unpacked state; the file does everything for you.

When you downloaded N1630S.EXE following the earlier steps, it wound up in your C:\ folder. It's a good idea when you unpack any file, however, to do so in a "temporary" folder; this will provide you with an extra measure of insurance against mixing up the new files with files from another program or with any data you may have lying around. This is a pretty basic procedure—if you have some proficiency in Windows, you'll already know how to do most of this.

Here's how to create a folder called Temp and move the Netscape archive file there:

1. On the Windows Desktop, double-click on the My Computer icon to display the My Computer window.

2. Locate the icon for drive C in the My Computer window, and double-click on it. A window will display the contents of your drive C.

3. From the menu bar in the C:\ window, select File ➢ New ➢ Folder. The New Folder folder will appear in the window.

4. Now type **temp** and press ↵. The name of the new folder will change to what you just typed.

5. We are now ready to move the self-extracting archive file into the folder we just created. Locate N1630S.EXE and click on it to highlight it. It should appear in reverse video.

6. From the menu bar, select Edit ➢ Cut. The name of the self-extracting archive file will become grayed out.

7. Now double-click on the Temp folder. A new empty window will appear showing the contents of the folder you've created.

8. Select Edit ➢ Paste from the menu bar to paste the Netscape archive from the Clipboard into the folder you created.

   Okay, you've got N1630S.EXE in a folder called Temp. Let's unpack this baby.

9. To unpack the self-extracting archive, double-click on N1630S.EXE.

A DOS window will appear. Because the self-extracting archive is, strictly speaking, a DOS program and not a Windows program, it must unpack itself in a DOS window. Once it is finished unpacking, the title in the title bar of the DOS window will change to Finished. Now, to close the window, click on the close box in the upper-right corner of the DOS window.

When the archive has finished unpacking itself (this should take only a few seconds), all the files that were in the archive will be in your Temp folder.

 If an error message pops up when you're unpacking files you've downloaded, it's probably because something went wrong in the downloading process. No big deal. Simply download the file again, and when you unpack it this time, everything will probably turn out just fine.

Now, with all those files on your machine and unpacked, you're ready to install Netscape.

Installing the Program

Here's what you do to install that neatly extracted Netscape program:

1. Click on the Windows 95 Start button to display the Start menu. From the menu, select Run. The Run dialog box will appear.

2. In the Open field of the Run dialog box, type **c:\temp\setup** and press ↵. After a brief *Please Wait* message, you'll see the blue background common to all Windows setup programs; then a dialog box will welcome you to Netscape's own Setup program.

3. Click on the Next button to proceed. The Netscape Navigator Destination Path dialog box will appear, as shown in Figure 11.2. Netscape's Setup program will put Netscape in a folder called C:\Netscape unless you tell it to do otherwise. It's best to let this happen, but if you really, really want to, you can type another folder name in the Location text box, and Netscape will wind up there.

4. Click on the Next button to proceed. A dialog box will appear asking if you wish to install CoolTalk.

5. Click on Yes to install CoolTalk (you can find out more about CoolTalk in Chapter 6).

Setup will now proceed on its own, copying Netscape and all its affiliated files to the folder you chose in step 3.

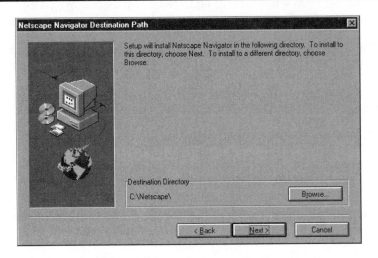

Figure 11.2: In the Netscape Navigator Destination Path dialog box, you should accept the default location for the Netscape files unless you have good reason to do otherwise.

6. When all this copying business is over, a dialog box will appear asking if you want to install the CoolTalk Watchdog program. The CoolTalk Watchdog program is useful only if you have a dedicated connection to the Internet, so if you are using a dial-up connection (as you do with an Internet service provider), select No.

7. A final dialog box will appear, confirming that Netscape was installed correctly and giving you the option of reading Netscape's README.TXT file. Select the dialog box's Yes checkbox and click on the Finish button to read the file. The README.TXT file contains important information about using Netscape; so we recommend that you read it. The file will open in the Windows Notepad. When you're done reading it, select File ➤ Exit from Notepad's menu bar to close Notepad.

If you don't want to read the file, remove any mark from the Yes checkbox by clicking on it, and then click on the Finish button to end the installation program.

The Windows Desktop will reappear.

Netscape is installed on your machine, just as we promised, but you still have to set up everything to work together properly. The next section, titled *Making a Netscape Navigator Connection*, shows you how to configure Netscape to work on your machine.

The Netscape program archive N1630S.EXE and all its component files are still in your Temp folder (or wherever you put them). It's always a good idea to have backups—copy N1630S.EXE to a different directory on your hard disk, just in case. Having done this, you can delete all the files in Temp and the folder itself.

◆ Making a Netscape Navigator Connection

Because Netscape Navigator is an Internet program, you need to start up your Internet connection before you can actually run Netscape. But most of what we're going to do now doesn't require you to be connected to the Internet. These sections are about *creating* the connection, not *using* the connection. First, we're going to start Netscape.

When you use Netscape to access the Internet, you have to engage in a two-step process that involves first starting up your Internet connection and *then* starting Netscape. In the procedure that follows, we're starting Netscape without first getting connected.

Starting Netscape Navigator

You can start Netscape Navigator in any of several ways:

- ◆ Double-click on the Netscape Navigator icon on your Desktop.

- ◆ From the Windows 95 Start menu, select Programs ➤ Netscape ➤ Netscape.

- ◆ Double-click on any Internet shortcut. Once Netscape is installed on your computer, Internet shortcuts may appear as Navigator icons on the Desktop, in other folders, in e-mail messages, or even in other applications' files. You can find out more about Internet shortcuts in Chapter 3.

Remember—to get connected and use Netscape to surf the Net, you have to start your Internet connection software and *then* start Netscape. But getting connected is not necessary in order to configure the software, as we're about to do....

Enhancing the Program's Look and Performance

Okay, we told you in the preceding sections that all you had to do was unpack the files and start up Netscape, and that's true. This is not to say you can't or don't have to configure Netscape; it's just that Netscape can start up and do some useful things before it is configured. You can configure Netscape (if you like) to make it work the way you want it to work.

Configuring Netscape is quick and easy. We've already done a little configuring earlier in the book, but we didn't make a big deal of it. In Chapter 3, we told you how to change the base font to make Netscape display text in a size and color that you like, and then we told you how to get Netscape to load inline images only on demand, speeding up Netscape's performance noticeably. In Chapter 12, we'll tell you how to configure Netscape to use external viewers and players for viewing video and playing sound. Here we're going to make some changes to enhance the cosmetics and performance of the program.

Making the Viewing Area Bigger

Controlling the look of the program is not just a matter of cosmetics; it can be a matter of making the viewing area larger and easier to work with. Above the document-viewing window and below the menu bar, you'll usually see a row of icons representing tools and features, a box showing the URL of the page you are currently viewing, and a row of directory buttons that take you to various Netscape Communications' home pages.

These are handy things to have around. If you want to see the Welcome to Netscape home page, you can simply click on the Home button on the tool box. If you want to view the document you were looking at just a second ago, you can click on the Back button on the tool bar, and so on.

If, however, you'd rather give the Web document you're viewing more room to breathe, you can turn off the tool bar, the Location box, and the directory buttons, in any combination, including all three (see Figure 11.3). Get this: You don't lose anything by turning them off; all their functions are still available on Netscape's menu bar.

Figure 11.3: The Netscape window on the left has the tool bar, the Location box, and directory buttons turned on. The window on the right has all three turned off, making the viewing area a lot bigger.

The tool bar, Location box, and directory buttons are all controlled by a "toggle switch" on Netscape's Options menu. That is, the same option on the menu turns each item both on and off; you can simply select the option once to turn an item off, and then select it again to turn it back on. Fiddle around with these options as you like to see what works for you.

When you've got Netscape's "face" configured to reflect your preferences, you can save your changes by selecting Options ➤ Save Options from Netscape's menu bar. If you don't save your choices, Netscape will go back to its usual configuration (with everything turned on the next time you start the program).

Getting Set Up for Mail and News

Looking past the surface, you might want to tweak a few things in the way Netscape works with mail and news servers. One of the nifty things you can do with Netscape, for example, is to e-mail a page that's caught your eye to a friend or a colleague. To do this, and to read and write articles to Usenet newsgroups, the program has to "know" where to find your Internet service provider's mail and news servers—the computers your provider uses to store and dish up mail and news.

What's Out There

You can learn all the ins and outs of using e-mail from *A Beginner's Guide to Effective E-Mail,* accessible via the URL
`http://www.webfoot.com/advice/email.top.html.`

To find out more about sending a page via e-mail and reading and writing Usenet news, turn to Chapters 2, 3, 4, and 7.

The Mail Server

Specifying the location of your Internet service provider's mail server is an important detail in setting up Netscape, because this is how the program "knows" where to send mail. This is yet another quick and simple Netscape operation. Just follow these steps:

1. From Netscape's menu bar, select Options ➤ Mail and News Preferences. The Mail and News Preferences dialog box will appear.

2. Along the top of the Mail and News Preferences dialog box, select the Servers tab. The contents of the dialog box will change to reflect this choice (see Figure 11.4).

3. In the Outgoing Mail (SMTP) Server text box, the presumed name of your provider's mail server appears as *mail.* (SMTP stands for *Simple Mail Transfer Protocol.*) Choose the appropriate address to enter from Table 11.1.

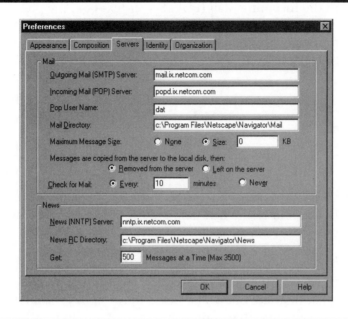

Figure 11.4: The Mail and News dialog box after it's been filled with e-mail information.

Table 11.1: Server Names for the Most Common Kinds of Connections

Connection	Outgoing Mail (SMTP) Server	Incoming Mail (POP) Server	News (NNTP) Server
Microsoft Network	mail.msn.com	mail.msn.com	news.msn.com
CompuServe WinCIM	mail.compuserve.com	mail.compuserve.com	news.compuserve.com
Netcomplete *or* NetCruiser	smtp.ix.netcom.com	popd.ix.netcom.com	nntp.ix.netcom.com

America Online does not support Netscape's E-Mail or News features, at least not yet.

4. In the Incoming Mail (POP) Server text box, the presumed name of your provider's mail POP server appears also as *mail*. (POP stands for *Post Office Protocol*.) Choose the appropriate address to enter from Table 11.1.

If you are accessing the Net via a provider other than those shown in Table 11.1, you'll have to find out the server names your provider uses.

5. Now click on the Identity tab along the top of the Preferences dialog box. The contents of the dialog box change to reflect your action.

6. In the Your Name text box, type your name—not your user name, but your real, true, human name.

7. In the Your E-mail text box, type your complete e-mail address.

8. If you want replies to messages that you send to go to an address other than the one you entered in the Your E-mail field in step 7, you can enter that address in the Reply-to Address field. If you want replies to your e-mail messages to go to your e-mail address, you can leave this field blank.

9. If you like, you can type the name of your organization (your company or school, perhaps) into the Your Organization text box.

10. You can also arrange matters so that the contents of a short file will be appended to every e-mail message you send.

This file is called a *signature* because it appears (like the signature on a letter) at the bottom of every message you send. A signature file can contain your name and e-mail address and maybe a little bit of information about yourself. It is considered very bad form on the Internet to create a signature file more than four lines in length.

To make a "signature" appear at the bottom of your messages, create a file in your word-processing program, save it as a text file with an appropriate filename, and then type that filename along with its path in the Signature File text box.

 The Your Name and Your E-mail text boxes must be filled in for you to be able to use either Netscape Mail or Netscape News, the e-mail and Usenet news features in Netscape. This is because your name and e-mail address will appear in the subject headers of messages you send using Netscape.

Once you've got this mail business set up correctly, you won't have to change it (unless you change Internet service providers). The same is true for news, which we'll cover next. You'll be using the same Mail and News Preferences dialog box that we just used to set up mail when you set up news in the next section; so leave the dialog box open.

The News Server

Usenet news looks like it's fully integrated into the Web when you use Netscape to access it, but it actually gets to your machine in an interesting way. Unlike the rest of the stuff on the Web, which is delivered to your machine from servers all over the world, Usenet comes to you from a news server machine that is maintained by your Internet service provider. On this machine are copies of Usenet news articles, which the service provider stores and forwards to you. Because of this structure, it's necessary to indicate on which machine your service provider is storing the stuff.

Follow these simple steps to tell Netscape which Usenet news server it can access and exactly where to find that server.

1. With the Mail and News Preferences dialog box still open (you were just using it to set up mail, right?), click on the Directories tab along the top. The contents of the dialog box will update to reflect your choice.

2. Now locate the News section at the bottom of the dialog box. In the News section's News (NNTP) Server text box, the presumed news server name appears as *news*. As you did when configuring mail, you should now look up the name of your news server in Table 11.1 and enter the appropriate name.

Just FYI: NNTP stands for Network News Transfer Protocol. This is the protocol for transferring news on the Internet, just as HTTP is the protocol for transferring hypertext documents on the Internet.

3. Click on the OK button, and the Mail and News Preferences dialog box will close. The Netscape window will reappear.

You're all set. You've got Netscape installed and ready to use. For the sake of form, though, let's look briefly at how to quit the program.

◆ Quitting Netscape Navigator

This is a handy piece of information that we don't want to neglect. When you're done with your travels for the day, simply do the following:

1. From Netscape's menu bar, select File ➤ Exit. This will quit Netscape, but if you happen to have your connection going, it will leave you connected to your Internet service provider, so, in that case...

2. Switch to your connection software—Windows 95 Dial-Up Networking or NetLauncher, for example—and disconnect from the Internet. The way you sever your Internet connection depends on the method and software you use to connect.

You'll be disconnected from your Internet service provider and free now to plant hydrangeas, tap dance 'til dawn, or whatever.

You're Set to Go

Bingo. You're all set up. You've installed your Internet connection software and Netscape, you know how to start Netscape and make it look the way you want it to, and you can access mail and news servers. If you like, you can turn to Chapter 1 for useful background information or to Chapter 3 to get started navigating with Netscape.

In the next and final chapter, we'll get Netscape to work with plug-ins and helper applications. These will enhance the interactivity of your Netscape adventure.

Get a Boost with Plug-Ins and Helper Apps

In your Web travels, you may have come across pages enhanced with various sorts of multimedia that Netscape couldn't quite handle on its own. A dialog box might have popped up announcing the need for some plug-in or helper application. If a Web site contains files other than text, HTML, and certain kinds of images, even the mighty Netscape may need a bit of help reading these files and integrating them into your experience of a given Web page. This is no weakness on the part of Netscape. Netscape Navigator's expandability—its capability to allow Web developers to invent and use new types of media and "introduce" them to Netscape via separate programs like these—is one of its great assets. Netscape can tell the difference between different kinds of files within any given Web page, recognize those for which it needs help, automatically launch the extra application needed, and start playing the file without much fanfare. Some helper apps and plug-ins even come pre-installed with Netscape. Others you will have to get and install the first time around, but Netscape will take care of things from there.

◆ What Are Plug-Ins and Helper Apps?

There are two kinds of add-on software you can use to enhance Netscape's ability to view or play different kinds of media files.

Plug-ins are a family of mini-applications built to work exclusively with Netscape—these tools detect a non-HTML component of a Web page like sound, video, and other media, and they combine that stuff with the text of the Web page to make regular old HTML documents much more interactive. Once you install a plug-in, you'll never think about it again, except maybe to say, "Hey, this Shockwave thing is right on." Plug-ins function as if they were a part of Netscape, such that whatever way-cool multimedia toy some crazy Webmaster conceives is displayed right in the Netscape window, without the necessity of any other application launching. If you've read Chapter 7 and started navigating virtual worlds with Live3D, Netscape's VRML viewer, then you've already seen how seamlessly plug-ins add their capabilities right into Netscape.

Helper applications (or helper apps for short) are stand-alone programs that play all kinds of sound and video files, for example. Every time you access a file on the Web—a plain old text file, a Web page, a sound clip, some software you want to install, or a multimedia movie—you're actually *downloading* that file. Netscape usually makes this practically invisible, but some kinds of files, like Adobe Acrobat documents, require Netscape to get help to deal with them. Once you have a helper app installed and you tell Netscape where it is on your hard drive, Netscape will "remember" that you have the helper app and will automatically launch it when it's needed. For example, when you click on a link that leads to a PDF file (an Adobe Acrobat document), Netscape will identify the file as such, download the file, and then launch the Adobe Acrobat player to help out with playing the file.

Dozens of helper apps are available as we write this book, and more than 100 plug-ins are available or in development. We're going to focus on some of the most popular (and most useful) plug-ins and helper apps that will make your Web experience a virtual carnival of sights, sounds, and interactivity.

Sound, video, and animation files can be *huge*, requiring a terribly long time to download (even over a T-1 line) and taking up enormous amounts of drive space when they get there. Conscientious Webmasters post the sizes of downloadable files, but be aware that some choose to disguise them as harmless hyperlinks. While plug-ins diminish these concerns, they don't eliminate them altogether. When you retrieve a file that requires a helper, such as an Adobe Acrobat file, the Saving Location dialog box will appear; you can click on Cancel anytime during the download if it seems to be too much for your system.

What's Out There

You can find a directory of all the plug-ins that work with Netscape by visiting the Netscape Components page at `http://home.netscape.com/comprod/mirror/navcomponents_download.html`. Netscape's guide to helper apps can be found at `http://home.netscape.com/assist/helper_apps/`. And Web user Jerry Baldwin provides a guide to Windows 95 plug-ins at `http://www.syspac.com/~jbaldwin/plugins.html`.

◆ Using the Software That Comes with Netscape

If you've installed the full version of Netscape, you already have several plug-ins and helpers on your hard drive and ready to use. (In the computer biz, you'd say that Netscape *ships with* this extra software.) The plug-ins that come with the full version of Netscape Navigator 3 offer capacity for speech, music, video, VRML, and other kinds of multimedia.

Regardless of what software you have, you need to have a sound card before you can hear anything emanating from your computer. If you don't know whether you have a sound card, contact the person or store who sold you the computer and ask 'em.

What Do You Want to Play Today?

To find out how many of what kind of plug-ins you have installed, from Netscape's menu bar, select Help ➤ About Plug-Ins. A page will appear listing the plug-ins in Netscape's Plug-ins folder. If you scroll through this list, you should find that you have the following plug-ins installed and ready to go:

The Plug-In Called	Recognizes the File Extensions	And Handles
QuickTime	MOV	QuickTime movies
Live3D	WRL	VRML worlds
LiveAudio	AU, AIFF, WAV, MIDI	Sound
LiveVideo	AVI	Microsoft video
Default Plug-In	None	Nothing

That Default Plug-In, the one that does nothing? It's there as a place-holder, with no real function. No one knows if it has any purpose—think of it as being like your appendix, and leave it alone, satisfied with the knowledge that it exists.

You can find out about using Live3D in Chapter 7. Right now we're going to tell you how to enjoy Web pages that talk, sing, and play movies. You don't have to do anything to get these toys, so let's forge into how to use them.

What's Out There

Netscape's Multimedia Showcase is an action-packed page that combines LiveAudio, LiveVideo, and Live3D all on the same page (`http://home.netscape.com/comprod/products/navigator/version_3.0/showcase/index.html`).

Go Multimedia Crazy with QuickTime

QuickTime is a versatile suite of software components that integrates with sound and high-quality video; a 3-D form called QTVR (QuickTime

Virtual Reality) is also available. The QuickTime plug-in comes with Netscape version 3, but there are some drivers that have to be installed for the plug-in to work. Figure 12.1 shows a very cute QuickTime animated worm.

QuickTime plays movie files of the file type MOV. With the Quick-Time plug-in, these files will play right in the Netscape window, but they may take a while to download. Further, the Netscape viewing area may look funny—blank, with a big Q where the movie will play—while the download is occurring. Hang tight; it's okay.

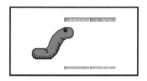  

Figure 12.1: *The Worm* is a tiny little QuickTime movie starring a tiny little worm.

Downloading and Installing the QuickTime Drivers

You can download the QuickTime drivers from Apple's Web site at `http://quicktime.apple.com/sw/sw.html`. Just tune your Web browser there and follow the easy download instructions. Be sure to download the version for Windows and to save it onto your Windows Desktop (that makes it easier to find when you are installing it). When you download QuickTime from Apple's site, you'll get a self-extracting archive file which contains the QuickTime files. It is this file you'll use to install QuickTime.

Installing the QuickTime drivers takes just a few minutes, and when you're done, you'll have all the drivers you need to work with the QuickTime plug-in; in the process, you'll also get the QuickTime Movie Player, the QuickTime Picture Viewer, and even an Uninstall/Reinstall program in case you change your mind once or twice. When you downloaded QuickTime from Apple's Web site, you got the self-extracting executable file QT32.EXE. We'll now use this file to install QuickTime on your computer.

1. You should have the file QT32.EXE on your Desktop (that's the file you downloaded from Apple's Web site). Double-click on its icon; a DOS window will appear and the file will unpack itself. (Because the self-extracting archive is a DOS program and not a Windows program, it must unpack itself in a DOS window.)

2. Once it is finished unpacking, the text in the title bar of the DOS window will change to Finished. Now, to close the window, click on the close box in the upper-right corner of the DOS Window.

3. Now you'll have another file, QT32INST.EXE, on your Desktop. Double-click on this file's icon, and the QuickTime Installer program will start, displaying first the QuickTime title and background, and the Begin Install dialog boxes.

4. The Begin Install dialog box asks you if you want to Install, Exit, or get Help. Click on the Install button to start installing QuickTime. The Check Existing Versions dialog box will appear.

5. In the dialog box, click on the Start button. A status window will appear showing the progress of the check.

6. When the check is finished, the Complete Install dialog box will appear, allowing you to choose Install, Exit, or Help. Click on Install, and a status window will appear again showing the progress of the installation.

7. When the installation is complete, the status window will close automatically, and the Success dialog box will appear, asking if you want to calibrate your QuickTime Movie Player. (Calibrating your player sets the speed and resolution of your Movie Player software.) Click on the Calibrate button to continue. The QuickTime Movie Player will start up, with a QuickTime movie (titled *Sample*) open.

8. Press the space bar to start the calibration process. A short movie will play. When it's finished, close the QuickTime Movie Player window by selecting File ➢ Exit from the menu bar. The window will close, leaving you at the Windows Desktop.

That done, you now have the QuickTime Movie Player and the drivers you need (all installed in C:\WINDOWS), and shortcuts to all the QuickTime applications in your Start Menu, under START\PROGRAMS\ QUICKTIME FOR WINDOWS. You can throw the now useless bits of installer that are still sitting on your Desktop (QT32.EXE and QT32INST.EXE) into the Recycle Bin.

According to Apple and Netscape, QuickTime movies, which are configured to play especially with the plug-in, should begin to play as soon as enough of the movie has been downloaded, rather than waiting for the entire thing to download. Unless you have a very fast connection, you will probably find that you still have quite a wait before the movie begins to play.

With the QuickTime files neatly installed on your computer, Netscape will be able to play QuickTime movies whenever it comes across them. Generally, you'll see QuickTime movies incorporated into Web pages in one of two ways:

◆ You'll see a hyperlink which goes to a QuickTime Movie file (QuickTime Movie files have the extension MOV). Clicking on one of these links will bring you to a new page which has a QuickTime logo in the center. Once the file is ready to be played (either when it has been completely downloaded to your computer or enough of it has been downloaded to allow it to start to play), the logo will be replaced by the first image in the movie.

◆ You'll see movies embedded into Web pages. These appear initially as QuickTime logos on the page until the movie is downloaded to your computer (or enough of the movie is downloaded to begin playing). Once the movie is ready to be played, the QuickTime logo is replaced with the first image from the movie.

Regardless of how the movie appears on screen, to play it, you have options:

◆ Some movies will appear with VCR Controls underneath them (Play, Stop, Fast Forward, and Rewind buttons, just like on a VCR).

◆ You can always right-click on the movie and from the pop-up menu that appears, select Play, Fast Forward, or Rewind to control the play of the movie.

To save a QuickTime movie for later viewing, right-click on the hyperlink to the movie and a menu will appear. From the menu, select Save Link As, and the Save As dialog box will appear. You can now pick a folder to save the movie into and start downloading it.

What's Out There

To find out all about getting QuickTime software, playing with QuickTime video, live events using QuickTime, and much more, visit `http://quicktime.apple.com/`. Samples of QuickTime audio, video, and QTVR can be found at `http://quicktime.apple.com/sam/sam.html`.

We visited the very helpful QuickTime Plug-In How-To Site at `http://www.MediaCity.com/~erweb/`.

VideoLinks is a great archive of QuickTime music videos and clips from popular TV shows and movies. Visit it at `http://members.aol.com/videolinks/`.

VH1's Digital Gallery holds QuickTime movies of many popular performers at `http://www.vh1.com/digigal.html`.

The Web Sings with LiveAudio

The Web is abuzz with sound files, and sound is about the easiest media to play (and the fastest to download). You do have to have a good sound card to get the most out of most sound files, which can include clips of speech, entire songs, sound bites from movies or TV shows, and any other recorded sound.

There are almost as many different kinds of sound file formats as there are kinds of sounds, and in days gone by you needed different sound players for each kind of sound file. For example,

The Extension	Indicated a Digitized Sound File That Was Developed
AU	By Sun for Unix workstations
AIFF	By Apple for Macintosh computers

The Extension	Indicated a Digitized Sound File That Was Developed
WAV	By Microsoft for Windows computers
MIDI	To represent musical notes that can be played back electronically on various musical instruments including the sound card in your computer

Now you can play any of them right from a Web page—all thanks to Netscape's LiveAudio plug-in.

QTVR: Apple's 3-D Video

Apple has its own 3-D virtual reality movie format, called QTVR. Right now, the QTVR player is available only for Windows 3.1 and Macintosh, but QTVR for Windows 95 and NT are in the works. Keep your eyes peeled at the URL `http://qtvr.quicktime.apple.com/` for a release date and then for download and installation instructions. If you try to view a QTVR movie without that software, it will most likely play as a regular QuickTime movie, minus the 3-D navigation.

 If you're offered a choice between two different kinds of sound files, choose WAV files over anything else—they'll generally sound better and download faster on your Windows PC.

When you click on a link that leads to a sound file with one of the extensions specified above, a sound player will appear. It may appear as part of the Netscape window, if the Webmaster specified that this should happen. Otherwise, a mini sound player will launch and conduct both the download and the playing of the file in a *separate* Netscape window. You can play the sound in this separate window as many times as you want, and you can always get to it by using the Window menu in Netscape's menu bar.

During the download, the LiveAudio Player will look blank—this player doesn't include status bars for either download time or play time. Below on the left is the LiveAudio player during a download; on the right is the player once the download is completed and ready for action.

What's Out There

There are lots and lots of sound archives on the Web, but two of the best are the Movie Sounds page, found at `http://www.moviesounds.com/`, and the SunSite music archive, at `http://sunsite.unc.edu/music.html`.

To download a sound file and save it to your hard drive, right-click on the link to that file. From the pop-up menu that appears, select Save Link As. The Save As dialog box will appear. Specify where you want your sound file to go, then click on Save. The sound file will appear on your Desktop, and you can play it with whatever sound players you happen to have.

Now you're ready to play nearly any sound file that comes your way. Simply click on a link to a sound file (usually marked as such), and Netscape's LiveAudio plug-in will do the rest. As the plug-in is playing the sound, you'll see a small window on screen which includes Stop, Play, and Pause buttons you can use to control the playback of the sound. When the sound is finished playing, you can either replay the sound by clicking on the Play button, or exit the player by clicking on the close box in the window's upper-right corner.

LiveVideo Makes Your Web Page a Video Player

AVI is a file format created for Windows that is similar to QuickTime's MOV format, and happily, Netscape's LiveVideo plug-in lets you watch AVI movies right in the Netscape window. Let's take a quick look at watching movies using Netscape and the LiveVideo plug-in for AVI movies.

If the Webmaster for a site with AVI movies has configured his or her pages to work with the LiveVideo plug-in, you'll see the first frame of the movie embedded in the Web page while the movie starts downloading. If this is not the case, a new (blank) Web page will appear while the video downloads.

Either way, you can click on a movie to play it, and click on it again to stop. When you click on a movie with the right mouse button, a set of controls will appear, including Rewind and Forward. What could be simpler?

To download a video file and save it to your hard drive, right-click on the link to that file. Select Save Link As from the pop-up menu that appears. When the Save As dialog box appears, specify where you want your video file to go, and click on Save.

What's Out There

You can find detailed information about LiveAudio at Netscape's LiveVideo page at `http://home.netscape.com/comprod/products/navigator/version_3.0/video/index.html`. A whole bunch of funky AVI movies await you at Protee's AVI site: `http://www.ganetweb.com/delmas/protee.htm`.

◆ Getting and Using Software from the Web

Any time you want to get a new plug-in or helper app, you'll follow a series of steps that is very similar from site to site. This process involves visiting the software producer's home page, downloading the software you want, and using an installer to set up the plug-in or helper app on your hard drive. In the case of plug-ins, the installation process configures

Netscape to work with the new software. This is also the case with many helper apps, but just in case, we'll show you how to set up Netscape to work with these applications. Finally, we'll give you lots of links so you can start using your new gadgets right away. By the time you run across a plug-in or helper app that we haven't covered, you'll be an old pro at getting and installing all kinds of Internet utilities.

Hear It Live with RealAudio

RealAudio, created by Progressive Networks, allows real-time broadcasting of sounds through a process called *streaming*. Instead of waiting for an entire sound file to download before you can play it, streaming allows the sound to be transmitted bit-by-bit over the Internet. As soon as you begin to download a sound file in the RealAudio format, the RealAudio player (which you might use in the form of the RealAudio plug-in) begins to play it. Concerts, political speeches, and the daily news can be broadcast live via the Internet—and so, with RealAudio, anyone can be a broadcaster. What's more, downloading recorded sound is even easier for people with slow connection speeds—you hear the sound as it's being played, and all the work has been done by the server on the other end.

Downloading and Installing RealAudio

Before you can use RealAudio, you have to download it from Progressive Networks' RealAudio Web site. Sometimes you'll encounter a Web page that includes RealAudio links and provides a convenient button for getting RealAudio so that you can get the full, rich audio impact of those links right away. Otherwise, you can go directly to the RealAudio site at `http://www.realaudio.com` to download the RealAudio software. When you do this, you'll be offered an option regarding where to put the software—on your Desktop is a good choice.

Getting RealAudio working with Netscape is a breeze. Whether you get the software via a RealAudio link on a Web page or by going to the RealAudio site, it will come with a program that installs both the RealAudio player and the RealAudio plug-in on your computer and configures Netscape to call on it. Here's how to set things up:

1. Find the RealAudio Installer (called RA32_201.EXE or something similar) that you downloaded from the RealAudio Web site. It will

be on your Desktop. Double-click on its icon, and a dialog box displaying the RealAudio license agreement will appear.

2. Read the RealAudio license agreement and click on the Accept button. The RealAudio Player Setup dialog box will appear, asking you to type in your name and (optionally) your company name. Do this, and when you're finished, click on Continue. Another dialog box will appear, asking you to verify the information you just typed. Click on OK. Another RealAudio Player Setup dialog box will appear, this time asking you to choose your modem connection speed.

3. In the dialog box's pull-down menu, select the speed of your Internet connection (28.8, T1, or whatever it is) and click on OK. Yet another dialog box will appear, asking you to choose between Express Setup and Custom Setup.

4. Unless you know enough about RealAudio to choose your own default settings, click on the Express Setup button. A series of dialog boxes will appear and disappear very quickly, advising you of the progress of the installation. In short order, a dialog box will appear telling you that the installation was completed successfully.

5. Click on OK. The RealAudio installer program will quit, the RealAudio player will launch, and you'll *hear* a message from Progressive Networks thanking you.

You now have the RealAudio player and the plug-in installed in Netscape's Plug-ins folder and all ready to go.

Using RealAudio

Playing sounds with RealAudio is a snap. (So to speak.) From here on out, any time you click on a link marked as RealAudio or a RAM file, the RealAudio player (Figure 12.2) will launch and begin playing a RealAudio sound file—no waiting required. You can hear live events or recordings of past live events—this is what folks in the biz refer to as "audio on demand."

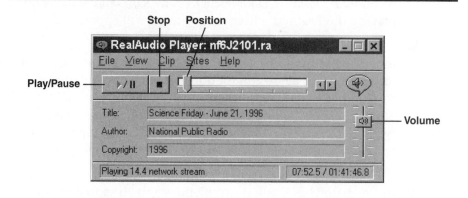

Figure 12.2: The RealAudio player starts playing live and on-demand sound files as soon as you start downloading them.

What's Out There

Tune in to Timecast, RealAudio's events directory, at
`http://www.timecast.com/`. RealAudio's home page, at
`http://www.realaudio.com/`, offers scads of live link listings, too. AudioNet, a RealAudio-friendly site for radio and sports fans, is at
`http://www.audionet.com/`.

Get Shocked with Shockwave

Macromedia's Shockwave was one of the first plug-ins created to work with Netscape. Now, with the new and improved Shockwave, you actually get three Shockwave plug-ins-in-one so you can view some of the most dynamic, visually (and aurally) appealing multimedia available on the Web. Shockwave files deliver CD-ROM-quality movies, games, and music, usually with fairly short download times. You do need a minimum of 16MB of RAM, but with this and the new plug-ins, you'll be able to experience the exciting interactivity of Director movies and games and Authorware presentations along with all the complex imagery of Freehand graphics, all from within Netscape's viewing area.

Downloading and Installing Shockwave

Getting the Shockwave software from Macromedia's site is easy—just download it from `http://www.macromedia.com`. It will come with an installation program. To install Shockwave:

1. Find the Shockwave Installer (called N32Z0003.EXE or something similar), which you downloaded from the Macromedia Web site, on your Desktop. Double-click on its icon, and the InstallShield Self Extracting EXE dialog box will appear, asking if you want to install Shockwave. Click on Yes, and a series of status windows will appear while the installer decompresses the files you downloaded.

2. Soon the Welcome dialog box will appear, advising you to quit all other open applications. Follow this wise advice, then return to the Welcome dialog box and click on Next. The Shockwave license agreement dialog box will appear.

3. Read this agreement, which essentially states that Shockwave is copyrighted and you agree not to sell it. If you accept those terms, click on the dialog box's Yes button. The Select Browser dialog box will appear.

4. From the choices provided, choose Netscape Navigator by selecting its radio button. Click on Next, and the Browser Location dialog box will appear.

5. The Browser Location dialog box asks you to verify the location of the Netscape files on your computer. If it's correct, proceed by clicking on the Next button. If it's incorrect (which it might be only if you have more than one copy of Netscape installed on your computer), you can select the Browse button to choose the directory where Netscape is installed, then click on Next. The Select Components dialog box will appear.

6. The Select Components dialog box lists the Shockwave plug-ins you are about to install:

   ◆ Shockwave for Authorware

   ◆ Shockwave for Director

   ◆ Shockwave for Freehand

Unless you have some compelling reason for not installing one of these plug-ins, leave all the choices selected. The Select Components dialog box also asks you to confirm the plug-ins folder you wish to use—because you've already specified the location of your Netscape directory, you can simply move on to confirm that you have enough disk space to continue. Click on Next, and the installation will begin.

7. The status bar will inform you of the installer's progress. When all the software is installed, a Setup Complete dialog box will appear. If you want to view the Readme files, select Yes. If not, deselect Yes. When you're ready, click on Finish. The installation program will close, leaving you at that familiar Windows Desktop once more.

The next time you launch Netscape, nothing more than a click on a link will cue Shockwave to do its magic automatically.

Using Shockwave

Some pages on the Web will load Shockwave files automatically, and others may ask you to click on a link to get "shocked." When a Shockwave movie is loading onto a Netscape page, a black or gray box will mark where the movie's going to appear. Then the action gets going. Shockwave is fully interactive—any time the Netscape cursor turns into a hand, you can click there and something (a sound, perhaps) will happen. Figure 12.3 shows Shockwave's own interactive home page.

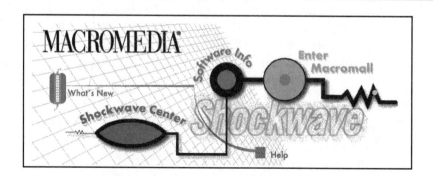

Figure 12.3: Macromedia's pages seem to come alive with electricity, thanks to Shockwave.

What's Out There

Explore Madeleine's Mind, at `http://www.madmind.com/`, to see (and hear) an all-Shockwave site. Shockwave's Epicenter gallery (`http://www.macromedia.com/shockwave/epicenter/`) offers access to hundreds of other sites that feature Shockwave.

Get Adobe Acrobat for High-Design Pages

HTML, for all its wonders, just doesn't have quite the flexibility your favorite desktop publishing software offers. Publishers who want to recreate the typographic and graphic sophistication of the printed page might find creating PDF (Portable Document Format) files that can be read with the Adobe Acrobat Reader to be just the ticket. And if you want to see those pages, from newspapers to training manuals, you'll need Acrobat.

Downloading and Installing Adobe Acrobat

You can download the latest version of Adobe Acrobat from Adobe's Web site, `http://www.adobe.com`. When you do so, be sure to get the version that will support your platform—Adobe makes versions for both Windows and the Macintosh. As usual, the download process will leave you with an installer program on your Desktop. Using the Acrobat Installer will get you the software you want and configure Netscape to open the reader automatically whenever you access a PDF file.

You can use this same general process to configure *any* helper apps that don't configure themselves automatically on installation.

1. Find ACROREAD.EXE, which you downloaded from the Adobe Web site, on your Desktop. Double-click on its icon, and the Electronic End User License Agreement dialog box will appear. Read the agreement, and if you accept the terms, click on the Accept button. The first in a series of Acrobat Installer dialog boxes will appear.

2. The dialog box will ask you to choose a location for your new software. The default location is C:\ACROREAD. This is a good place, so click on the Install button. Another Acrobat Installer dialog box will appear, reminding you to print out your registration card and send it in. (You can also register online, at `http://www.adobe.com/acrobat/register.html`). Click on OK, and a dialog box will appear, asking you to personalize your copy of Acrobat.

3. In the spaces provided, type your name (and organization, if any). When you're ready, click on OK. A status dialog box will appear while the installer does its thing.

4. When the installation is complete, the status dialog box will close. A final dialog box will inform you that the installation is complete. Click on OK. The dialog box will close, leaving the Windows Desktop visible, with the Adobe Acrobat folder on it.

We aren't *quite* ready to start using Acrobat with Netscape yet—we first have to configure Netscape to use the Acrobat Player.

Adobe is hard at work developing a new version of Adobe Acrobat that will include a Netscape plug-in, authoring tools, and expanded capabilities. Keep an eye on Adobe's site at http://www.adobe.com for more news.

Configuring Netscape to Use the Adobe Acrobat Reader

Although you just installed the Adobe Acrobat Reader, Netscape doesn't yet "know" about that software—you have to configure Netscape to recognize and work with Adobe Acrobat files. This is a straightforward process:

1. Start Netscape. (No need to get connected to the Internet.) From Netscape's menu bar, select Options ➤ General Preferences. The Preferences dialog box will appear.

2. Click on the Helpers tab, which is along the top of the Preferences dialog box. The Preferences dialog box will update to reflect your choice (see Figure 12.4).

3. In the Preferences dialog box's File Type list, locate the entry for `application/pdf` (you may have to look over the entire list to find it, the list is not in alphabetical order) and click on it once.

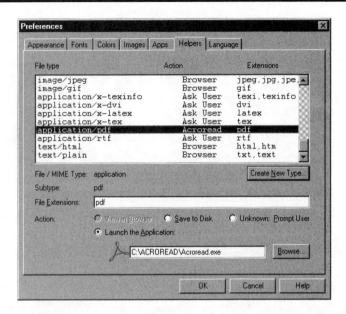

Figure 12.4: Netscape's Preferences–Helpers dialog box, with Adobe Acrobat selected.

4. In the Action section, which is near the bottom of the window, click on the Launch the Application radio button. Then, in the text box right below the radio button, type **c:\acroread\acroread.exe**.

5. Click on OK to close the Preferences dialog box. The familiar Netscape window will be visible.

That's all there is to it. Netscape is ready to display Adobe Acrobat files as you cruise the Web, and you're set for total reading enjoyment.

Using Adobe Acrobat

Now whenever you click on a link that goes to a PDF file, Netscape will transfer that file to your computer, and in an automatic process, the Adobe Acrobat Reader will launch and open the files you downloaded. You'll see a viewing window containing the text, graphics, and (perhaps most importantly) fonts that the designer intended you see (Figure 12.5).

Figure 12.5: The Truly Electronic Times publishes in PDF format so that everyone who reads it with Adobe Acrobat will see the same layout and design.

What's Out There

Peruse the Truly Electronic Times at
`http://sunsite.unc.edu/nppa/epw71/stories/ssignment7.html`, or
TimesFax, a daily digest of *The New York Times,* at `http://nytimesfax.com/`.
3-D games in PDF format are available at Mazeworld,
`http://www.ep.cs.nott.ac.uk/~pns/mazeworld/`. For more lovely PDF
pages, look into Adobe Acrobat's Cool Sites gallery
(`http://www.adobe.com/acrobat/coolpdf.html`)

◆ More Than a News Service: PointCast

PointCast network feeds you the latest news, weather, sports, stock
quotes, and links literally up to the minute, if you're connected to the
Internet (Figure 12.6). It also operates as a cool screen saver, so even
when you're not connected, all this floats by in a slick presentation that
sorely tempts you to sit down and read whenever you pass your machine.
PointCast also includes links to the Net. PointCast's Internet news button, for example, opens PointCast Viewpoint, an online magazine, as a
Web page in Netscape's viewing area. Best of all, PointCast is completely
customizable—you decide which news you need and which items you
can live without, and PointCast delivers the goods.

Figure 12.6: PointCast's weather area is very, very cool.

 PointCast is so smart it upgrades itself. If the hard-working folks at the PointCast Network get ahead of you (version-wise), you don't have to do a thing. When you connect to the PointCast Network, or if you click on the Update button in the PointCast browser, PointCast checks with home base to make sure that your software and the newest software are the same. Let's hear it for *technology*.

Downloading and Installing the PointCast Network

You can download the PointCast software right from PointCast's Web site at **http://www.pointcast.com**. When you do this, you may have to specify where the software should go—put it on your Desktop for now. An installer will appear. Let's install the PointCast software. You don't need to have your Internet connection running to use the installer.

1. Go find PCNINSTL.EXE (the installer) now and double-click on its icon. The Select Destination Directory dialog box will appear.

2. In the dialog box's text box, specify the directory in which PointCast will reside. The default directory is C:\PCN, and that's a fine choice. Click on the OK button. A dialog box will appear informing you that the directory you just selected does not exist. Not to worry—click on the Yes button and the directory will be created. The PointCast License Agreement dialog box will appear.

3. Read the PointCast license agreement. If you accept the terms, click on the Agreed button. The Registration Information dialog box will appear.

4. In the dialog box, you will be asked to supply your e-mail address, the country in which you live, your age group, and your gender. If you wish PointCast not to share any of this information with other companies, check the box labeled *Check here if you wish not to disclose this information.* Click on Continue. The United States ZIP Code dialog box will appear.

5. In the dialog box, type your 5-digit ZIP Code and click on Continue. A dialog box titled *Installing* will appear, with a status bar to indicate the installation's progress.

6. When installation is complete, the PCN Personalization dialog box will appear. If you would like to indicate your favorite topics now, click on Personalize PCN and do so. (You can always personalize PointCast later if you prefer.) Click on the Launch PCN button.

or

To launch PointCast with the preset news topics in place instead, click on the Launch PCN button.

You'll find that installing PointCast also leaves you with a nice, automatically created shortcut on your Desktop. You can double-click on this shortcut to launch PointCast any old time. This will not, however, start your Internet connection, so what you'll see is the most recently updated news (which may be several days old if you haven't been online in a while). To get more recent information, start your Internet connection first and then launch PointCast.

Using PointCast

Using PointCast is extremely intuitive, and the specifics change with frequent updates to the software, so forgive us for not detailing that subject.

Here, instead, are tips for using the PointCast browser (which operates basically the same whether you're using the stand-alone version or the plug-in) and the PointCast SmartScreen screensaver.

Reading PointCast News

◆ To "change the channel," simply click on the button bearing the name of the channel that contains the news you want to read. The table of contents area will change to reflect your choice. You can use the scroll bar to browse the list of available articles. Often there are file tabs that let you have more choices within each channel.

◆ To view tabs that appear "off" screen, you can click on the right- and left-arrow buttons above the table of contents area.

◆ To read an article, double-click on the news icon next to its title.

◆ When you run the mouse over any article in the news viewing area, the cursor will take the form of a magnifying glass. To maximize a news article, simply click on it. To minimize it, click on it again.

◆ To view channels that are not onscreen, you can use the up- and down-arrow buttons that appear below the channel buttons. Clicking on them scrolls you through the list of available channels. To select a channel, simply click on its button.

◆ To access PointCast's Help viewer, (what else?) click on Help.

◆ To launch or return to Netscape, click on the Netscape Now button near the bottom of the button bar.

◆ Next to the Netscape button is an arrow-shaped button with which you can toggle the size of the button bar.

Customizing PointCast

Pointcast's appeal is in its customizability. You can change your personalization and other options without even being online. Access any of the following areas by clicking on the buttons that appear on the main PointCast window.

Personalize   You can personalize PointCast so that it will display only certain types of information—maybe you want to know about Internet companies in the news but not telephone companies. Or you may want the baseball scores to appear in the sports section but not the hockey scores. To change your Personalization information at any time, click on the Personalize button. The Personalization dialog box will appear, with a handy tab for every channel.

Options   To change how PointCast accesses the Internet, click on Options. The Options dialog box will appear. From the tabs at the top of it, you can select SmartScreen (to get screensaver options); Update (to select a schedule for automatic updates); Internet (to modify your dial-up connection information); or Proxies (useful only if your Internet service provider uses proxy connections).

PointCast's SmartScreen Screensaver

PointCast's SmartScreen Screensaver launches automatically whenever your computer is idle; you can set the amount of time before SmartScreen's will launch by clicking on the PointCast windows' Options button. When SmartScreen launches, it displays the news that was current the last time you downloaded it. Depending on how often you tell PointCast to update, it may automatically dial your Internet connection and download fresh news. To display the full story for any news item, simply click on it. To bypass PointCast and return to what you were doing, click on any blank space. Clicking on an ad will launch Netscape and send you to that advertiser's site. The ticker at the bottom of SmartScreen is also clickable; you can adjust the speed and direction of the ticker tape by dragging it with the hand that the cursor turns into.

You're All Set

So—you're a master Web navigator and burgeoning Web publisher after reading the earlier chapters in this book, and now you even know how to get and use viewers and players to augment your Netscape experience. You're ready to proceed full steam ahead into your World Wide Web travels using Netscape.

Bon voyage!

Internet Service Providers

If you need to set up an account with an Internet service provider so that you can get started with Netscape, this is the place for you. This appendix lists providers that supply the type of service you need to use Netscape.

As mentioned previously in this book, the difference between Internet service providers and commercial online services traditionally has been that Internet service providers provide access to the Internet but not content, while commercial online services (CompuServe and America Online, for example) provide their own selected and specially developed content to their subscribers—perhaps including Internet access as one of the services they provide. If you want to get your Internet access via one of the commercial online services, your best bet is to use the software on the CD that comes with this book or get your hands on one of the disks those companies tuck into magazines and give away at trade shows.

When you're shopping around for an Internet service provider, the most important questions to ask are (a) Is this a SLIP or a PPP account? (either is fine, although PPP is somewhat better) (b) What is the nearest local access number? (c) What are the monthly service charges? and (d) Are there setup and/or hourly usage fees?

What's Out There?

Two good sources of information about Internet service providers are available on the Internet itself:

◆ The List is a comprehensive directory of Internet service providers worldwide, searchable by country, area code, and name. You'll find The List at `http://thelist.com`.

◆ Yahoo's list of Internet service providers is also extensive and easy to use. It's at `http://www.yahoo.com/Business_and_Economy/Companies/Internet_Access_Providers/`.

◆ In the United States

In this section we describe Internet service providers that have local access phone numbers in most major American cities. These are the big, national companies. Many areas also have smaller regional Internet providers, which may offer better local access if you're not in a big city.

Opening an account with any of the providers listed here will get you full access to the World Wide Web along with full-fledged e-mail service (which allows you to send and receive e-mail). You'll also be able to read and post articles to Usenet newsgroups.

Netcom   Netcom On-line Communication Services is a national Internet service provider with local access numbers in most major cities. Netcom's Netcomplete or NetCruiser software will give you point-and-click access to the Internet. Netcomplete software is available on the CD that comes with this book or with a very good book (*Access the Internet!*, by David Peal and Jennifer Kirby, Sybex, 1996) that shows you how to use the software. To contact Netcom directly, phone (800) 353-6600.

Performance Systems International   (PSI) offers local access numbers in many U.S. cities and an expanding international presence. To contact PSI directly, phone (800) 82P-SI82.

UUNet/AlterNet   UUNet Technologies and AlterNet offer Internet service throughout the United States. They run their own national network. To contact UUNet and AlterNet directly, phone (800) 900-0241.

In Canada

Listed here are providers that offer access to Internet service in the areas around large Canadian cities. For information about local access in less-populated regions, get connected and check out The List.

UUNet Canada   (416) 368-6621

Internet Direct   (604) 691-1600

Big and Small Internet Service Providers

In this appendix we focus on the big, national service providers, but smaller, more local providers are also an important option to consider. Both the big guys and the little guys have advantages, which parallel the advantages you might find in, say, a national retail chain and a small local shop. For example, a big service provider offers POPs (points of presence, or local phone number to dial in to) all over the place. So if you travel a lot and want to have local Internet access across the country (or around the world), a national provider may be for you. However, lots of other people are also dialing in—the sheer volume of usage may mean you have difficulty connecting sometimes. With all those people to attend to, the big service providers sometimes have trouble getting around to customer service.

Local providers, on the other hand, offer access to a smaller geographical area but can be easier to dial into; often they can also give you more personal attention than the big guys can. Frequently, a local Internet service provider makes special services available to attract and keep its users. For example, DNAI, a small but mighty service provider in the San Francisco Bay Area, offers all sorts of utilities that help users set up and monitor their Web sites at no extra cost. This is just the sort of thing that's a major convenience but that a bigger service provider might not want to get into. You can reach DNAI at (510) 649-6110.

◆ In the United Kingdom and Ireland

The Internet is *international*. Here are some service providers located and offering service in the United Kingdom and Ireland.

EUNet GB Ltd.	44 1227 266 466
Easynet (UK)	44 171 209 0990
Ireland On-line	353 1 855 1739

◆ In Australia and New Zealand

Down under in Australia and New Zealand the Internet is as happening as it is in the Northern Hemisphere; here are a couple of service providers for that part of the world.

Connect.com.au (Australia)	61 3 528 2239
Actrix (New Zealand)	64 4 499 1122

Get Connected, Get Set, GO!

Selecting an Internet service provider is a matter of personal preference and local access. Shop around, and remember—if you aren't satisfied at any point, change providers.

B

Spots on the Web You Won't Want to Miss

Along the Infobahn, there are many places you'll want to visit. Here to get you started are some hip, happening, and useful sites we've seen on the Web in our own travels. We've categorized this stuff for your convenience.

◆ The "Best" of the Web

The Web's got its own lineup of "Best of" awards, bestowed upon outstanding Web sites by a variety of authorities and amateurs. These lists can be an interesting browsing experience; take a look at some of them just for kicks.

What's Out There

You can see winners of the "original" Best of the World Wide Web competition through the URL `http://wings.buffalo.edu/contest/`.

c|net's very own view of what's best on the Web can be seen at `http://www.cnet.com/Content/Features/Special/Awards/index.html`.

GNN's "best" is at `http://gnn.com/wic/botn/index.html`.

◆ Arts and Entertainment

The arts are terrifically well represented on the Web—from graffiti to the Louvre, from the blues to *The Tempest*, from architecture to Tinseltown, and all sorts of products of the American entertainment dream machine.

Art Crimes: The Writing on the Wall   ...Is it art or is it entertainment? Here you'll find hundreds, if not thousands, of graffiti images from around the world, organized by city.

What's Out There

The handwriting's on the wall at `http://www.gatech.edu/graf/index.html`.

Blue Highway   The Blue Highway is all about the blues, from well-crafted profiles of the great blues masters and their lives to images and sound files.

What's Out There

Get the blues at `http://www.vivanet.com/~blues/`. And whether you're a big-time music fan or just a Web wanderer, dig deep into alternative music at the Internet Underground Music Archive (`http://www.iuma.com`).

The Electric Postcard   During the writing of this book, one of the most fun moments we had was testing this site. We sent each other charming Web postcards (see Figure B.1), then we sent them to friends, and then we wished even more of our friends had Web browsers so that we could keep up the good time.

Your machine must have the appropriate sound capabilities (lots o' memory along with a sound card, drivers, and maybe even speakers) to play sound files.

Tokyo Billboard
J. Donath

To whom should this postcard be sent (email address, please)?
dat@netcom.com

Figure B.1: Drop us a postcard, send us a line! You can send electric postcards.

Games Domain   Games Domain is (simply put) far and away the best resource for lovers of computer games of all kinds. It offers fast access to up-to-date, authoritative information, and it covers FAQs, walk-throughs, and links to other game-related sites. A gamer could spend all his or her days just browsing here, if not for the call of the game…

Leonardo   *Leonardo*, the print publication, is a journal that covers the fusion of art, music, science, and technology. *Leonardo*'s Web site covers the same topics, with an overview of the medium and viewable images and downloadable sound files created by artists and musicians using the arts and technology in innovative ways.

What's Out There

The arts and technology merge in *Leonardo's* online version at
`http://www-mitpress.mit.edu/Leonardo/home.html`.

Internet Movie Database   For the starstruck or the plain old curious, a searchable, indexed database of movie-related stuff might be just the ticket. Query it by the name of an actor or actress, the title of a film, a genre, or a quote from a movie. You can also get a listing of the Academy Award winners in many key categories, dating all the way from 1920.

What's Out There

The now venerable Movie Browser database is at
`http://www.msstate.edu/Movies/`. And if you're interested in film sites, check out a few more: CimemaSpace, at
`http://cinemaspace.berkeley.edu/` is a terrific site for film studies; the Early Motion Pictures site from the Library of Congress at
`http://lcweb2.loc.gov/papr/mpixhome.html` is an archive of old films; and Cinemaven, at `http://www.uspan.com/mavin.html/`, is great for reviews of current feature films. Gaze on all that glitters by visiting *Mr. Showbiz* at `http://web3.starwave.com:80/showbiz/`. Closer to home, you can find out where the latest flicks are playing in your neighborhood by looking in on `http://www.777film.com`.

The Scrolling Mystery Theater

A melding of time-honored entertainment traditions with new technology, the Scrolling Mystery Theater presents an interactive...*experience. The Moving Face* (Figure B.2) is the current offering as of this writing. As a tale of intrigue unfolds, you can peruse the text for clues, or take a look at hint-ridden documents in an online dossier, or talk via e-mail with actors playing the characters in the story (including Woof the dog).

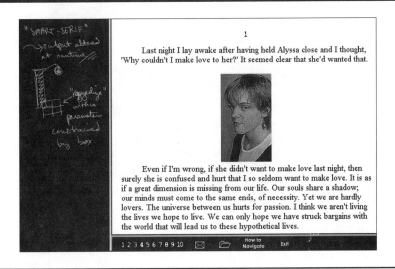

Figure B.2: *The Moving Face,* an interactive mystery theater experience with literary pizzazz

What's Out There

Take in a moving mystery experience at `http://www.fiction.com`.

The Spot

We loved the *Real World* on MTV and have to admit a soft spot for that sort of peek-into-the-everyday-life type of entertainment, but even if we were just fans of good stories (which we also are), we would have loved the Spot, shown in Figure B.3.

What's Out There

You can find out what's up in the lives of a bunch of hip, cool, and groovy housemates at the Spot. Its URL is `http://www.thespot.com/`.

Figure B.3: Stop in at the "spot" every week to stay current.

◆ Computers and the Net

So maybe you want to upgrade your modem? Find free software to enhance your Internet abilities? Reconfigure and upgrade your entire computer system? All you need to know is where to go for all the technical and product-specific information you'll ever need.

Cryptography, PGP, and Your Privacy   Privacy on the Net has become a major concern in the past couple of years. The Cryptography, PGP, and Your Privacy site will provide you with all the background you'll need to understand these issues. It will also give you a place to get involved in grassroots electronic activism if you care about privacy.

What's Out There

To find out about privacy issues as they might affect you, pop in at
`http://world.std.com/~franl/crypto.html`.

The Dilbert Zone   Dilbert is the consummate Silicon Valley nerd, whose adventures in techno-employment are undeniably real to those of us who've been in the industry.

What's Out There

The Dilbert Zone is at `http://www.unitedmedia.com/comics/dilbert`.

Linux: A Unix-Like Operating System for Your PC   If you're interested in fiddling around with a Unix clone on your PC (Intel 386, 486, or Pentium), you can find out all about the Linux operating system and its champions at a terrific Web site.

What's Out There

The Linux site serves up background information and how-to documents at `http://www.linux.org`. Don't leave DOS without it.

For more on Linux, which is a terrific operating system that's no picnic to install but a real delight to use, check out Sybex's *The Complete Linux Kit* by Daniel A. Tauber. You'll discover the ins and outs of installing and using Linux, and you'll even get a copy of the software on a convenient CD-ROM.

Sun and Java Technology   Sun, the folks who bring you Java and HotJava, have a happening site where you can find all the latest about these products and everything else Sun wants you to know. (See Figure B.4).

What's Out There

The Sun will be in your eyes when you visit the Java site at `http://java.sun.com`.

Java(tm): Programming for the Internet

Figure B.4: Check out the Sun site on Java to get the Java development skinny.

◆ Education

The Web started as a tool for research and academia; so plenty of the stuff on it appeals to those in education circles.

AskERIC ERIC is the Educational Resources Information Center; AskERIC (see Figure B.5) is a Web site that's packed with resources for education. Find out about conferences, curricula, funding, reference tools, professional organizations—it's pretty much all here.

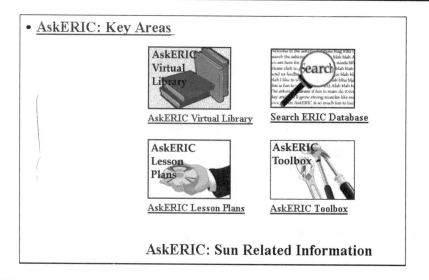

Figure B.5: AskERIC about education.

What's Out There

Learn about AskERIC's fantastic resources for K-12 educators at the URL `http://ericir.syr.edu`.

Web 66, an outstanding source of information for K-12 educators, is at `http://web66.coled.umn.edu/`. MegaMath offers fun math activities for kids (honestly!) at `http://www.c3.lanl.gov/mega-math/index.html`. And the classic interactive frog dissection is at `http://curry.edschool.virginia.edu/~insttech/frog`.

EdWeb A great site that focuses on the use of technology and the Internet as tools in educational reform, this is a wonderful resource for anyone interested in the future of education.

What's Out There

Get into the swing of education's future by visiting EdWeb at the URL `http://edweb.cnidr.org:90`.

Human Languages With links to just about every human language, including Esperanto (the artificially created universal human language) and even some we've never heard of, this site can truly be called comprehensive.

What's Out There

Languages are described, discussed, translated, and even pronounced at `http://www.willamette.edu/~tjones/languages/Language-Page.html`.

A Professor's Guilt List for English Lit Majors From Alcott to Yeats, this site provides a list of all the works of literature a self-respecting English major must have under his or her suspenders. Constructed by an actual professor, this is a great resource for everyone who reads and enjoys English lit.

What's Out There

Read up on great writing by following the list provided by a professor of English Lit at `http://www.next.com/~bong/books/GuiltList.html`.

Stanford University   The Stanford University site has many links that will help those at Stanford, those thinking of going to Stanford, and those who just want Stanford information.

What's Out There

You can look into Stanford and what's happening there via the URL `http://www.stanford.edu/`.

U.S. Geological Survey   The U.S. Geological Survey (USGS) boasts as one of its purposes the publishing of information about the United States' mineral, land, and water resources, which it has done through traditional means for many a decade. Now the USGS has a Web server. If you live in earthquake country, you'll want to size up the seismic activity stuff—some nifty maps show up-to-date earthquake information (see Figure B.6).

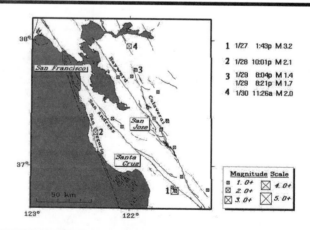

Figure B.6: If you live in earthquake country (or if you're just curious), you'll want to check out the USGS's cool maps.

Many schools from K-12 to universities have their own Web sites, where you can find out about student activities and classes and even take a virtual tour. To find a school that interests you, search the Web using the tools described in Chapter 8.

◆ Food and Beverages

A veritable feast of Internet sites cover food and beverage topics. You can trade recipes with others around the world, find out about nutrition, learn to make medieval food or home-brewed beer, linger for a while at a cybercafe, or investigate restaurants in your city or another. Bon appétit!

Cafe Orbital   The primary site at Cafe Orbital is in French; appropriately so, because this is a virtual French cafe, where you can hobnob with your virtual pals or peruse pages yourself while sipping coffee at your keyboard. There is an easy link to an English translation of the site; so for those of us who lack the French language, there's hope.

Epicurious   A Condé Nast publication, Epicurious incorporates those two grand dames of food magazines, *Bon Appétit* and *Gourmet*. There's nothing stodgy about *Epicurious*. Its graphics are tasty; its content delectable. You can get a look at it in Figure B.7.

Taste Epicurious for yourself at `http://www.epicurious.com`.

copyright© 1996 concenet

Figure B.7: Epicurious serves up delicious graphics and delectable feature articles on food and dining.

The URL Minder (`http://www.netmind.com/URL-minder/URL-minder.html`) will track changes in your favorite Web sites and notify you when they occur.

Virtual Vineyards Virtual Vineyards (see Figure B.8) is a wine shop run by a very knowledgeable and un-snobby wine expert. Here you can get advice, bone up on wines and vintages, and purchase what strikes your fancy.

Figure B.8: The Virtual Vineyards opening banner

◆ Government and Politics

The Clinton administration showed a strong interest in the Net when it promoted the Information Superhighway. The U.S. and world government have an increasing presence on the Web; a broad range of grassroots activism can also be heard and seen.

George   Billing itself as having been the first magazine to attempt simultaneous paper/Web launch, JFK Jr's political rag is the behind-the-scenes, hip, people-are-politics, Washington-insider's view of American government and its various facets. *George*'s look is shown in Figure B.9.

Figure B.9: *George* bills itself as the first magazine to have launched in print and online simultaneously.

Thomas: Congress's Legislative Database　Thomas, the Congressional database service, makes available information about the House and Senate, the e-mail addresses of all members of Congress, and (especially juicy) the full text of legislation beginning with the 103rd Congress.

What's Out There

Thomas will tell you what's happening in Congress if you stop in at `http://thomas.loc.gov/`. And while you're toddling around, tour the White House interactively by checking in at `http://www.whitehouse.gov`.

The Right Side of the Web　On the *right* side of the political coin, you can check out a site (see Figure B.10) devoted to convincing liberals of the correctness of the ultraconservative viewpoint.

What's Out There

To find out about the more conservative views expressed on the Web, go to the URL `http://www.clark.net/pub/jeffd/`.

Figure B.10: Farther down the page, Reagan's smiling face graces the Right Side of the Web.

Socialist Party USA Cybercenter   On the *left* side of the Web is an informative site about the Socialist viewpoint, where a tongue-in-cheek history of socialism is featured along with the article "How to Be a Socialist."

What's Out There

If you're interested in the political left, you can learn more about socialism at `http://sunsite.unc.edu:80/spc/index.html`.

Supreme Court Decisions   A project of Cornell's Legal Information Institute (LII), the Supreme Court Decisions document provides a searchable database of recent Supreme Court decisions (from 1990 on), indexed by topic.

What's Out There

A searchable database of Supreme Court decisions is available at the URL
`http://www.law.cornell.edu/supct/supct.table.html/`.

◆ Health and Wellness

The Web is heaven for information seekers; those who want to find out
about health, wellness, disorders, and diseases might look here before
trekking off to the public library.

Healthwise   A remarkable site packed with information about health
matters, Healthwise features Go Ask Alice, which is itself a terrific
resource. Here, you can ask a health-related question anonymously, and
the answer of professionals and peers is posted publicly. That means the
questions are candid and the answers are informative to all.

What's Out There

You can ask Alice about what ails or interests you at Healthwise. The URL is
`http://www.columbia.edu/cu/healthwise/`.

HyperDoc: The National Library of Medicine   Here's the World-
Wide-Web way to look into the National Library of Medicine, part of the
U.S. National Institutes of Health in Bethesda, Maryland. The library
houses more than 4.5 million books, journals, reports, manuscripts, and
audiovisual materials (see Figure B.11), making it the largest medical
library in the world.

What's Out There

Everything you ever wanted to know about Western health and medicine (and
perhaps even alternatives) can be learned at: `http://www.nlm.nih.gov/`.

Figure B.11: Be sure to stop by the History of Medicine exhibit at the National Library of Medicine.

World Health Organization   Headquartered in Switzerland, the World Health Organization is an international organization dedicated to "the attainment by all peoples of the highest possible level of health."

What's Out There

The World Health Organization provides loads of information on the Web by publishing its newsletters at the URL `http://www.who.ch`.

◆ News and Weather

The advent of the Web has made a new world for journalism. You'll find that some news services, such as Pointcast and CNN Interactive, take striking advantage of the new possibilities.

CNN Interactive   The news according to CNN Interactive (see Figure B.12) is definitely *interactive*. You can, for example, read news articles, sports briefs, and movie reviews in the form of text, but you can also actually see and hear brief interviews with key figures and preview films in the form of video and audio clips. For an innovative experience of news on the Web, turn here.

What's Out There

Pick up the daily news at CNN's interactive site: `http://www.cnn.com`.

Figure B.12: CNN on the Web is a truly interactive experience.

The *New York Times*   Here's an example of a news service that seeks to recreate its paper version online. The *New York Times*, in one of its Internet versions, uses Adobe's Acrobat reader (see Chapter 12) to provide the news in a layout that looks essentially like the print version of the paper. You don't have to pay for the Adobe Acrobat software needed to read the online *Times*; it comes with the "paper."

What's Out There

The *New York Times* will arrive on your machine in a form that looks much like the actual paper when you go to `http://nytimesfax.com`. Another, more "traditional" Web-site version of the *Times* is at `http://www.nytimes.com/`.

All the News All the Time

Any number of news services and publications make their content available online; we describe a few in this appendix, but there are so many that you'll probably want to look for your favorites and bookmark them. Here are a few more:

News Provider	Its URL
AP on trib.com	`http://www.trib.com`
ClariNet	`http://www.clarinet.com`
Financial Times	`http://www.usa.ft.com`
Reuters	`http://www.reuters.com`
Mercury Center Web	`http://www.sjmercury.com`

Some of these services charge a fee; some ask you to "subscribe" in a quick process that simply tells them who you are. (They generally use this info as a marketing survey.) Some narrow their online focus to news about business and/or technology. All are worthwhile.

Pathfinder   Pathfinder is the big, comprehensive site where Time Warner makes available many of its publications, including *Time*, *Money*, *Fortune*, and more popular-culture oriented rags such as *People*, *Entertainment Weekly*, and *Vibe*.

What's Out There

Make your way to Time Warner's Pathfinder site at `http://www.pathfinder.com`.

Pointcast is a wonderful online news service that comes in the form of a plug-in to Netscape. See Chapter 12 for more on Pointcast and other plug-ins.

The Weather Net Index   Whether its general weather trend information, specific prognostications, or storm tracking that interests you, here you'll find links to sites that will get you on your way.

What's Out There

Weather's cleared up for you at `http://cirrus.sprl.umich.edu/wxnet`.

◆ People Everywhere

The Web is global; so you can find plenty about cultures other than your own. Curious about Russia? Vietnamese business ventures in the U.S.? Indigenous peoples? Women, gays, and "minorities" in the U.S.? It's all here on the Web.

Amnesty International   Amnesty International is an international human rights organization whose site publishes information about how to contact the group and what membership involves.

What's Out There

For human rights developments, turn to Amnesty International at `http://www.organic.com/Non.profits/Amnesty/index.html`.

African/Black Resources   At the African/Black Internet Resources site, you'll find an index with abstracts of literally hundreds of things on the Net having to do with African and Black studies. Another great resource is the African-American Culture and History site, with sections on colonization, abolition, migration, and the WPA, and a major exhibition on the impact of African-American culture on the American identity (see Figure B.13).

Gender Issues Directory   This great starting point for the exploration of such issues as the ability of women to break into and succeed in the

What's Out There

Links to hundreds of African and Black studies sites are at
`http://www.sas.upenn.edu/African_Studies/Home_Page/other.html`.

African-American culture and history is exhibited by the Library of Congress
at `http://lcweb.loc.gov/exhibits/African.American/intro.html`.

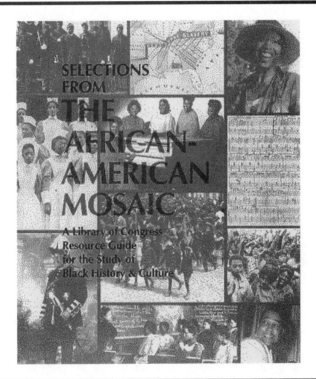

Figure B.13: The Library of Congress' African-American culture exhibit is an
especially rich resource.

world of computers and computer science also publishes information on
gender studies, women, and feminism in general. There are many links to
other sites on the same topics.

What's Out There

Women in computing and other gender-focused topics are discussed at
`http://www.cpsr.org/dox/program/gender/index.html`.

Indigenous Peoples' Literature   At this highly informative but somewhat graphically dull site, you'll find guides to Native American languages and a broad range of articles about the current indigenous nations of North America.

What's Out There

Native American cultures and languages are the topic at
`http://web.maxwell.syr.edu/nativeweb/`.

Islamic Architecture in Isfahan   Renowned for its lush, picture-book quality, this site presents a photographic history of Islamic architecture. The text is informative, the photography superb, the layout inviting.

What's Out There

Explore Islamic architecture at
`http://www.anglia.ac.uk/~trochford/isfahan.html`.

Maximov   This complete reference to the Russian government includes contact information for 5500 members of that government, including the President's Administration, Federal Government, Parliament, and Judiciary, as well as the Administrations and Legislatures of the Russian Federation. Mikhail Gorbachev is quoted as saying that the print version is "An indispensable companion—authoritative and up to date" that he "uses every day." Maximov's home page is shown in Figure B.14.

What's Out There

A complete guide to the Russian government is available at the URL
`http://www.maximov.com/`.

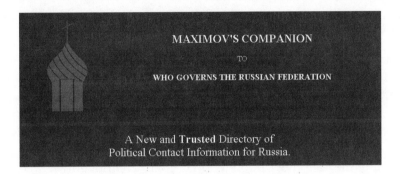

MAXIMOV'S COMPANION

TO

WHO GOVERNS THE RUSSIAN FEDERATION

A New and **Trusted** Directory of
Political Contact Information for Russia.

Figure B.14: Maximov is known as a complete guide to the Russian government.

The Vietnamese Professionals Society
For information about Vietnamese people the world over (but mainly in the U.S.), this is a great place to start. Like a central meeting hall, this site includes links to other sites, as well as translations of professional journals, listings of meetings, newsletters, Vietnamese software programs, and a wealth of other gems.

What's Out There

Vietnamese people and people interested in the Vietnamese can find out more at `http://www.webcom.com/~hcgvn/`.

Lesbians, Gays, and Bisexuals on the Web
The Society and Culture: Sex site provides paths to a host of lesbian, gay, and bisexual resources, ranging from pages on Domestic Partnership and Same Sex Marriage to the "CyberQueer Lounge."

What's Out There

To find out more about lesbian, gay, and transgender topics, look for the URL `http://www.yahoo.com/Society_and_Culture/Lesbians__Gays_and_Bisexuals/General_Interest/`.

◆ Personal Finance

Money's the name of the game—where to get it, how to maximize it, and what to do with it. (Spend it? Save it?) Here are some sites to consult on these topics.

Consumer Information Center   You'll get all sorts of basic information about personal finance at this site, provided by a U.S. government organization, the Consumer Information Center. (We thought we were going to find buying advice for retail goods here, but it's much more than that.)

What's Out There

Get the lowdown on all sorts of finance matters at the Consumer Information Center at `http://www.pueblo.gsa.gov/`.

The *Financial Times*   That long- and well-known international publication, the *Financial Times*, has gone online, and lucky for us. You'll find top stories on Asia, the Americas, and Europe, along with stock-market indexes presented with a 30-minute delay.

What's Out There

Get financial facts and news at either the *Financial Times* U.S. site at `http://www.usa.ft.com` or the British site at `http://www.ft.com`.

Mortgage Calculator   A convenient-to-use mortgage amortization form (see Figure B.15), created by an individual with an interest in the topic, offers you the opportunity to work out the numbers involved in financing a home.

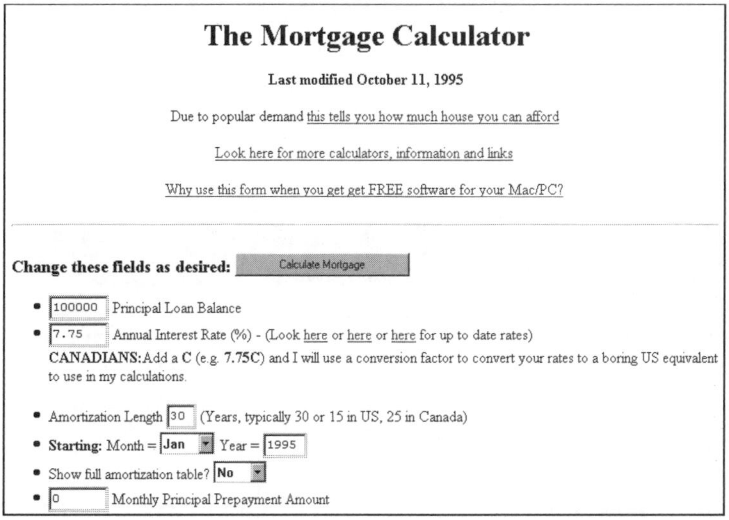

Figure B.15: Figure what your monthly and lifetime mortgage payments will be.

What's Out There

Work out the numbers for your home financing at the URL
`http://ibc.wustl.edu/mort.html`.

◆ Publishing and Literature

To many people, the creation of Web technology is as big a deal as the invention of the printing press. Wide-scale electronic distribution of attractively laid out information is now a reality. Let's look at how a sampling of publishers and information providers (both professional and amateur) are using this new medium.

See the *Zines* section at the end of this chapter for the scoop on alternative electronic publishing, including a description of a terrific literary zine, *Enterzone*.

BookWire   Both book lovers and publishing pros will love this comprehensive Web site (see Figure B.16). Start with the online *Publishers Weekly* bestsellers list and then go on to the links to reviews. More links take you to libraries, publishers, booksellers, news, and even a daily cartoon by Mort Greenberg.

What's Out There

Open up the pages at `http://www.bookwire.com/` to find out what's happening in the publishing world. The Pulitzer Prize's background and the current awardees are yours to read at `http://www.pulitzer.org/`.

Figure B.16: BookWire's a terrific starting place for publishing news.

Complete Works of William Shakespeare   As browsable, searchable, and cross-referenced as the works themselves, this online collection is the creation of an MIT grad student, Jeremy Hylton. There's even a hypertext glossary built into each of the Bard's works.

What's Out There

The Bard's complete works are set before you and searchable at the URL `http://the-tech.mit.edu/Shakespeare/works.html`.

Mississippi Review   Literary reviews—small, carefully edited journals of writing with literary merit—are the gems of contemporary writing, offering newcomers a place to get their breaks and well-known writers a place to publish shorter works. The *Mississippi Review* is a prestigious example of the literary journal.

What's Out There

Contemporary short fiction is showcased for your reading pleasure at `http://sushi.st.usm.edu:80/mrw/`.

Urban Diary   Is it art or is it lit? This hybrid of narrative and collage sometimes looks like typed and scribbled notes on gridlined paper, sometimes like doodles on a calendar page, sometimes like...well, like someone's underground diary (see Figure B.17). An obvious plot line never develops, but, hey, that's the nature of postmodern fiction.

What's Out There

A really unusual experience awaits you at `http://gertrude.art.uiuc.edu/ludgate/the/place/urban_diary/intro.html`.

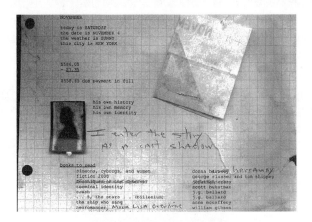

Figure B.17: Is it art or is it lit?

♦ Science and Technology

The Web, and in fact the Internet, started as a research tool, though of course it's grown into much more than that. You can see the effects of these beginnings in the wide range of information available about sciences both "hard" and "soft."

MIT Media Lab   Where better to look into computers, science, and technology than at that granddaddy of science and technology academia, the Massachusetts Institute of *Technology*?

What's Out There

You'll get direct access to the MIT Media Lab through the URL
`http://www.media.mit.edu/`.

NASA Information Services via the World Wide Web   Voyage
here for information about upcoming space shuttle missions, access to
the many images made public from the Hubble Space Telescope, and a
peek into NASA's strategy for the future. Also very cool, very fresh, is the
"live" map of NASA centers around the country (see Figure B.18).

What's Out There

Space, the final frontier, is yours to explore through the NASA Information
Services home page. Its URL is `http://www.nasa.gov/`.

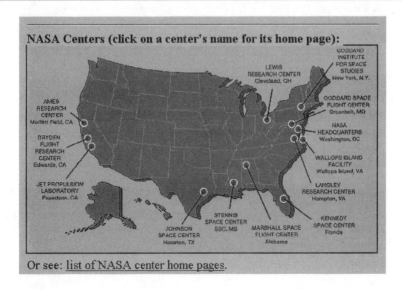

Figure B.18: To find out what's up at any NASA center in the country, simply click
on the name of that center in this map.

◆ Sports

From the major leagues to the minors, to the oh-so-minors and even the fantasy leagues, sports are all over the Net.

Create Your Own Sports Page   Another great gizmo from those fun-loving guys at MIT, this is a long list of sports links from which you can pick and choose those that interest you most and create a customized sports page. You just point and click. The result is a set of links on a page with its own URL.

Remember to bookmark the customized sports page you create. If you don't, you'll never remember its self-generated URL, and you'll have to do the whole business of creating it over again.

What's Out There

Create your very own customized sports page via the URL
`http://tns-www.lcs.mit.edu/cgi-bin/sports/create-form`.

ESPNet Sports Zone   College and professional sports are covered big time here, with up-to-date scores, feature articles, and player interviews. There's a charge for the whole shebang (including the broadcast of basketball games with audio), but there's also plenty here you don't have to pay to view.

What's Out There

Big, better, and busting the mold, ESPNet Sports Zone is at the URL
`http://espnet.sportszone.com`.

The 1996 Olympic Games   A timely site devoted to developments in the 1996 Olympics, this site will keep up with some or all of the actual events as they occur and afterward will provide a record of the events. (See Figure B.19.)

Figure B.19: Keep up with Olympic developments at this site.

GNN Women's Basketball   The GNN Sports Center covers women's basketball, offering scores, schedules, player spotlights, and features. You'll also find an archive of past news, the AP Top 25 poll, and more.

◆ Travel

Not only can you travel around the Web—you can use the Web to plot your travels around the world or just around town. The Internet offers all kinds of travel information and services, ranging from stuff about how to get there to what to expect and do once you arrive.

Foreign Languages for Travelers   It's always best to learn a few phrases (such as "Where is the bathroom?") before you travel to a new country.

What's Out There

Expand your foreign language vocabulary at `http://www.travlang.com/languages/`.

Preview Media   Great vacation information and travel package bargains are available via the Preview Media site (see Figure B.20). Here you'll find a thoughtful range of insider descriptions and background on locales (we never knew before that Cancun was chosen for development into a resort based on a *computer study*). Check out Find-a-Trip, a nifty questionnaire that helps you focus your ideas and select a travel destination.

What's Out There

View vacation wonderlands via the Preview Media travel site at the URL `http://www.vacations.com`. (Note the *s* in *vacations*.)

Rough Guides   Rough Guides appeared first in print, then on TV, and now they're on the Web. In a special deal with Wired Ventures, the folks who bring you *Wired* and *HotWired*, the very hip, cool, and groovy British travel guides for the masses are available online, with the usual *Wired* flair for the marriage of graphics and content.

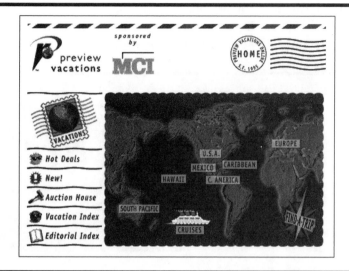

Figure B.20: The postcard-motif graphics are almost as attractive as the deals at Preview Media's travel site.

What's Out There

Journey via Rough Guides to hip, cool, groovy world travel at `http://www.hotwired.com/rough/`.

◆ World Wide Weirdness

We hardly know what to say about some of this. Anybody can publish a home page, and sometimes you'll run into the strangest, most wigged-out stuff in the world.

 Keep in mind that things change on the Web at the whim of the folks who publish there. Pages (and the pages they're linked to) will change and vanish to reflect the times.

The Squat   A (very quirky) response to the famous and popular the Spot, which we describe elsewhere in this chapter, the Squat changes the real-life locale to a trailer park in the backwoods of Missouri. There the cast of six acts out lives filled with lazing, guzzling, and just plain lousy living. The Squat's apparent in Figure B.21.

Hey, Com'on in!

(If ya can stand the smell)

Figure B.21: The Squat is an even quirkier response to the already quirky Spot.

What's Out There

Look in on the Squat, a "this-is-*real*-life" response to the Spot, at `http://theory.physics.missouri.edu/~georges/Josh/squat/welcome.html`.

The Surrealism Server   Time bends across a molten landscape.... We aren't even going to tell you what you'll find at the Surrealism server— just that it's weird and wacky and, well, *surreal*.

What's Out There

It's surreal, and it's at the Surrealism server, which you'll experience at `http://pharmdec.wustl.edu/juju/surr/surrealism.html`.

◆ **Zines**

Defined by the kind of quirkiness that's so fashionable on the Net and the streets of our cities, zines are all the rage. Anyone can publish an electronic magazine to be distributed via e-mail or the Web; all it takes is a viewpoint you want to make known and a little computer know-how.

What's Out There

Several newsgroups are devoted to e-zine and Web zine talk. Make your way via your newsreader to `alt.zines`, `alt.ezines`, and `alt.etext` to check them out.

Enterzone   *Enterzone* provides a thoughtful selection of not just fiction, poetry, and essays, but also photography, paintings, and even interactive art forms.

What's Out There

Enterzone presents writing and artwork of true merit at the URL `http://www.ezone.org.ez`.

geekgrrl   One of the more famous zines, *geekgrrl* conjures images of hip feminists of the '90s speaking up, articulately and engagingly, in print.

What's Out There

Catch up with *geekgrrl* at `http://www.next.com.au/spyfood/geekgirl`.

Wired* Magazine and *HotWired   *Wired* was an immediate smash when it was launched in 1993. Devoted to the cybernaut subculture, this rag is high-tech with an attitude. Its progeny, *HotWired*, was launched online in late 1994 and was also a smash success. (See Figure B.22.)

To access *HotWired*, you'll have to go through the simple hoops of setting up a (cost-free) account. Just follow the on-screen directions the first time you jump into the *HotWired* world; you'll have your free account in a moment or two, and you won't have to go to any trouble at all next time.

What's Out There

Get *HotWired* via the Web server for this journal of the cybernaut subculture. The URL is `http://www.hotwired.com`.

Figure B.22: *HotWired*, the online progeny of *Wired* magazine

Factsheet Five   Billing itself as "your guide to parallel culture," *Factsheet Five* offers zine reviews, online catalogs, and even journals and articles on electronic publishing issues.

What's Out There

Get *Factsheet Five* at `http://www.well.com/conf/f5/f5index2.html`.

John Labovitz's comprehensive list of zines can be seen at the URL `http://www.meer.net/~johnl/e-zine-list/`.

There's also a great e-zine FAQ (Frequently Asked Question list) at `http://www.well.com/conf/f5/ezines.faq`.

Zine Terminology

There are *e-zines,* and there are *Web zines.* What's the diff? Well, an e-zine might be considered by the new elite as the e-mail forerunner of the Web zine, but to the e-zine underground, it's a wider-range medium. (Believe it or not, not everyone has a Web browser.) The earlier forerunners of e-zines and Web zines might be the fold-and-staple variety of alternative magazines that are (still to this day) photocopied rather than printed. Zines are a low-cost way to publish what you think the world wants or needs to know. In publishing, printing costs are a terrible burden; so the lower you can get your printing costs, the less funding you need to start your own rag. Where else can you get the low-cost/high distribution bang for your buck but on the Net? You too can be a publisher. (See Chapter 9.)

Word   With some stunning graphics and its own quirky viewpoint, *Word* more or less defines the height of zine culture. It's worth a glance if only for the clever use of art and layout (see Figure B.23).

What's Out There

Word, an online zine with inspiring layout and its own viewpoint, is at `http://www.word.com/`. Also of interest: *Suck* (`http://www.suck.com`) and *Salon* (`http://www.salon1999.com`).

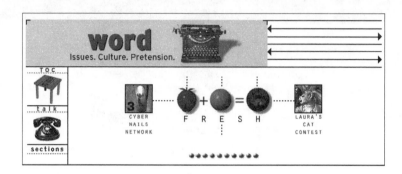

Figure B.23: Visually, *Word* is striking.

One Thing Leads to Another

Things change. The Web changes all the time—new stuff appears there daily, and part of the wonder of Web exploration is accidentally coming across the unexpected, the unusual, or even the outrageous as you tinker about. After looking through this appendix, you should have some ideas about the range of stuff that's available. Cruising the Web is your game now—have a grand old time.

What's on the CD

Inside the back cover of this book you'll find a CD containing tools and software that will get you started surfing the Internet. You'll get:

- ◆ A customized What's Out There page linking you to millions of entertaining and useful Web sites, along with an online glossary
- ◆ A number of popular connectivity options that will make getting online a simple and convenient process

Let's take a look at each of these items in turn.

◆ The What's Out There Page

All of the many, many Internet sites discussed in this book (and then some) are linked to a customized Web page included on the CD. We call it the What's Out There page, because, obviously, it links you to all the great stuff we've pointed out in the What's Out There boxes throughout this book. It also links you to an online glossary.

You can make the What's Out There page the start-up home page you'll see when you start Netscape, or you can keep it nearby for convenient reference. In either case, you'll get quick access to a wide array of Internet resources, including:

◆ Search tools and directories—such as Alta Vista, HotBot, Excite, InfoSeek, and Yahoo—that will enable you to find what you seek on the Internet in a jiffy and be your entry point to literally millions of Web pages

◆ Sources of free and inexpensive software that will enhance your Internet capabilities

◆ Publishing tools and resources that will get you started and help you to refine and even publicize your own Web publications

◆ Hand-selected sites on topics such as Arts and Entertainment, Computers and the Net, Personal Finance, Sports, Travel, Zines, and more

You can quickly find terms that are defined in the online glossary by selecting Edit ➤ Find from Netscape's menu bar and typing the term of interest into the dialog box that appears.

The What's Out There home page takes advantage of Netscape's frames, providing easy navigation and a lot of information packed into a comprehensive layout (see Figure C.1).

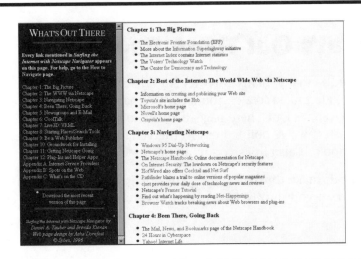

Figure C.1: The What's Out There page makes exploring the Internet easy.

The What's Out There page actually (and technically) consists of six inter-linked HTML and graphic files that are stored in a single folder on the disk. All you have to do is copy the folder to your hard drive (a simple task with Windows 95) and launch Netscape, and then you can view the page. Read on for easy instructions.

Copying the Home Page onto Your Hard Drive

The first part of this process is to copy the home page folder to your hard drive.

1. Insert the CD into your CD-ROM drive. (We'll assume you're using drive D: here, but if you use drive F:, just change D: to F: in the instructions that follow.)

2. From your Desktop, double-click on the My Computer icon to display your computer's hard disk and drives.

3. Double-click on the CD-ROM drive icon to display the contents of the What's Out There CD. You'll see a folder named WOT.

4. Copy the WOT folder to your hard drive by clicking on it and dragging it to the drive C: icon.

That's all there is to it. Now let's take a look at your new home page.

Launching Netscape and Looking at the Page

Now that the files are stored on your hard drive, you can use Netscape to view the What's Out There page.

Although you don't have to be connected to the Internet to view the page, you do need to be connected to follow many of its hyperlinks, because they point to sites all over the Net.

1. Launch Netscape. (See Chapter 3 if you need more details.)

2. From the menu bar, select File ➤ Open File. The Open dialog box will appear.

3. Click on the Look In pull-down list and select your hard drive (in our case, it's drive C:) to make its contents visible in the dialog box's big text area. (See Figure C.2.)

4. Double-click on the WOT folder to open it.

5. Double-click on HOMEPAGE.HTM (see Figure C.3). The Netscape N icon will become animated, and the What's Out There page will appear on your screen.

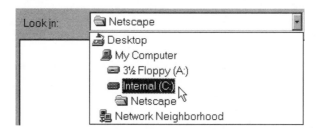

Figure C.2: Select your hard drive from the pull-down list.

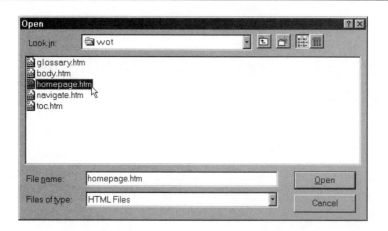

Figure C.3: Double-click on the file named HOMEPAGE.HTM to open the What's Out There page.

If you open the page using a browser that doesn't support frames (or a version of Netscape earlier than 2.0), you won't be able to see the thing. Instead, a message will appear saying that the page is viewable only using a frames-capable browser such as Netscape version 2.0 or later.

Navigating the Page

The What's Out There page takes advantage of frames, a terrific design effect instituted by Netscape. Each frame is actually the result of a distinct HTML file; both frames are displayed in one viewing window—it's as if several Web pages were combined into one screen. In fact, it isn't *like* that—it *is* that. Pages that use frames present new options for navigating around. For helpful information about how to get around this particular page, click on the How to Navigate link in the page's left frame.

Making the What's Out There Page Your Home Page

You can keep the What's Out There page on your hard disk and open it, whenever you like, to use as a reference source, while retaining some other page as your start-up home page. Or you can make the What's Out There page your start-up home page—that is, the page that automatically appears each and every time you launch Netscape. We went over this in Chapter 3, but let's take a quick look at the process again.

1. Launch Netscape.

2. Open the What's Out There page using the instructions in the *Launching Netscape and Looking at the Page* section earlier in this appendix.

3. A URL beginning with the phrase `file:///` will be visible in the Location text box near the top of the Netscape viewing window. Click on the URL to highlight it. (See Figure C.4.)

Figure C.4: Here you can see the location of the file for the What's Out There page, appearing in the familiar format of a URL.

4. From the menu bar, select Edit ➤ Copy (or press Ctrl+X) to copy the page's location to the Clipboard (the page location will remain stored there until you are ready to use it in a moment in step 7).

5. Select Options ➤ General Preferences. The Preferences dialog box will appear.

6. Click on the Appearance tab at the top of the dialog box. The dialog box will change to make that set of preferences visible (see Figure C.5).

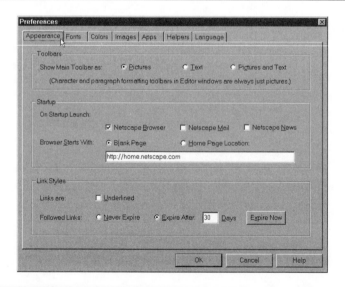

Figure C.5: The Preferences dialog box

7. In the Startup section of the dialog box, select the Home Page Location button, click in the text box under it, and then press Ctrl+V to paste in the location of the What's Out There page (you copied it to the Clipboard in step 4, remember?). It'll look like Figure C.6 when you're done.

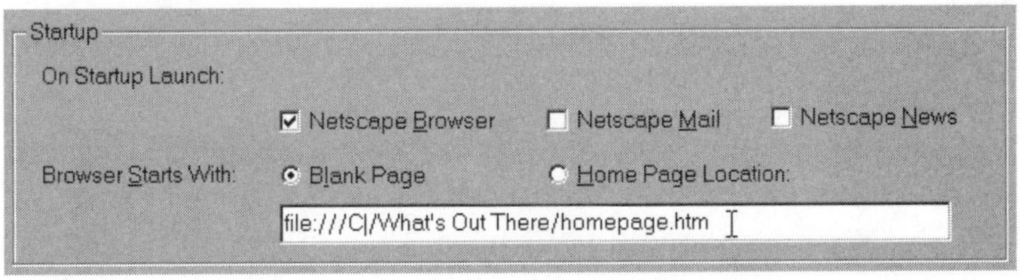

Startup
On Startup Launch:

☑ Netscape Browser   ☐ Netscape Mail   ☐ Netscape News

Browser Starts With: ⦿ Blank Page   ○ Home Page Location:

file:///C|/What's Out There/homepage.htm

Figure C.6: Paste in the location of the What's Out There page.

8. Click on the OK button at the bottom of the Preferences dialog box.

9. From Netscape's menu bar, select Options ➤ Save Options to save the change you just made.

Now, each and every time you start Netscape, the What's Out There page will be your launch point.

You can add your favorite links to the What's Out There page using the HTML skills you learned in Chapter 9. Read on to find out more.

Adding Your Own Links to the Page

As your Web exploration expands, you may want to add your own newly discovered hyperlinks to the What's Out There page. You can keep adding stuff and expanding the page all you like, customizing it for your own purposes. All you need is some basic HTML know-how (which you have if you've gone through the exercises in Chapter 9 of this book). The home page files are fully customizable, and you can make any changes to them you want.

 The What's Out There home page is a document whose copyright is held by Sybex. You can copy and customize the document for your own use, but you may not copy or distribute the document for the use of others.

 It's always a good idea to make changes to your important files on *copies*, not on the original files.

The HTML file that contains the hyperlinks to Internet sites is called BODY.HTM. It is stored on your hard drive in the WOT folder. To add your own links, simply open BODY.HTM using your word processor (or you can use an HTML editing programs included on the CD, add hyperlinks where you would like them to appear in the page (see Chapter 9 for details), and then save and close the document. The next time you open the What's Out There page using Netscape, your links will appear.

Of course, making more sophisticated changes in the home page requires more HTML expertise—that's the sort of thing you'll want to get into only if you have some serious HTML experience.

 You can get an updated version of the What's Out There page by clicking on the <u>Download</u> the latest version... link.

◆ Netcom's Netcomplete

Netcomplete is a suite of Internet access software and services from Netcom Communications, a well-known Internet service provider that offers access via local phone numbers in most of the big U.S. cities. Netcomplete, designed to work with (and *only* with) Windows 95, provides an easy point-and-click interface that makes surfing the Internet a breeze.

To install Netcomplete, open the NETCRUZ folder on the CD and double-click on SETUP.EXE. The program will install itself; during the process a series of dialog boxes will open and close as various files are copied to your machine. When installation is complete, a sign-up procedure will be launched automatically; get out your credit card and follow the simple steps laid out before you to register for Netcom's Netcomplete service.

You're asked for a registration code. Type **92015.**

This is all very easy—when you're done, turn to chapters 10 and 11 to learn how to set up and use Netscape with Netcomplete.

What's Out There

Netcom's home page contains information about all of its services; visit it at `http://www.netcom.com`.

◆ Netcom's NetCruiser

Netcom Communications (described in the preceding section) also offers NetCruiser Internet access software for Windows 3.1. This option gives you easy point-and-click access to the whole Internet; NetCruiser has been extremely popular (especially with beginners) since its inception in 1994. With NetCruiser, as with Netcomplete, your access will be Netcom's network of local access telephone numbers throughout major U.S. cities.

To install NetCruiser, open the NETCOM folder on the CD and double-click on SETUP.EXE. As the program installs itself, a series of dialog boxes will open and close and various files will be copied to your computer. Then a sign-up procedure will be launched; have your credit card handy and follow those steps that appear before you to register for NetCruiser service.

You'll be asked for a registration code. Type **92015**.

When you're finished, turn to chapters 10 and 11 to set up and use Netscape with NetCruiser.

◆ CompuServe's WinCIM

CompuServe is a popular commercial online service that offers its own content along with Internet access to its subscribers. CompuServe has been known in the past for content that is more business-oriented where competitor America Online is more entertaining, but there are distinct signs of a shift in this equation. WinCIM is the special CompuServe software that lets you explore CompuServe (and the Net via CompuServe).

To install WinCIM on your computer, open the WINCIM folder on the CD and double-click on SETUP.EXE. As files are copied to your machine, a series of dialog boxes will appear and close. Then you'll be stepped through the sign-up process; keep your credit card nearby during this simple procedure.

At some point you'll be asked for a code, which you can get from the card you'll find packaged with the CD.

When you've got CompuServe up and running, turn to chapters 10 and 11 for the scoop on running Netscape with the WinCIM software.

What's Out There

Find out more about CompuServe via the Web at http://www.compuserve.com.

Surf's Up!

You've got everything you need to surf the Internet with Netscape Navigator. You've got the skills, the software, and even the convenient What's Out There page. You're on your way....

Index

Note to the Reader: Throughout this index **boldface** page numbers indicate primary discussions of a topic. *Italic* page numbers indicate illustrations.

Meet tomorrow's deadlines today!

Sybex has just what you need...

Always Asking Colleagues and Friends for Help?

Use Sybex's new ABCs series instead. By skipping the long drawn-out introductions, you get right into the really useful information. With a task-oriented approach, these new ABCs help you maximize your effectiveness and save valuable time.

Available Now at a Bookstore Near You.

SYBEX®

©1996 SYBEX® Computer Books

The ABCs of Word for Windows 95
Guy Hart-Davis
0-7821-1877-1, $19.99

The ABCs of Excel for Windows 95
Gene Weisskopf
0-7821-1875-5, $19.99

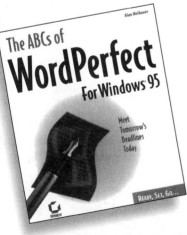

The ABCs of WordPerfect for Windows 95
Alan Neibauer
0-7821-1876-X, $19.99

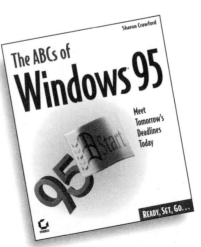

The ABCs of Windows 95
Sharon Crawford
0-7821-1878-X, $19.99

The ABCs of Microsoft Office for Windows 95
Guy Hart-Davis
0-7821-1866-6, $19.99

◆ Surf Savvy with the What's Out There CD

It's easy to find what's out there on the Net with the help of this book and its companion CD. Sure, the book shows you how to get and use Netscape, but it also shows you what's out there that can add dimension to your Internet experience. And on the CD you'll find an easy-to-use Web page with tons of links to:

- ◆ Directories and search tools such as Alta Vista, Excite, and Yahoo that provide an entry point to literally millions of Web pages
- ◆ Sources of free and inexpensive software that will enhance your time online
- ◆ Publishing tools and resources that will get you started and help you to refine and even publicize your own Web publications
- ◆ Hand-selected sites on topics such as Arts, Business, Sports, Travel, and Zines

There's software on the CD, too! You'll find a variety of the most popular connectivity options: Netcomplete, NetCruiser, and CompuServe—so you can get online and start surfing in a snap.

With this book/CD combo, you'll get quick access to thousands of rich Internet resources. See Appendix C for easy installation instructions for the What's Out There CD.

Customer Service and Support

For Netscape technical support, call (800) 320-2099 or send e-mail to `client@netscape.com`.

SYBEX